SOUL EATER

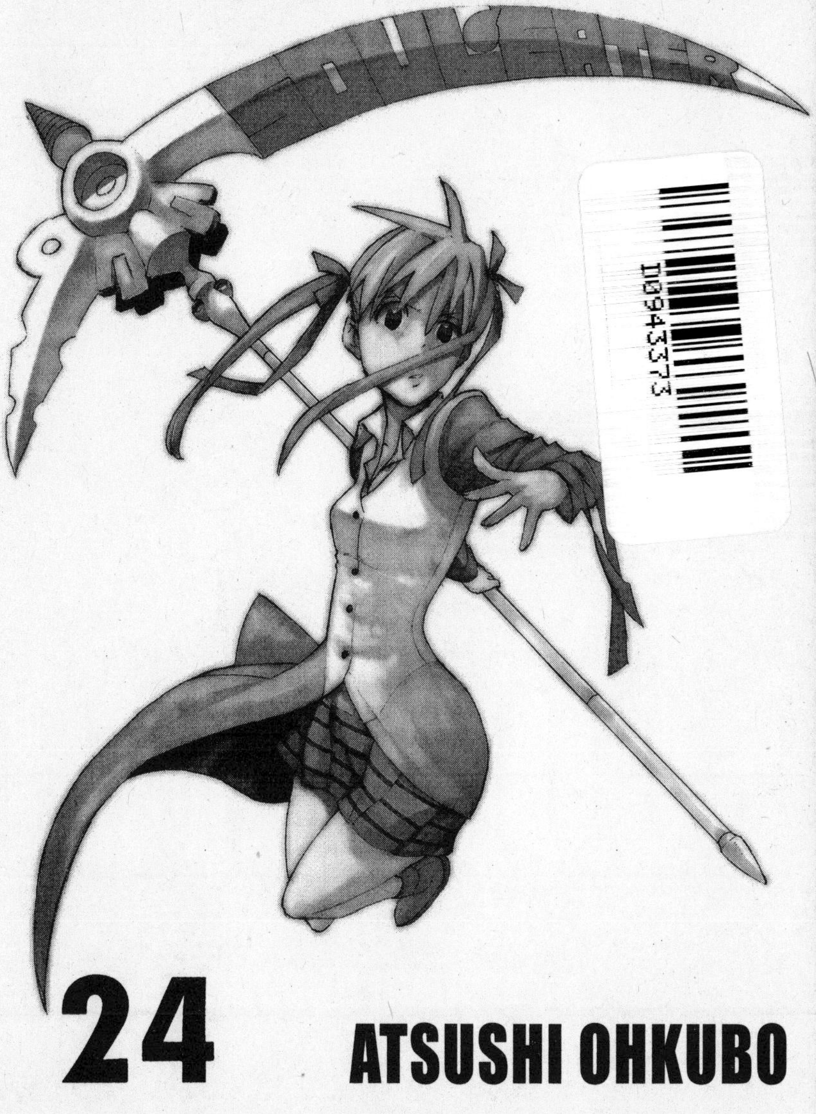

24

ATSUSHI OHKUBO

SOUL EATER

vol. 24

by ATSUSHI OHKUBO

Kishin Asura has manifested on the moon

SOUL EATER 24

CONTENTS

WITH THE WITCHES BACKING US UP, WE'VE WIPED OUT THE CLOWNS...

ONLY ASURA THE KISHIN REMAINS...

I SOWED THE SEEDS OF THIS FATE...

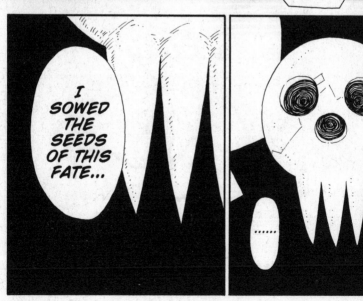

......

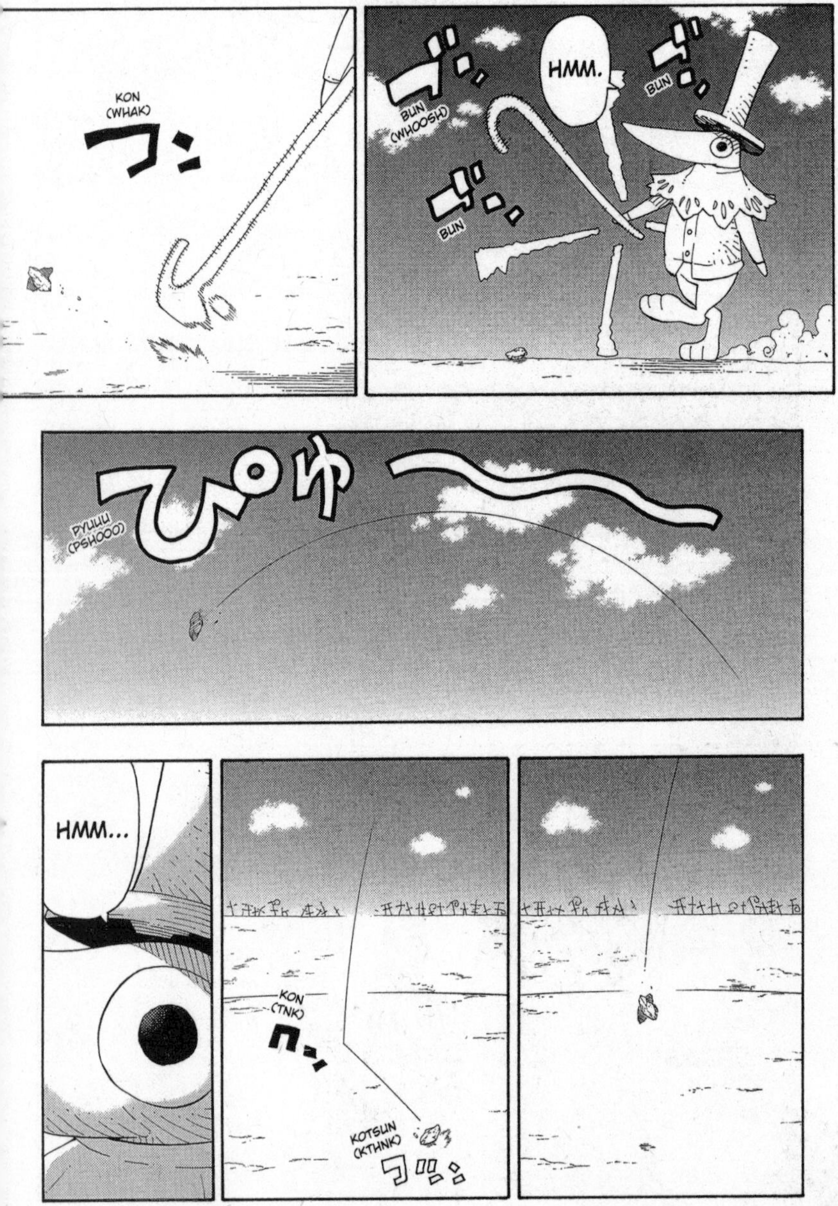

HMM.
BUN (WHOOSH)
BUN
BUN
KON (WHAK)
コン
PYUUU (PSHOOO)
ぴゅ〜〜
KON (TNK)
KOTSUN (KTHNK)
HMM...

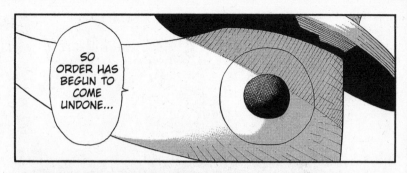

SO ORDER HAS BEGUN TO COME UNDONE...

......
THE DEATH ROOM IS A SPACE THAT REFLECTS THE ORDER OF THE WORLD...

IT IS VERY SENSITIVE TO THE ONSET OF MADNESS.

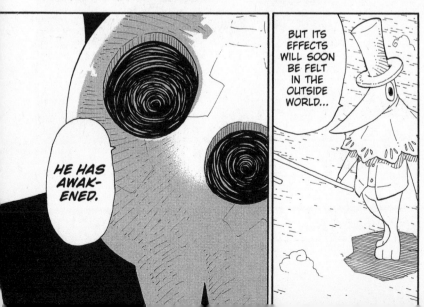

BUT ITS EFFECTS WILL SOON BE FELT IN THE OUTSIDE WORLD...

HE HAS AWAK-ENED.

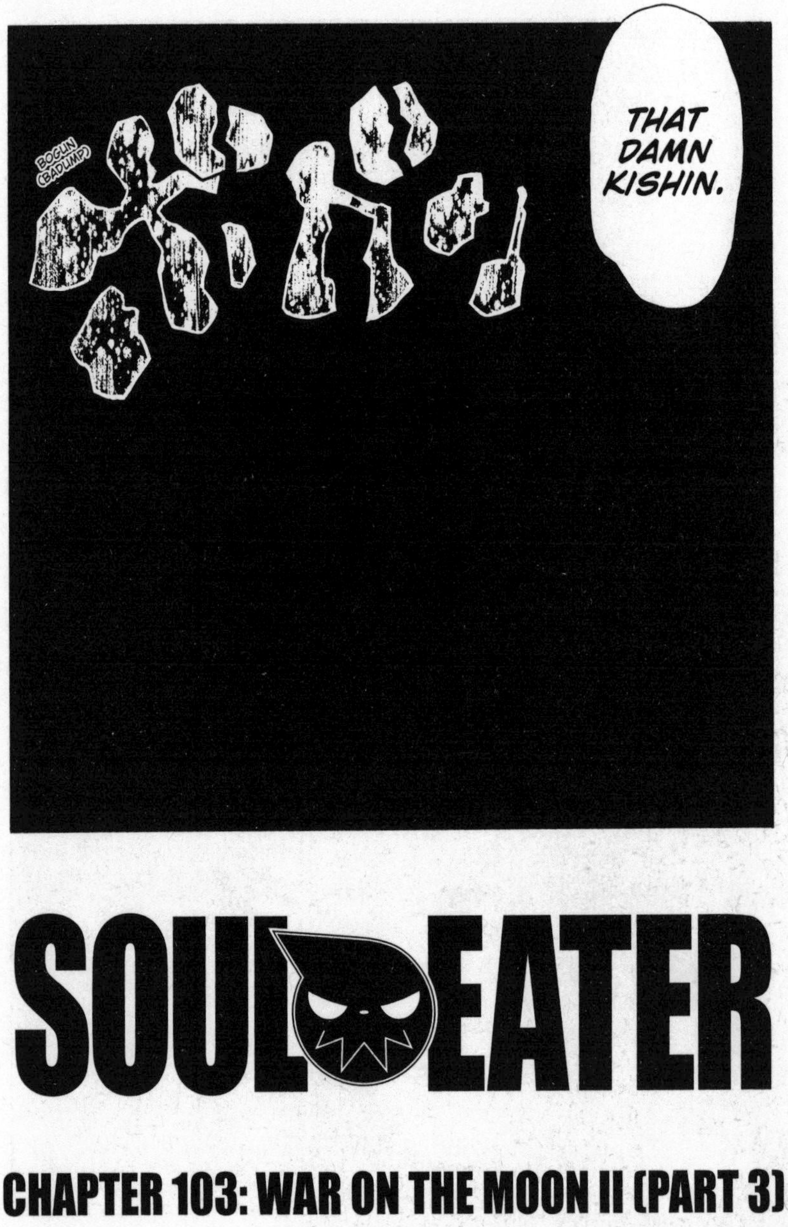
THAT DAMN KISHIN.
BOGUN (BADUMP)

SOUL EATER

CHAPTER 103: WAR ON THE MOON II (PART 3)

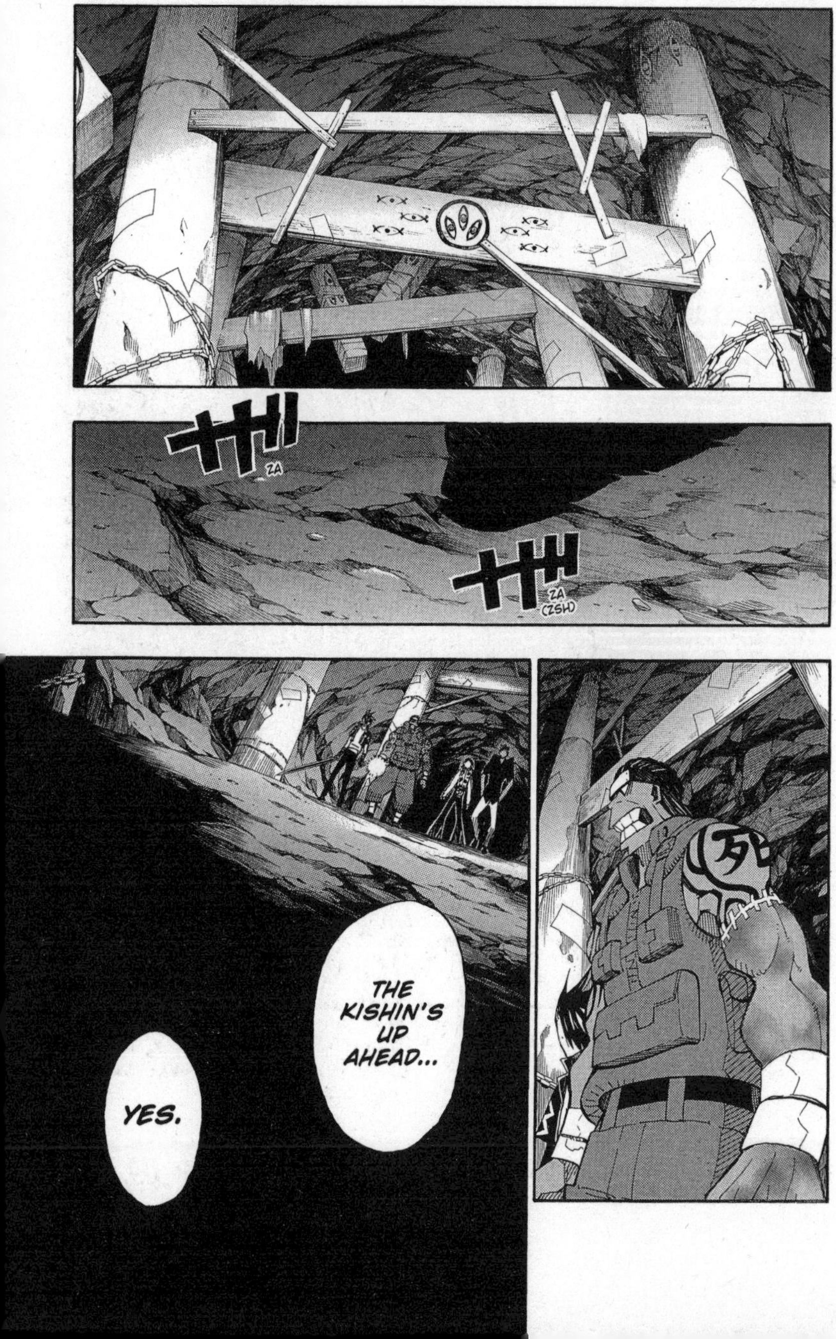
ZA
ZA
(ZSH)
THE KISHIN'S UP AHEAD...
YES.

BOGUN (BADUMP)

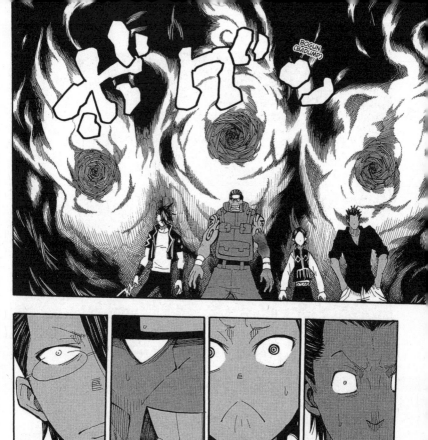

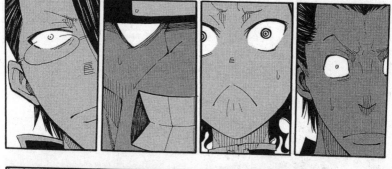

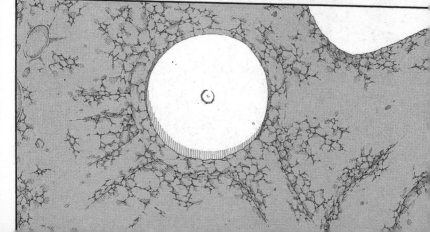

HERE IT COMES...
BOGUN

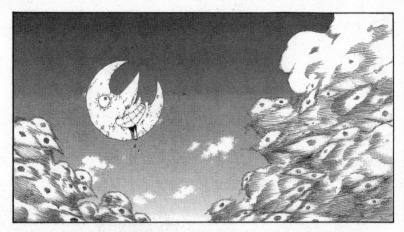

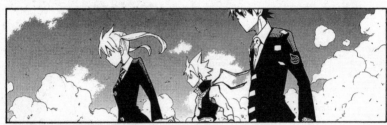

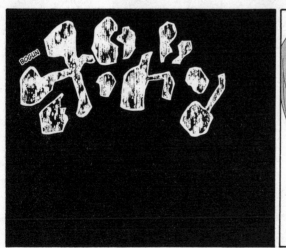

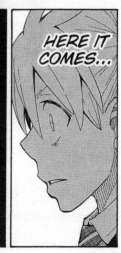

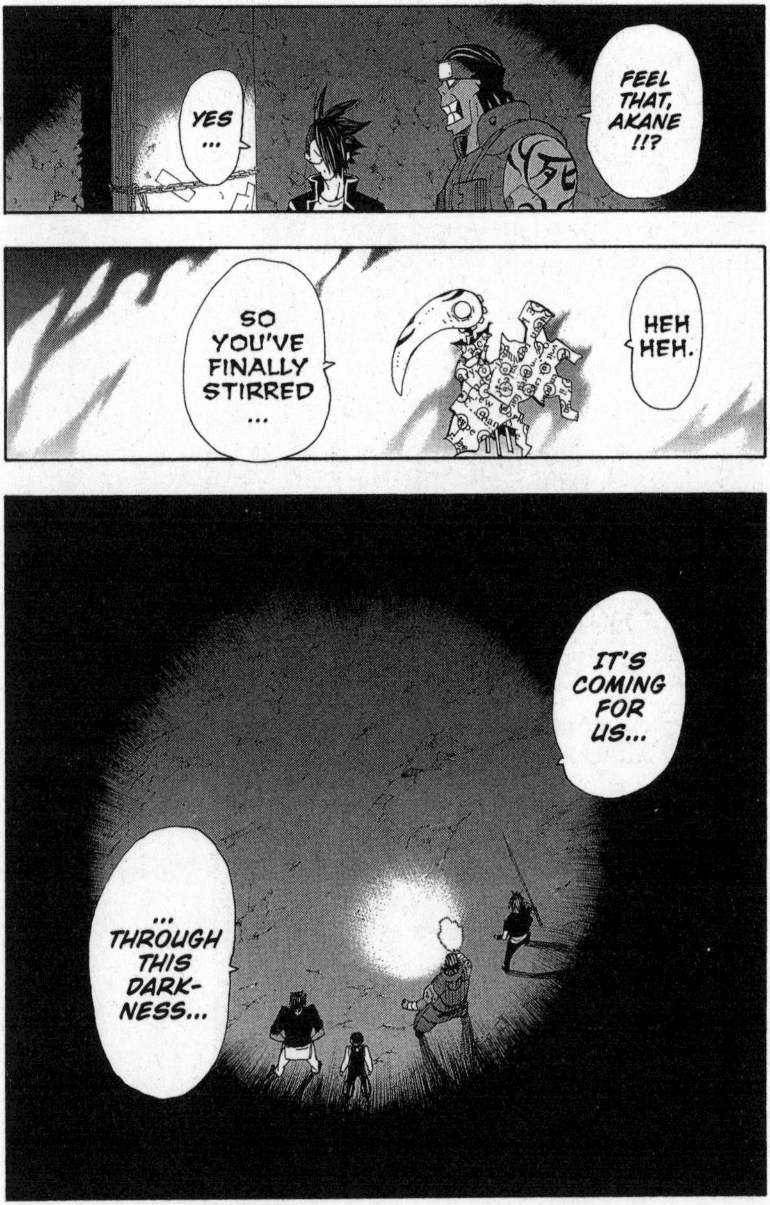
FEEL THAT, AKANE !!?
YES ...
HEH HEH.
SO YOU'VE FINALLY STIRRED ...
IT'S COMING FOR US...
... THROUGH THIS DARK-NESS...

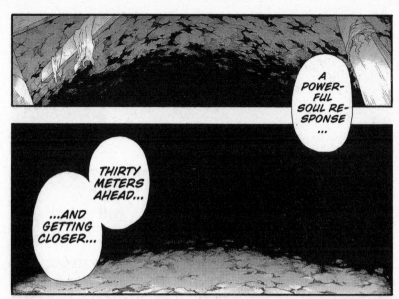

A POWER- FUL SOUL RE- SPONSE ...

THIRTY METERS AHEAD...

...AND GETTING CLOSER...

TARA (DRIP)

TWENTY METERS.

FIF- TEEN...

TEN...

KASHA (KSHAK)

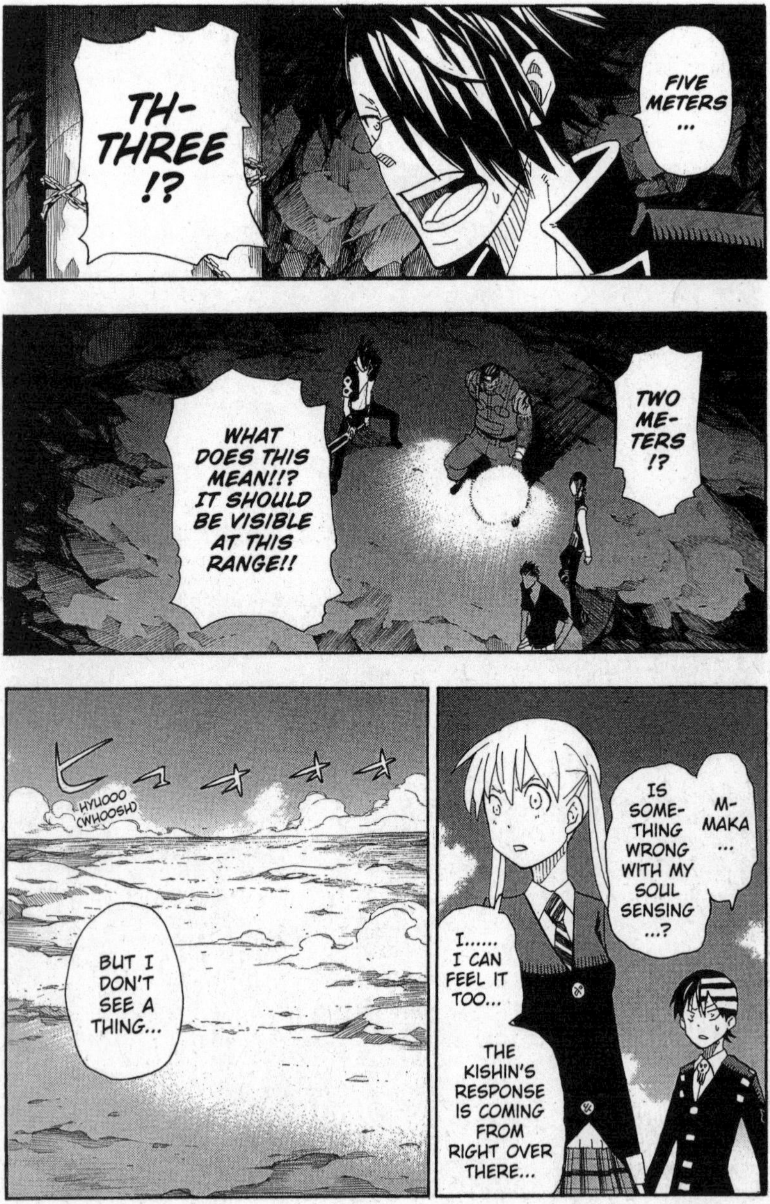
FIVE METERS ...
TH-THREE !?
TWO METERS !?
WHAT DOES THIS MEAN!!? IT SHOULD BE VISIBLE AT THIS RANGE!!
M-MAKA ...
IS SOMETHING WRONG WITH MY SOUL SENSING ...?
I...... I CAN FEEL IT TOO...
THE KISHIN'S RESPONSE IS COMING FROM RIGHT OVER THERE...
HYUOOO (WHOOSH)
BUT I DON'T SEE A THING...

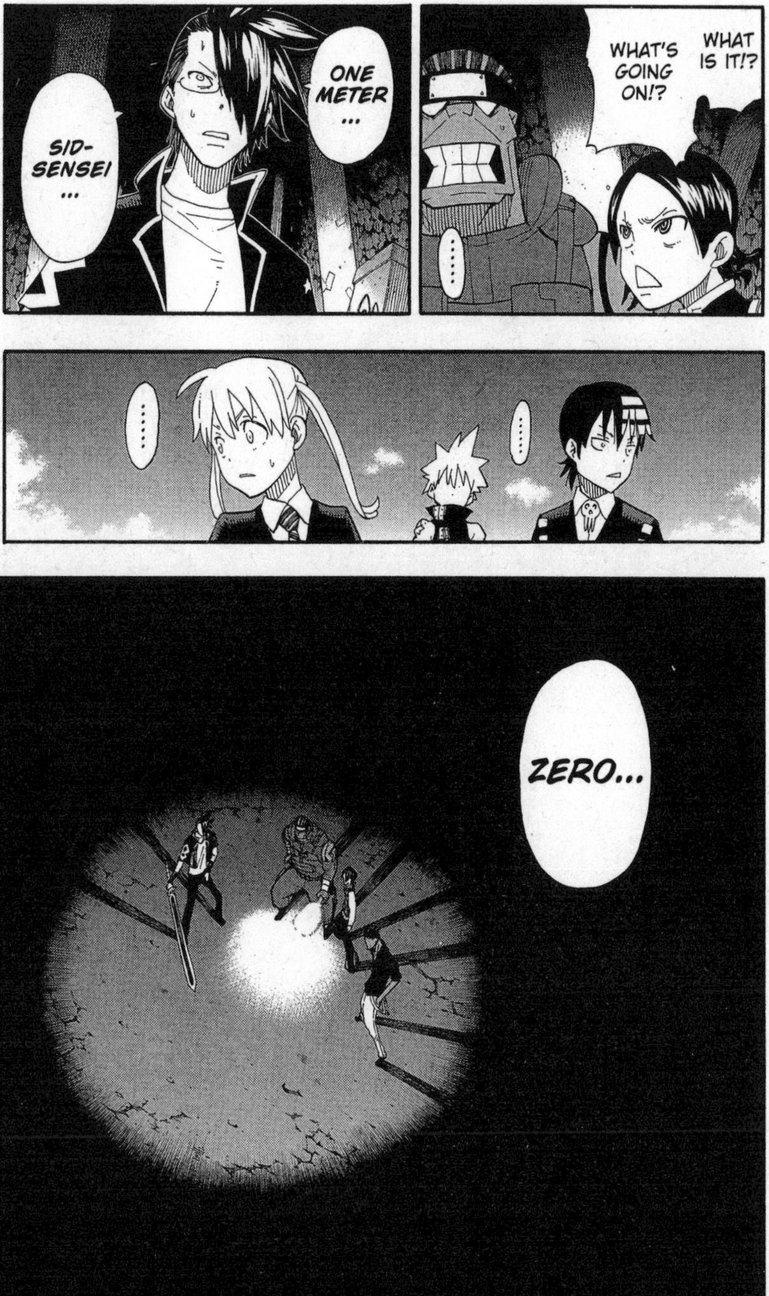
WHAT IS IT!?
WHAT'S GOING ON!?
......
ONE METER ...
SID-SENSEI ...
......
......
ZERO...

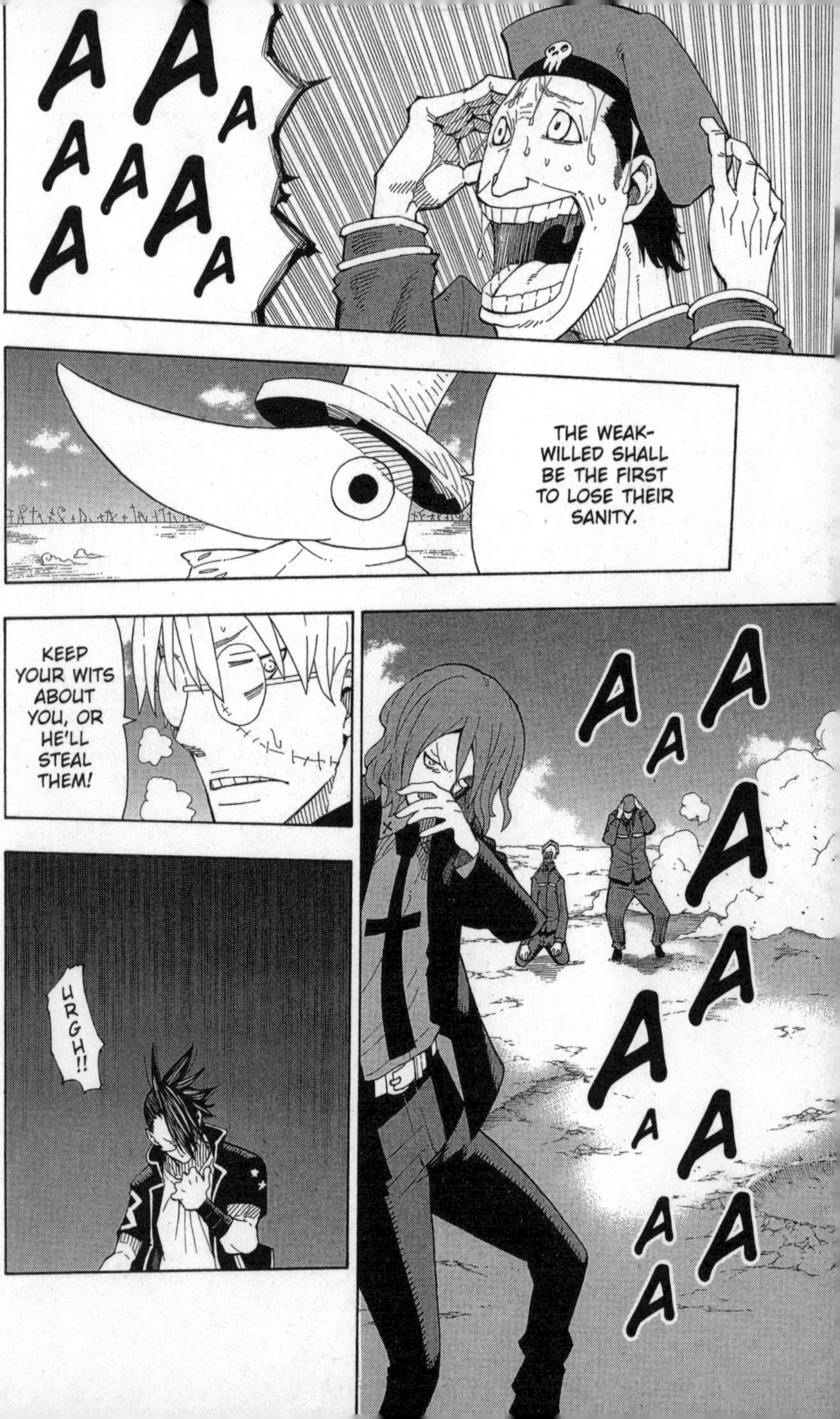
AAAAAAAAAA
THE WEAK-WILLED SHALL BE THE FIRST TO LOSE THEIR SANITY.
AAAAAAAAAAAAAA
KEEP YOUR WITS ABOUT YOU, OR HE'LL STEAL THEM!
URGH!!

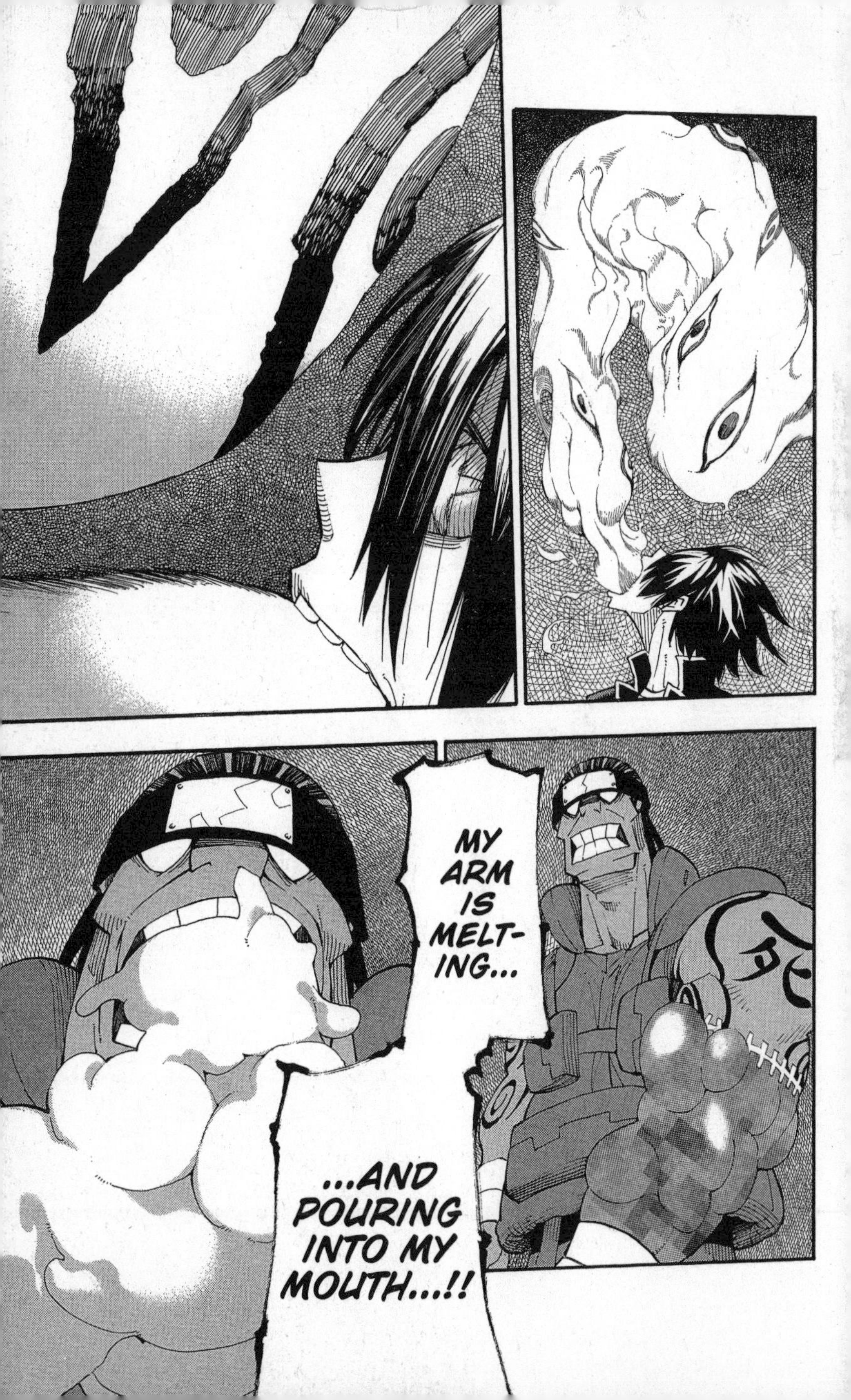
MY ARM IS MELTING...
...AND POURING INTO MY MOUTH...!!

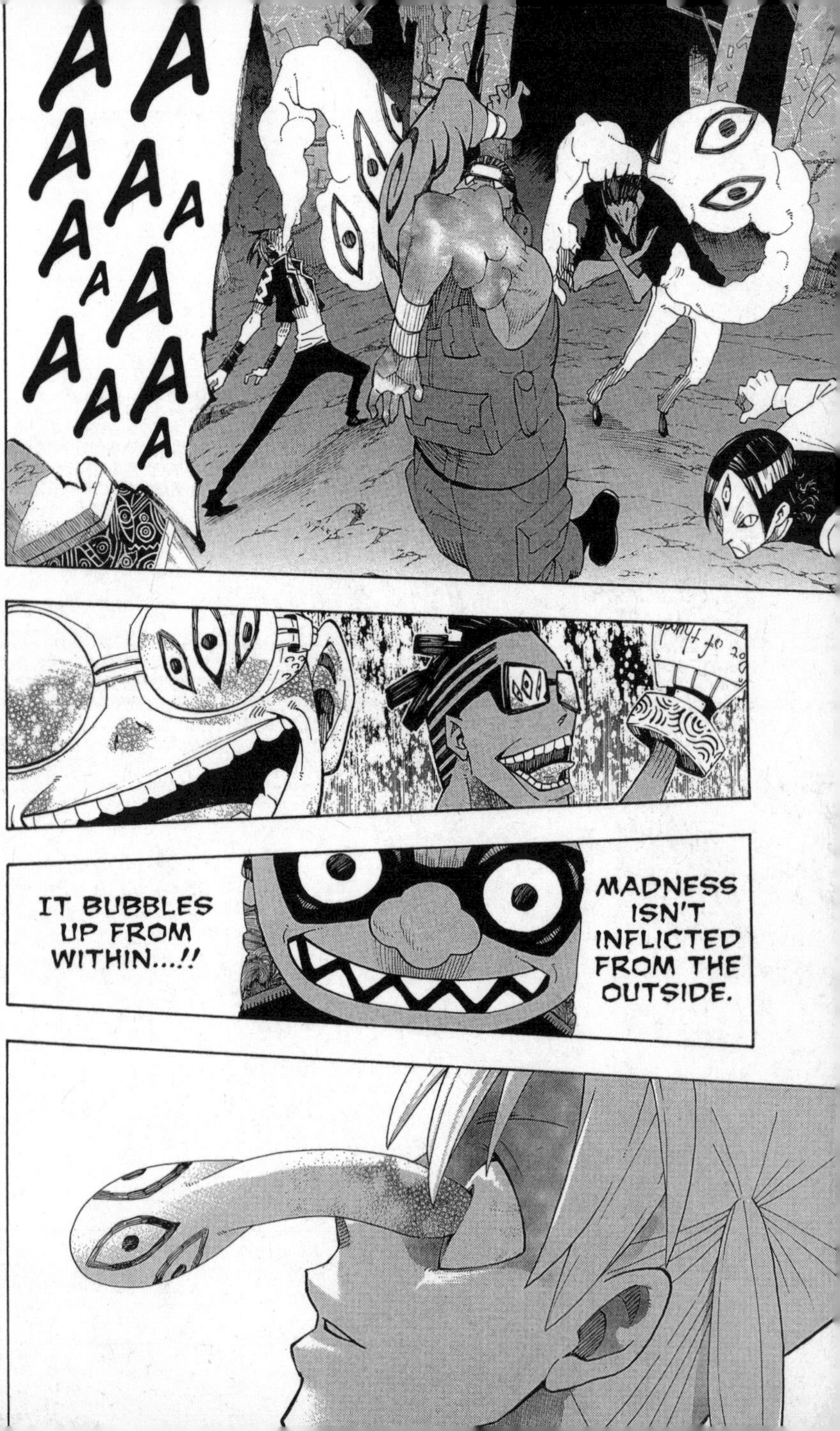
AAAAAAAAAAAAAAA
MADNESS ISN'T INFLICTED FROM THE OUTSIDE.
IT BUBBLES UP FROM WITHIN...!!

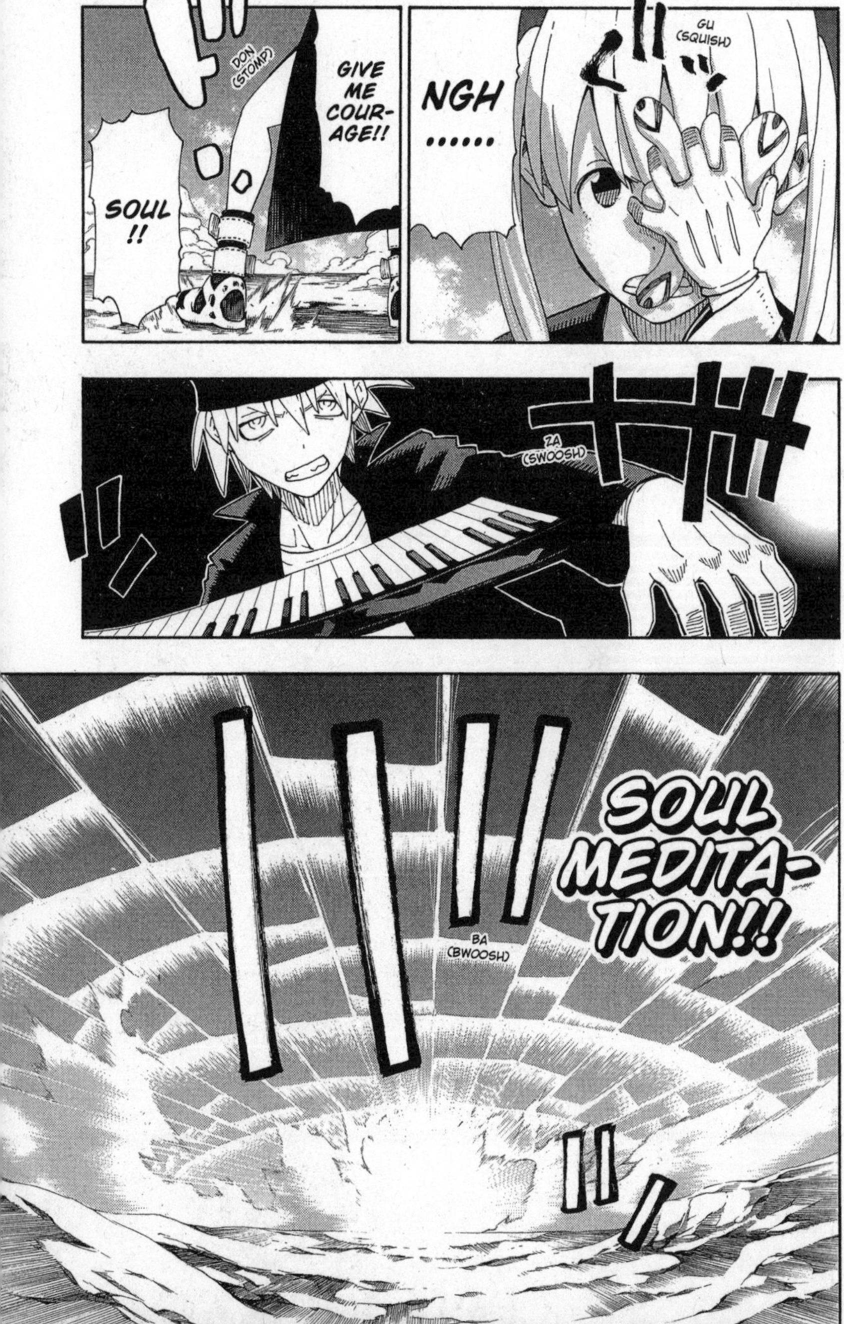
GU (SQUISH)
NGH ......
GIVE ME COURAGE!!
DON (STOMP)
SOUL !!
ZA (SWOOSH)
SOUL MEDITATION!!
BA (BWOOSH)

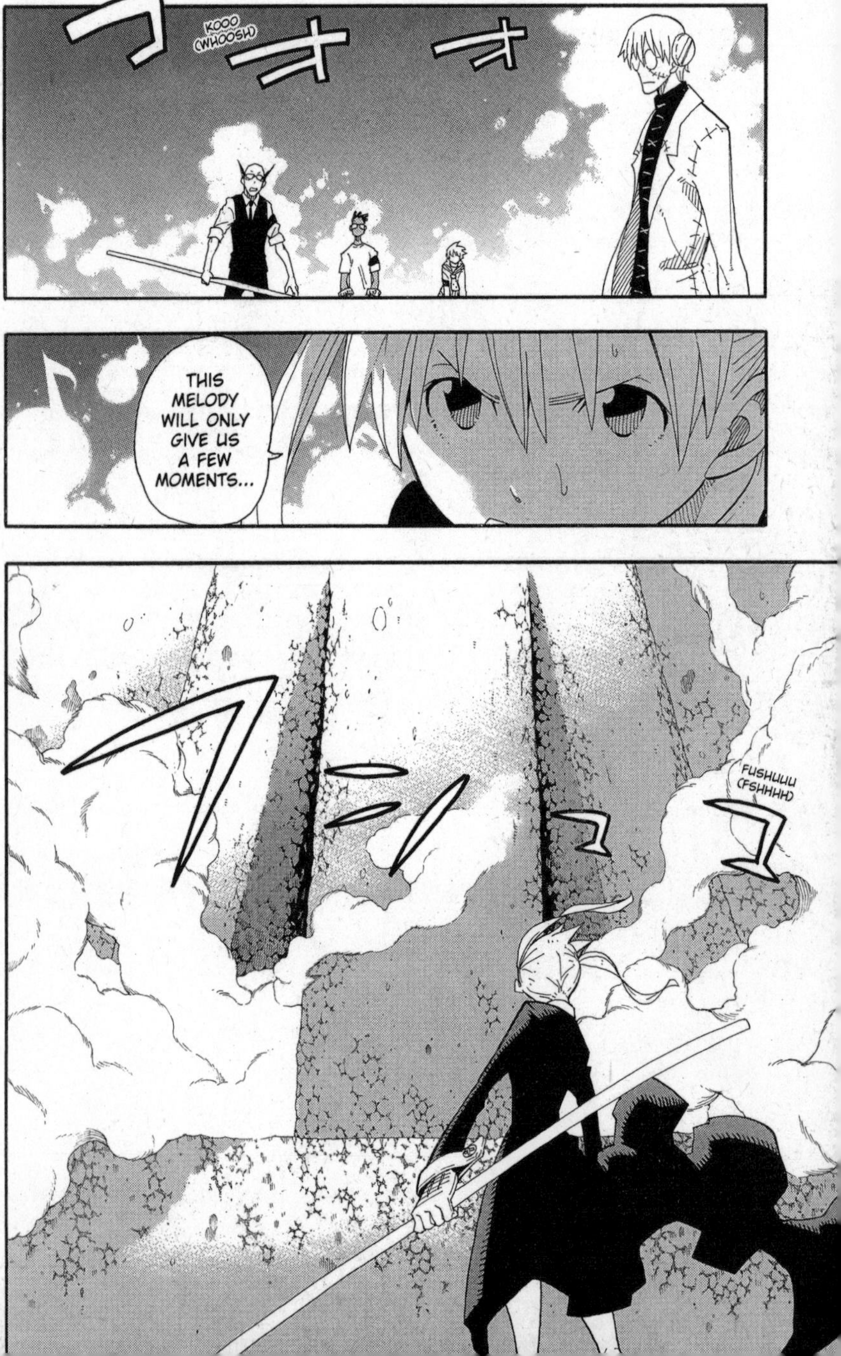
KOOO
(WHOOSH)
THIS MELODY WILL ONLY GIVE US A FEW MOMENTS...
FUSHUUU
(FSHHHH)

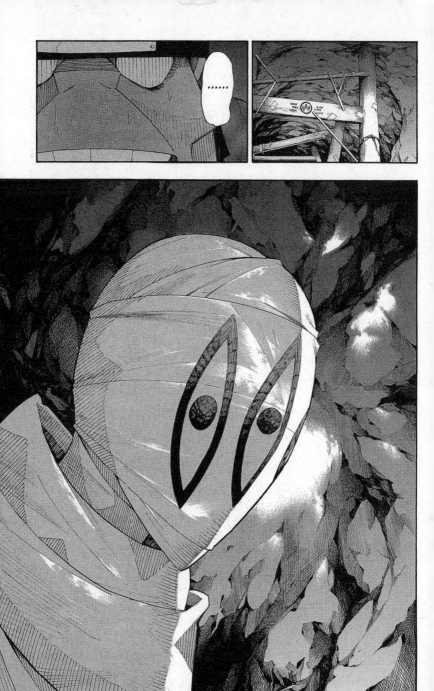

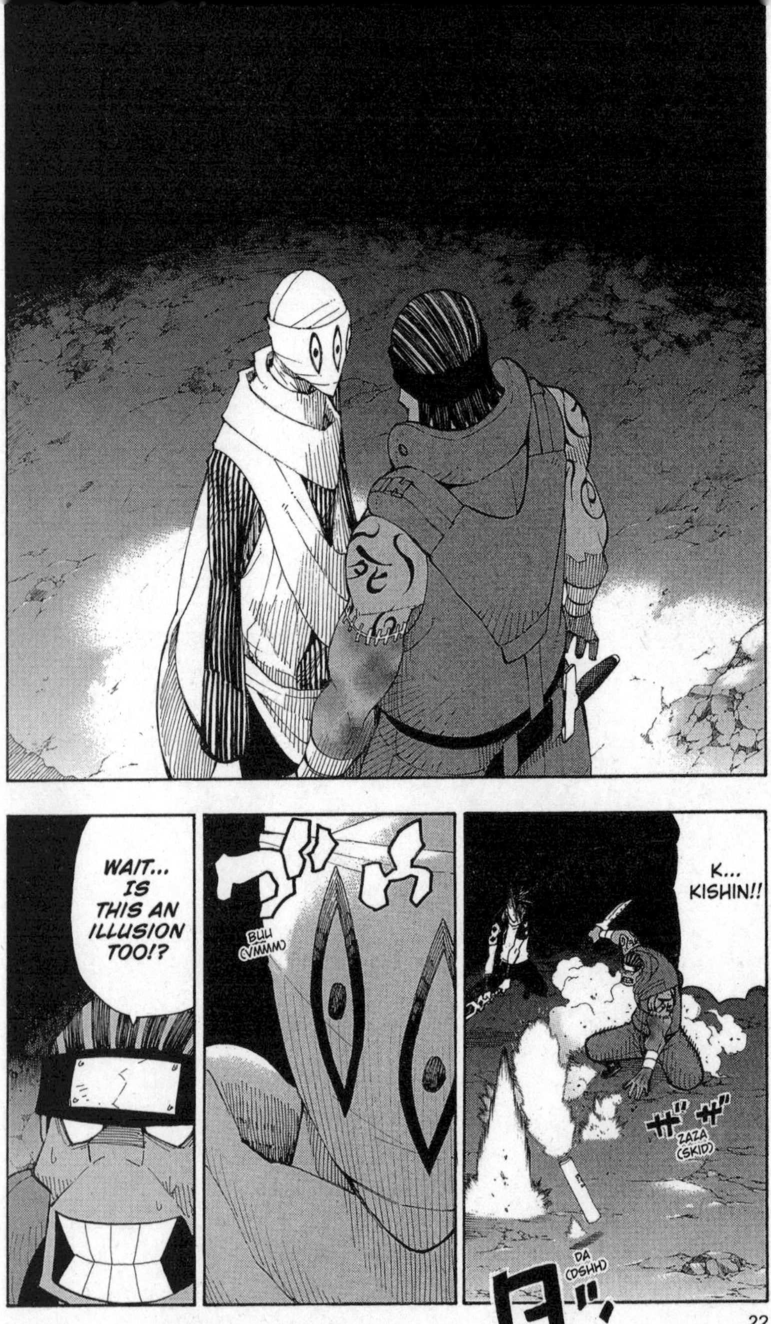
K... KISHIN!!
ZAZA (SKID)
DA (DSHH)
BUU (VMMMM)
WAIT... IS THIS AN ILLUSION TOO!?

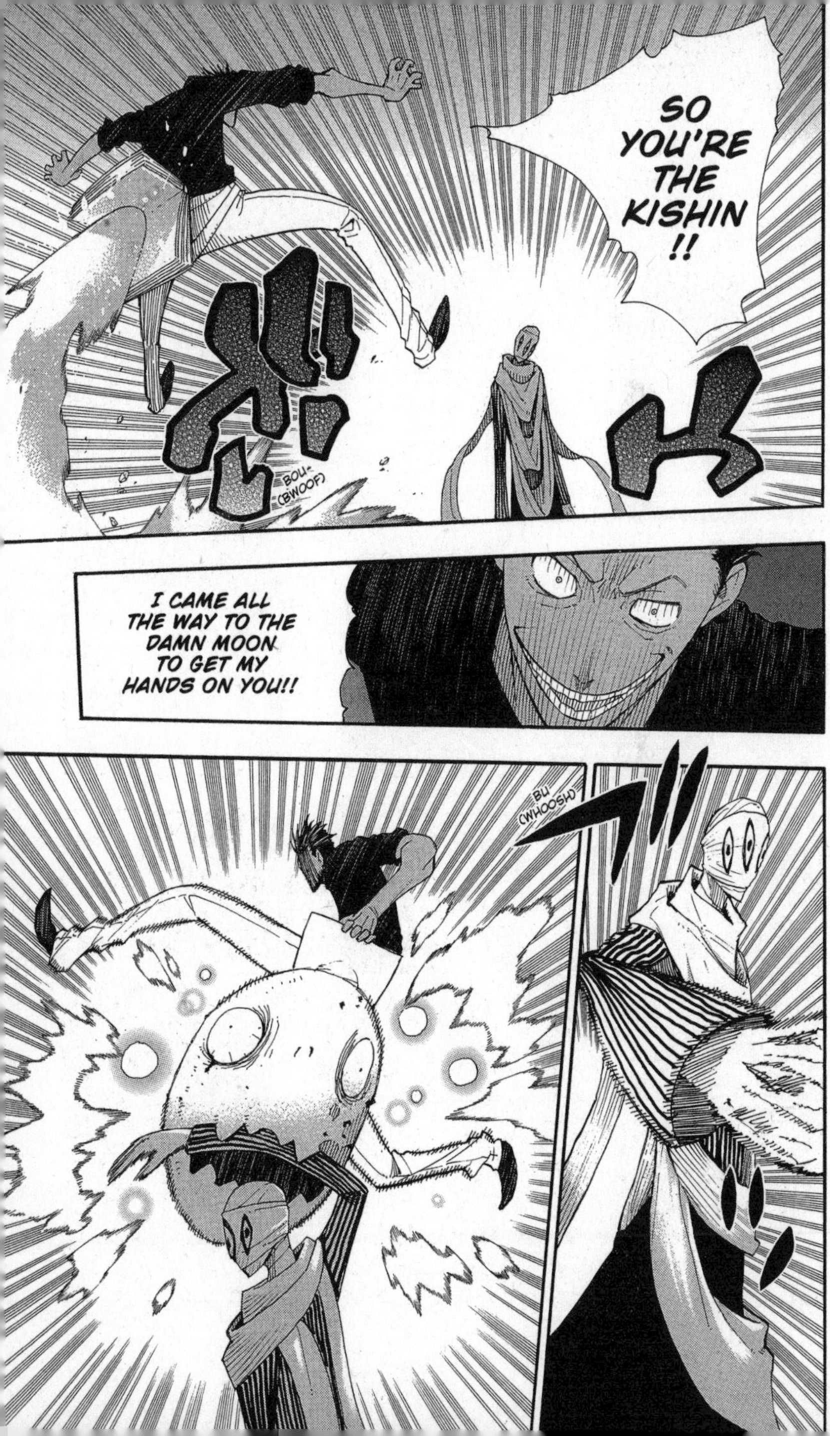
SO YOU'RE THE KISHIN !!
BOU- (BWOOF)
I CAME ALL THE WAY TO THE DAMN MOON TO GET MY HANDS ON YOU!!
BU (WHOOSH)

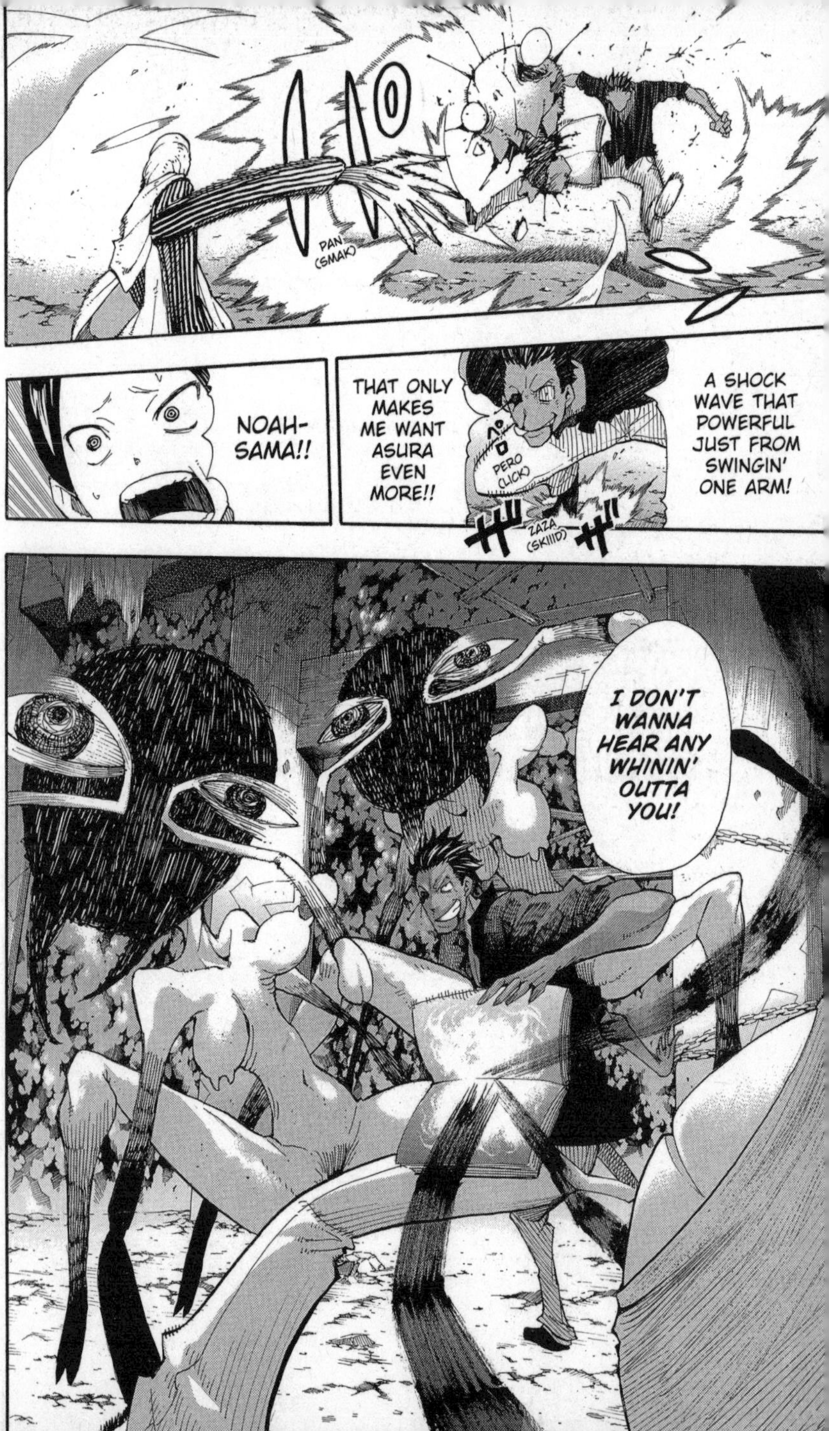
PAN
(SMAK)
A SHOCK WAVE THAT POWERFUL JUST FROM SWINGIN' ONE ARM!
THAT ONLY MAKES ME WANT ASURA EVEN MORE!!
PERO
(LICK)
ZAZA
(SKIIID)
NOAH-SAMA!!
I DON'T WANNA HEAR ANY WHININ' OUTTA YOU!

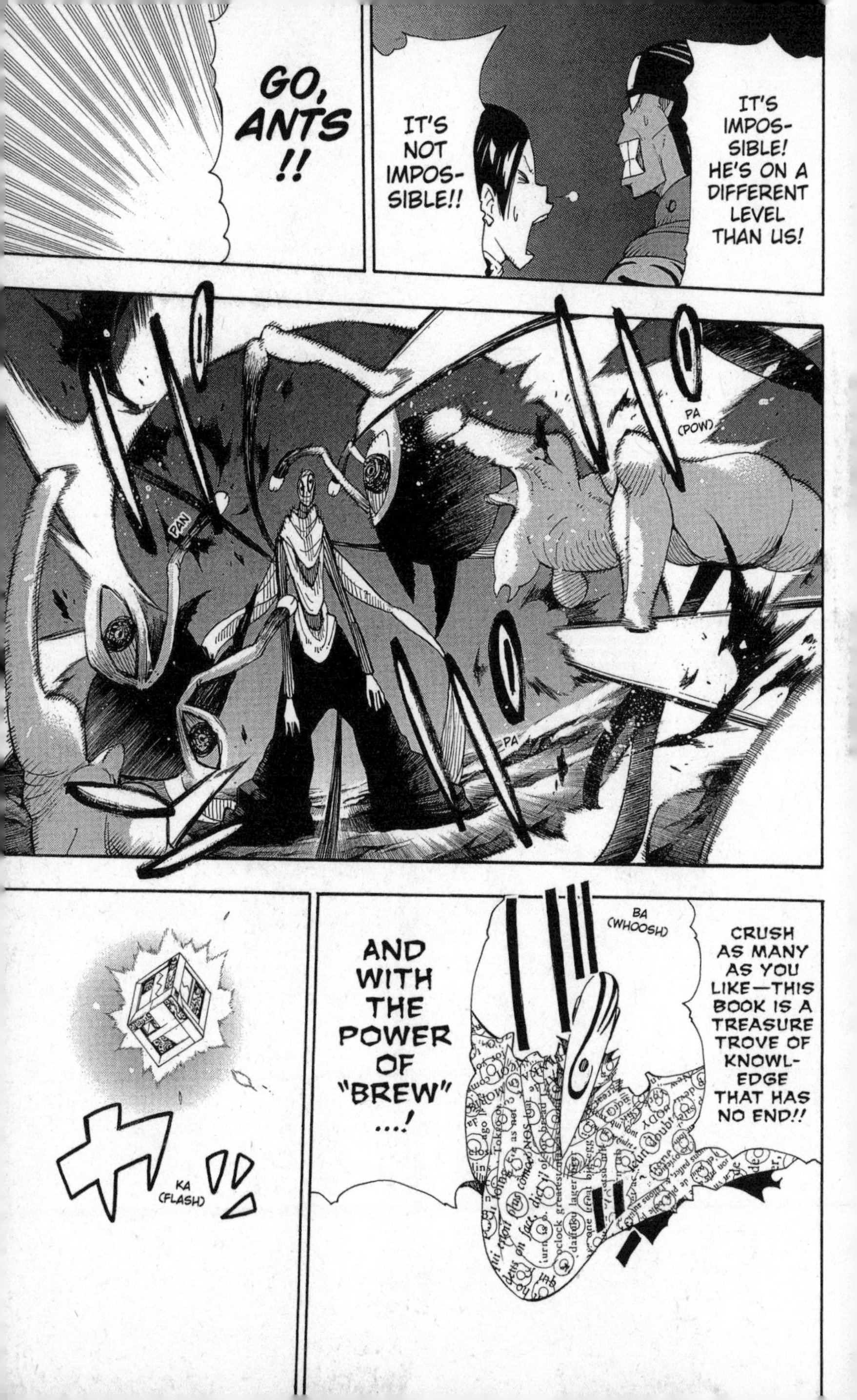
IT'S IMPOSSIBLE! HE'S ON A DIFFERENT LEVEL THAN US!
IT'S NOT IMPOSSIBLE!!
GO, ANTS!!
PA (POW)
PAN
PA
CRUSH AS MANY AS YOU LIKE—THIS BOOK IS A TREASURE TROVE OF KNOWLEDGE THAT HAS NO END!!
BA (WHOOSH)
AND WITH THE POWER OF "BREW"...!
KA (FLASH)

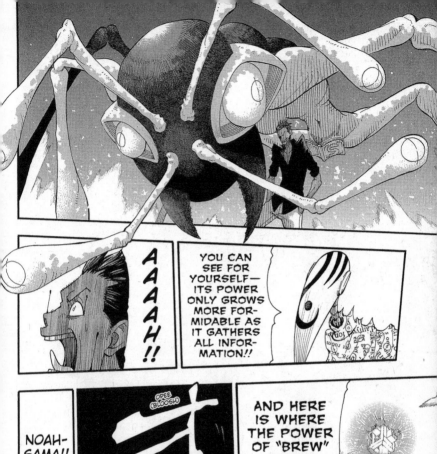

AAAAH!!

YOU CAN SEE FOR YOURSELF— ITS POWER ONLY GROWS MORE FORMIDABLE AS IT GATHERS ALL INFORMATION!!

NOAH-SAMA!!

OPEE
(BLOOSH)

AND HERE IS WHERE THE POWER OF "BREW" TRULY SHINES! IT ABSORBS ALL INFORMATION AND RECOMBINES IT TO GIVE BIRTH TO NEW KNOWLEDGE!!

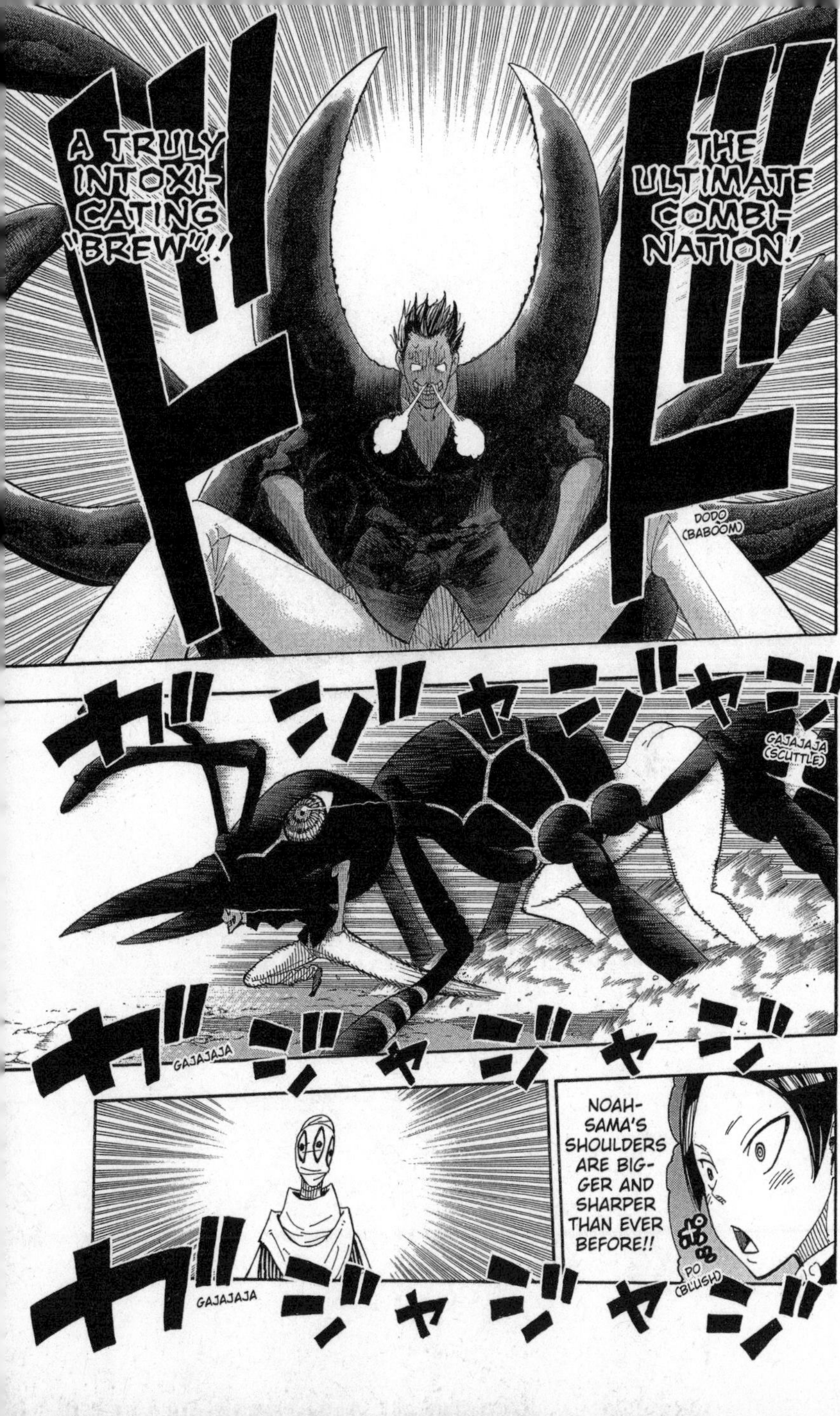
THE ULTIMATE COMBI-NATION!
A TRULY INTOXI-CATING "BREW"!!
DODO (BABOOM)
GAJAJAJA (SCUTTLE)
GAJAJAJA
NOAH-SAMA'S SHOULDERS ARE BIG-GER AND SHARPER THAN EVER BEFORE!!
PO (BLUSH)
GAJAJAJA

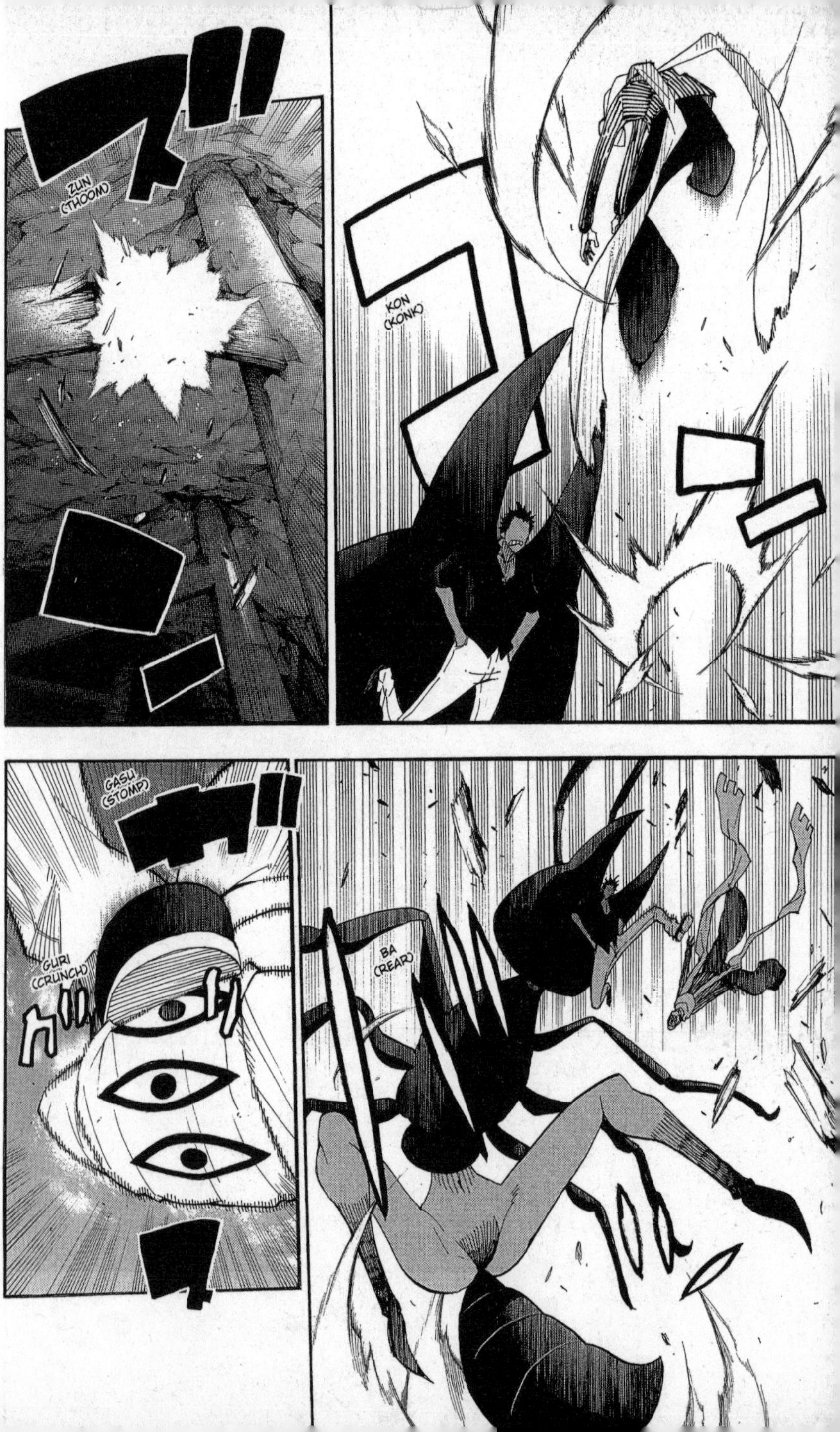
KON (KONK)
ZUN (THOOM)
BA (REAR)
GASU (STOMP)
GURI (CRUNCH)

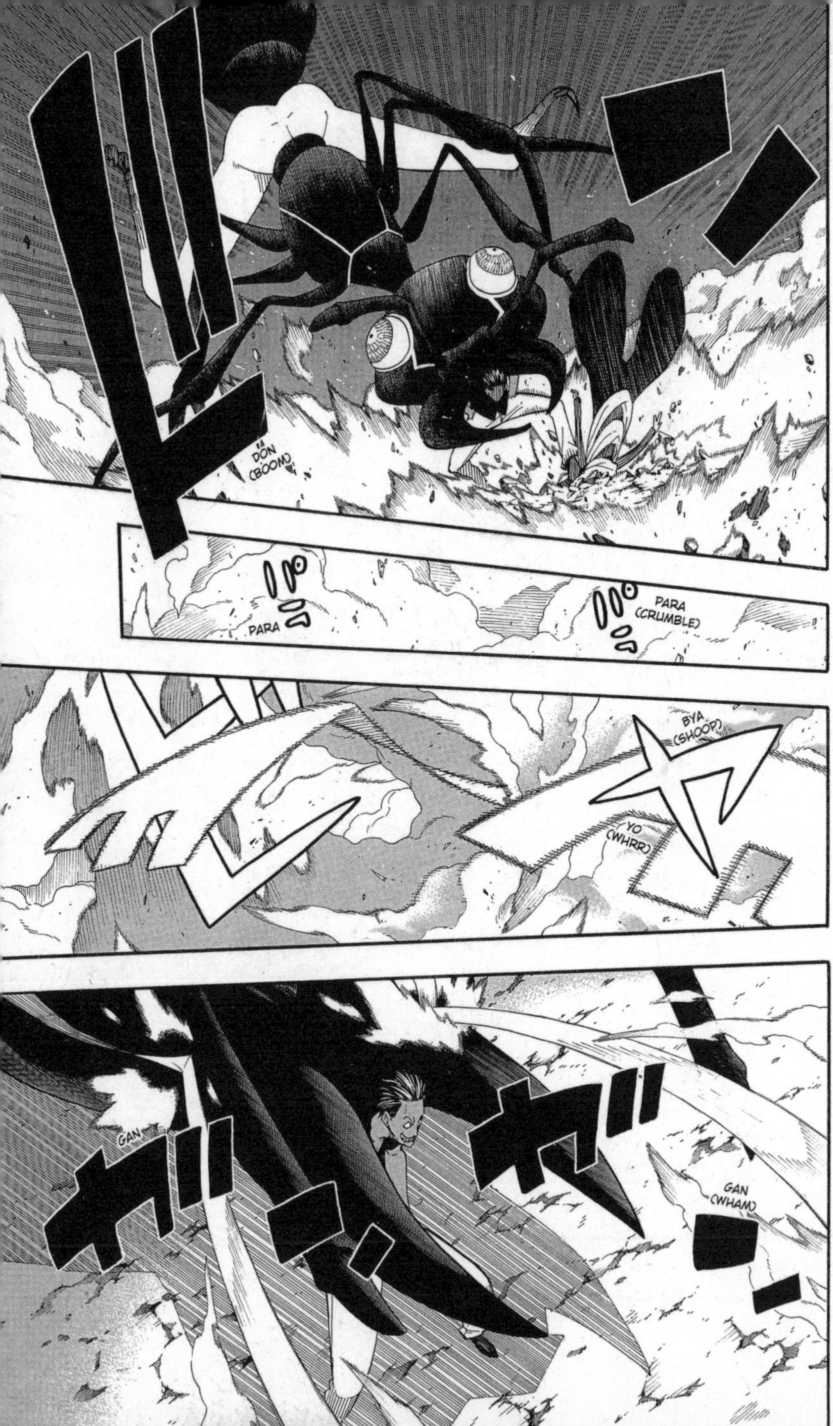
DON (BOOM)
PARA (CRUMBLE)
PARA
BYA (SHOOP)
YO (WHRR)
GAN (WHAM)
GAN

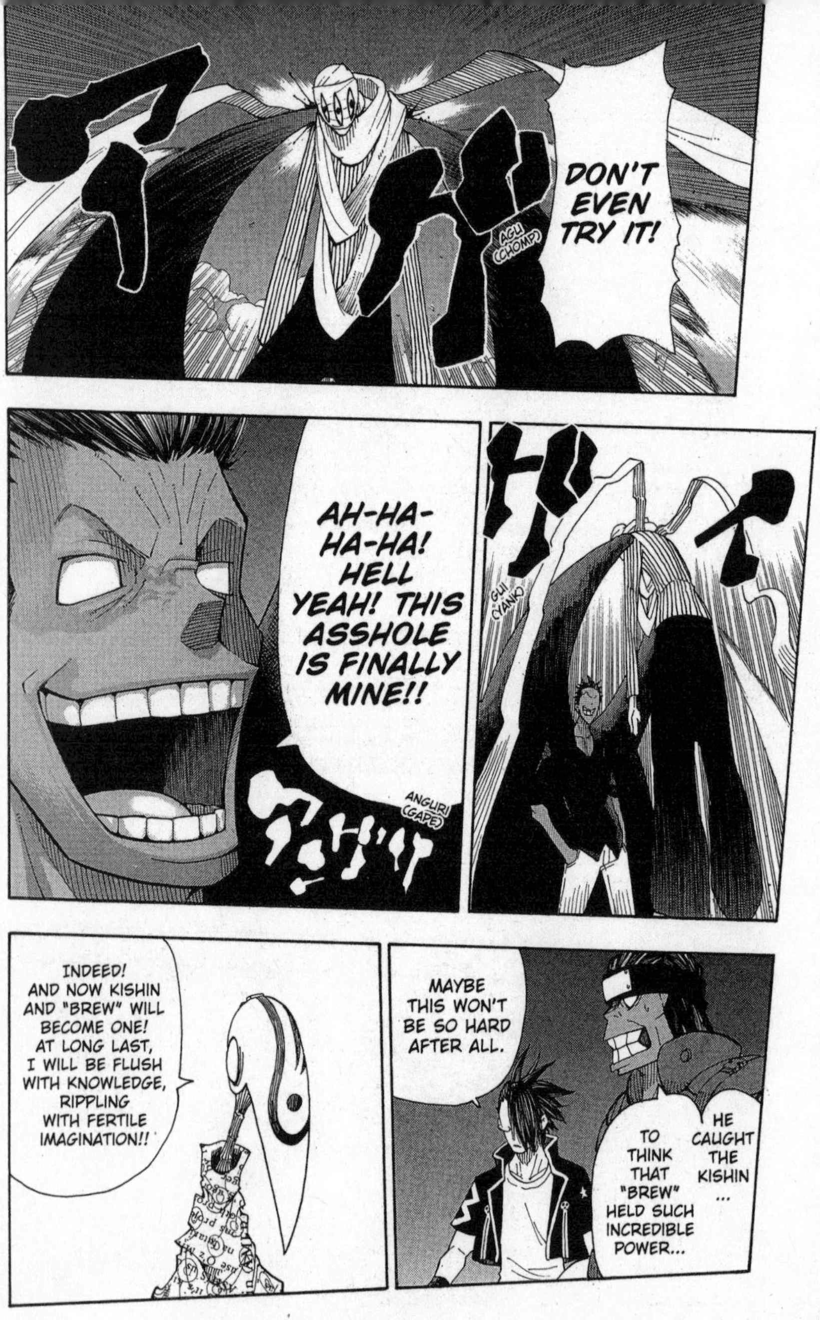
DON'T EVEN TRY IT!
AGU (CHOMP)
GUI (YANK)
AH-HA-HA-HA! HELL YEAH! THIS ASSHOLE IS FINALLY MINE!!
ANGURI (GAPE)
MAYBE THIS WON'T BE SO HARD AFTER ALL.
HE CAUGHT THE KISHIN...
TO THINK THAT "BREW" HELD SUCH INCREDIBLE POWER...
INDEED! AND NOW KISHIN AND "BREW" WILL BECOME ONE! AT LONG LAST, I WILL BE FLUSH WITH KNOWLEDGE, RIPPLING WITH FERTILE IMAGINATION!!

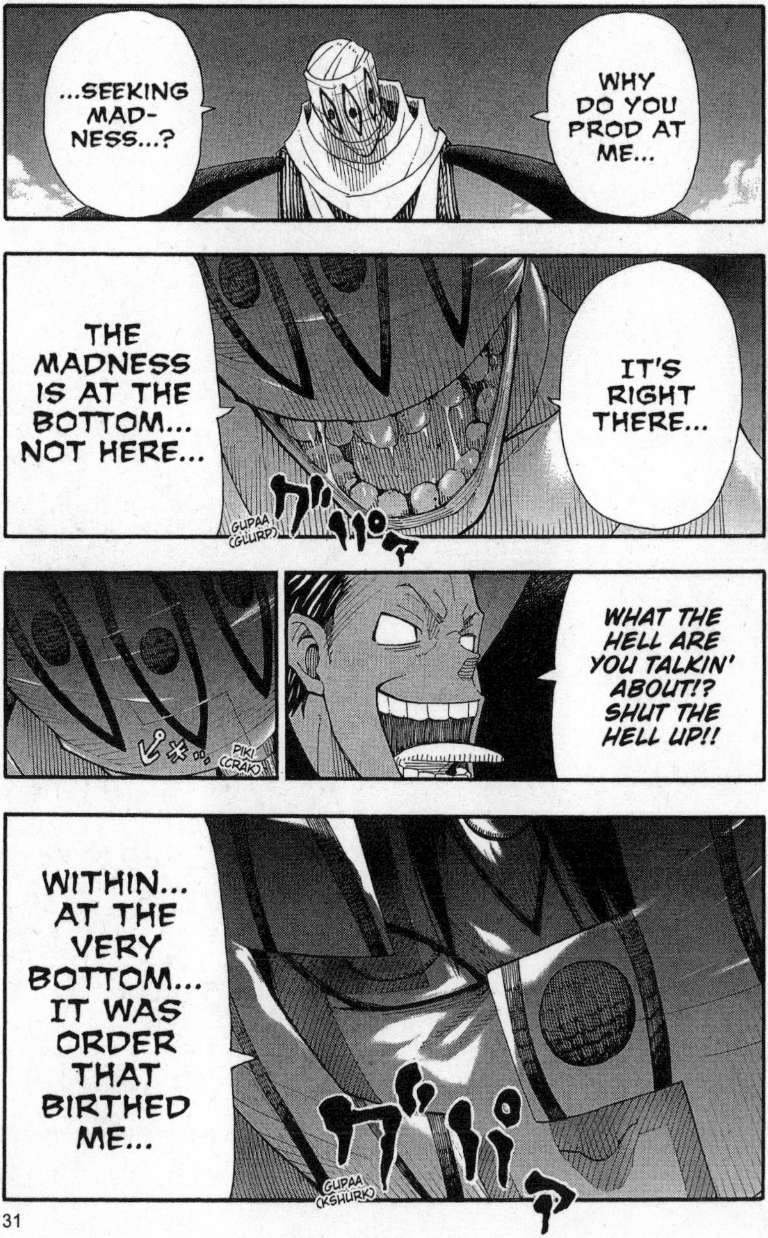
WHY DO YOU PROD AT ME...
...SEEKING MADNESS...?
IT'S RIGHT THERE...
THE MADNESS IS AT THE BOTTOM... NOT HERE...
GUPAA (GLURP)
WHAT THE HELL ARE YOU TALKIN' ABOUT!? SHUT THE HELL UP!!
PIKI (CRAK)
WITHIN... AT THE VERY BOTTOM... IT WAS ORDER THAT BIRTHED ME...
GUPAA (KSHURK)

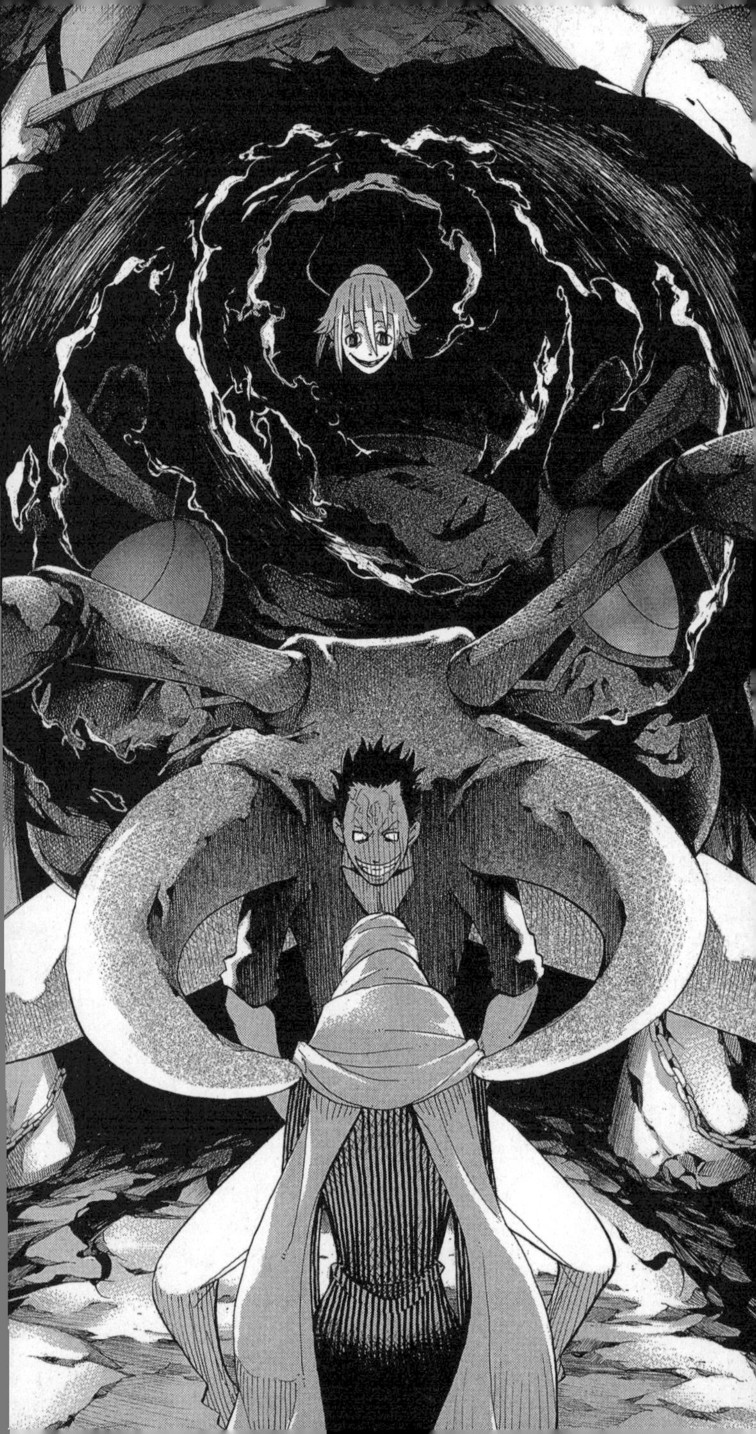

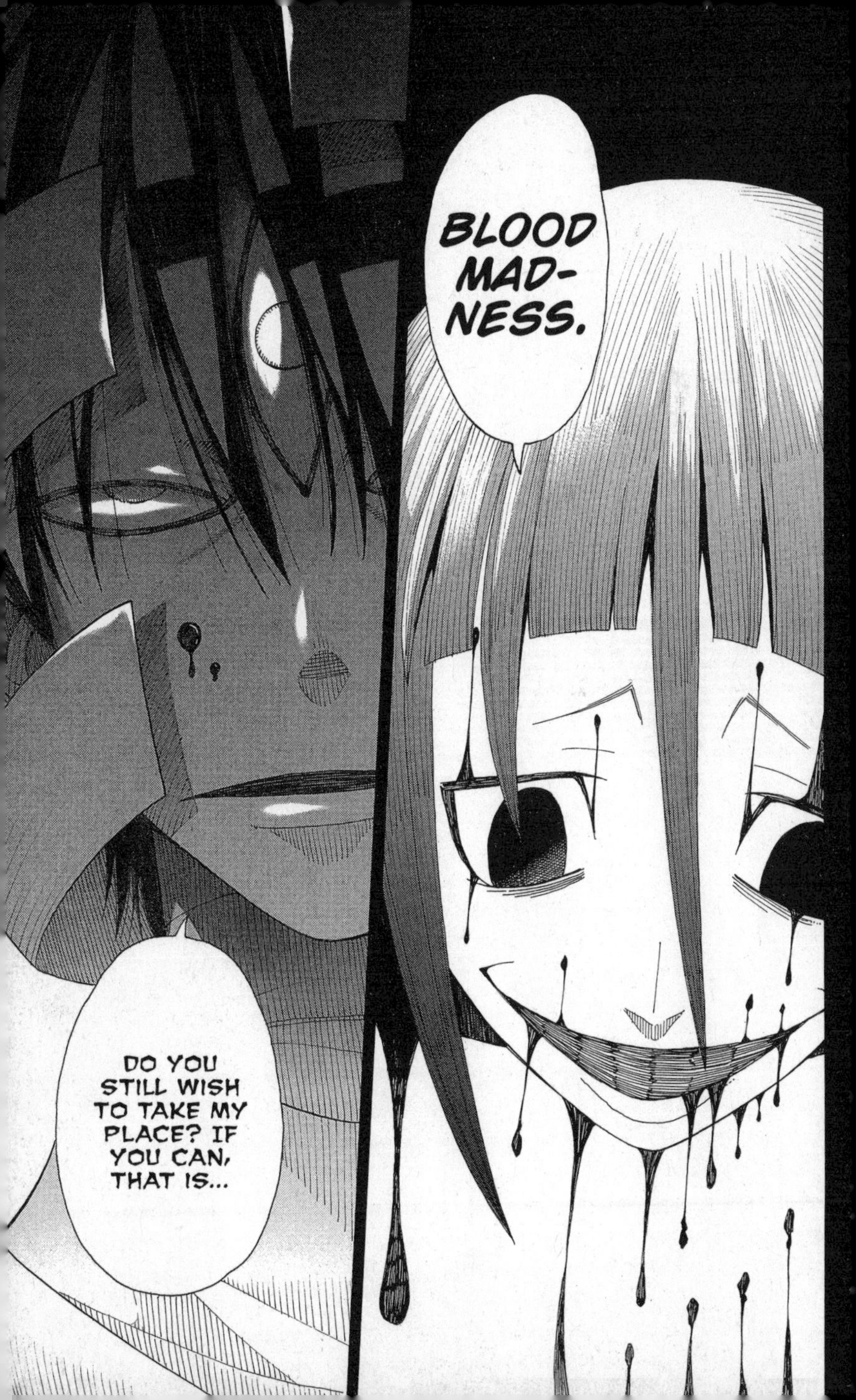
BLOOD MAD-NESS.
DO YOU STILL WISH TO TAKE MY PLACE? IF YOU CAN, THAT IS...

SOUL EATER

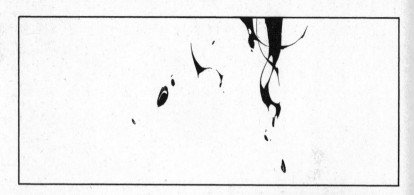

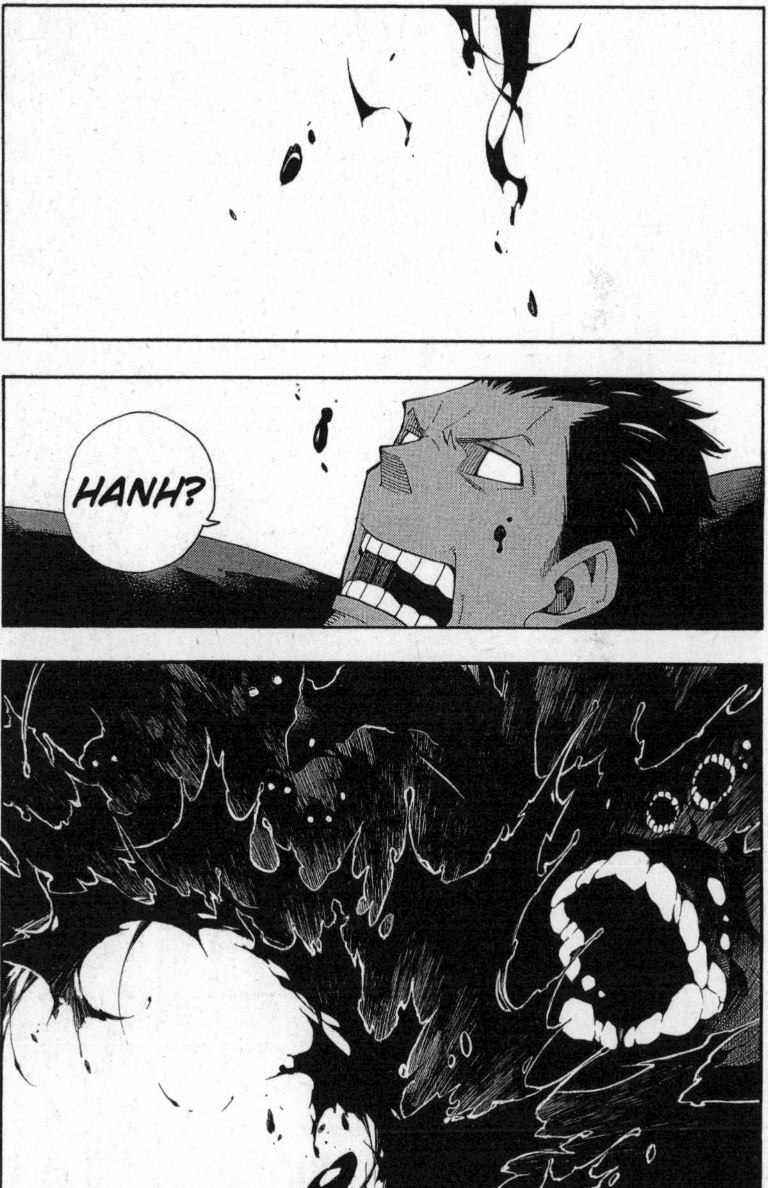
HANH?

SOUL EATER

CHAPTER 104: THE DARK SIDE OF THE MOON I

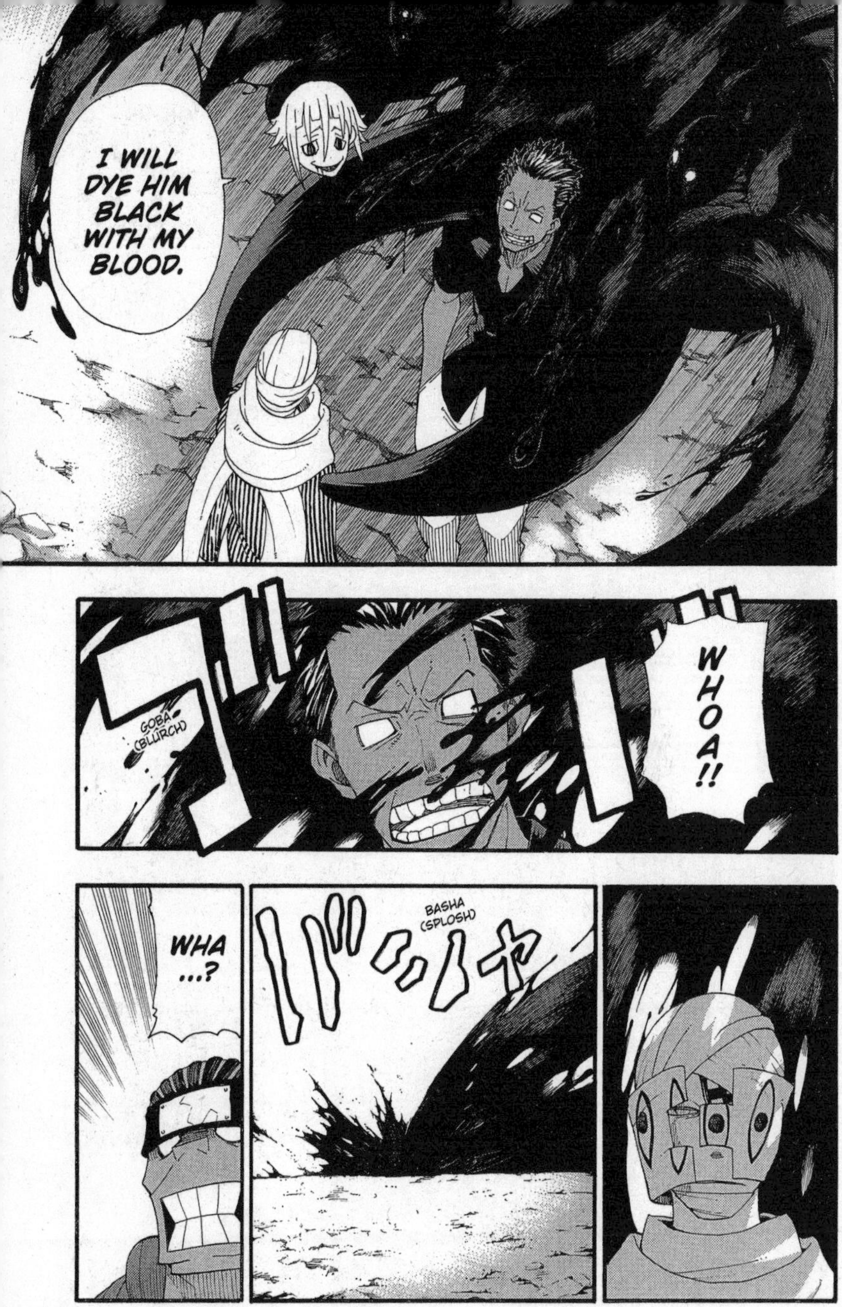
I WILL DYE HIM BLACK WITH MY BLOOD.
WHOA!!
GOBA (BLURCH)
BASHA (SPLOSH)
WHA ...?

GO ON— MELT.

WH- WHAT IS THIS !?

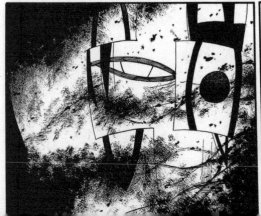

GWAAH!?

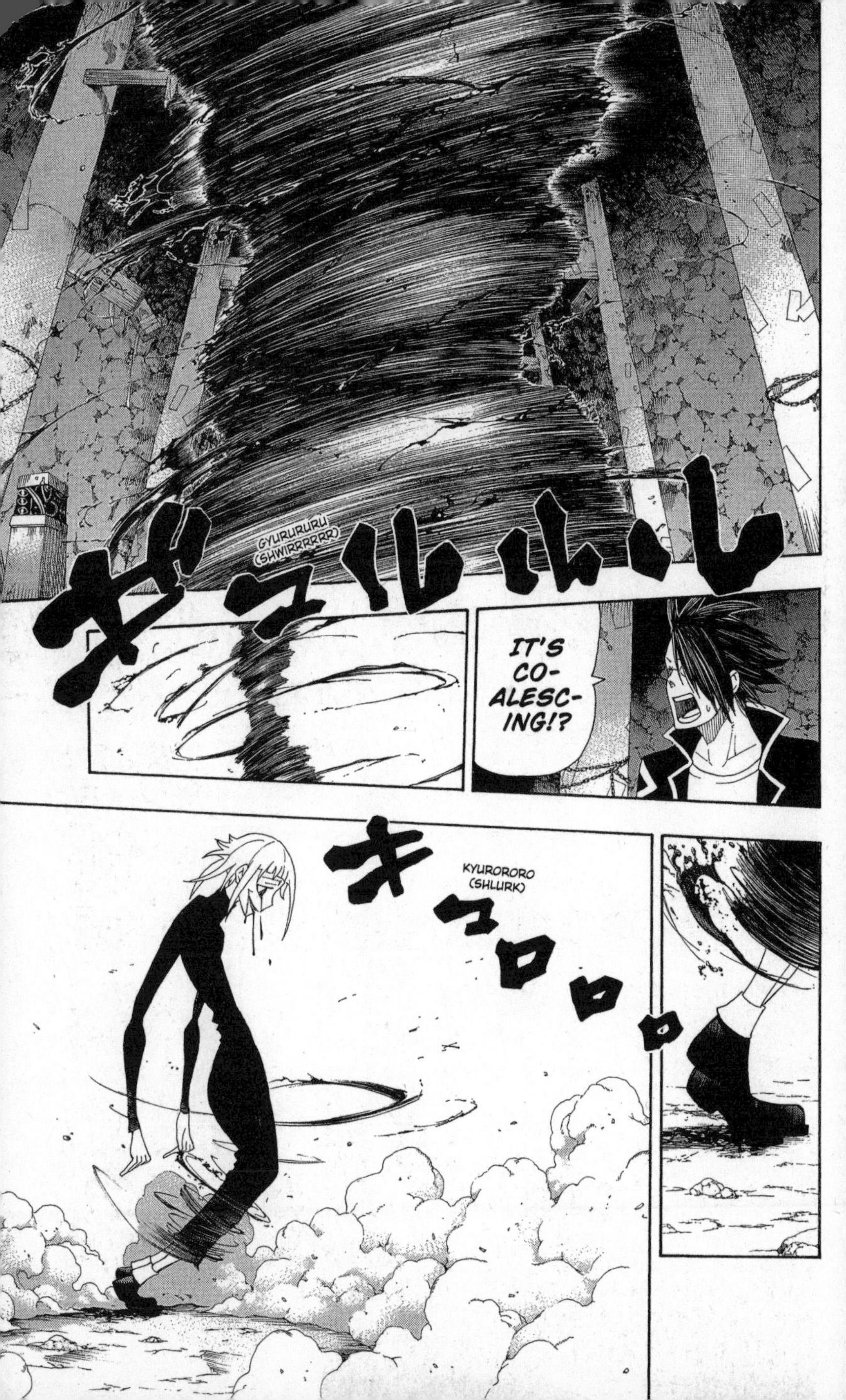
GYURURURU (SHWIRRRRRR)
IT'S CO-ALESC-ING!?
KYURORORO (SHLURK)

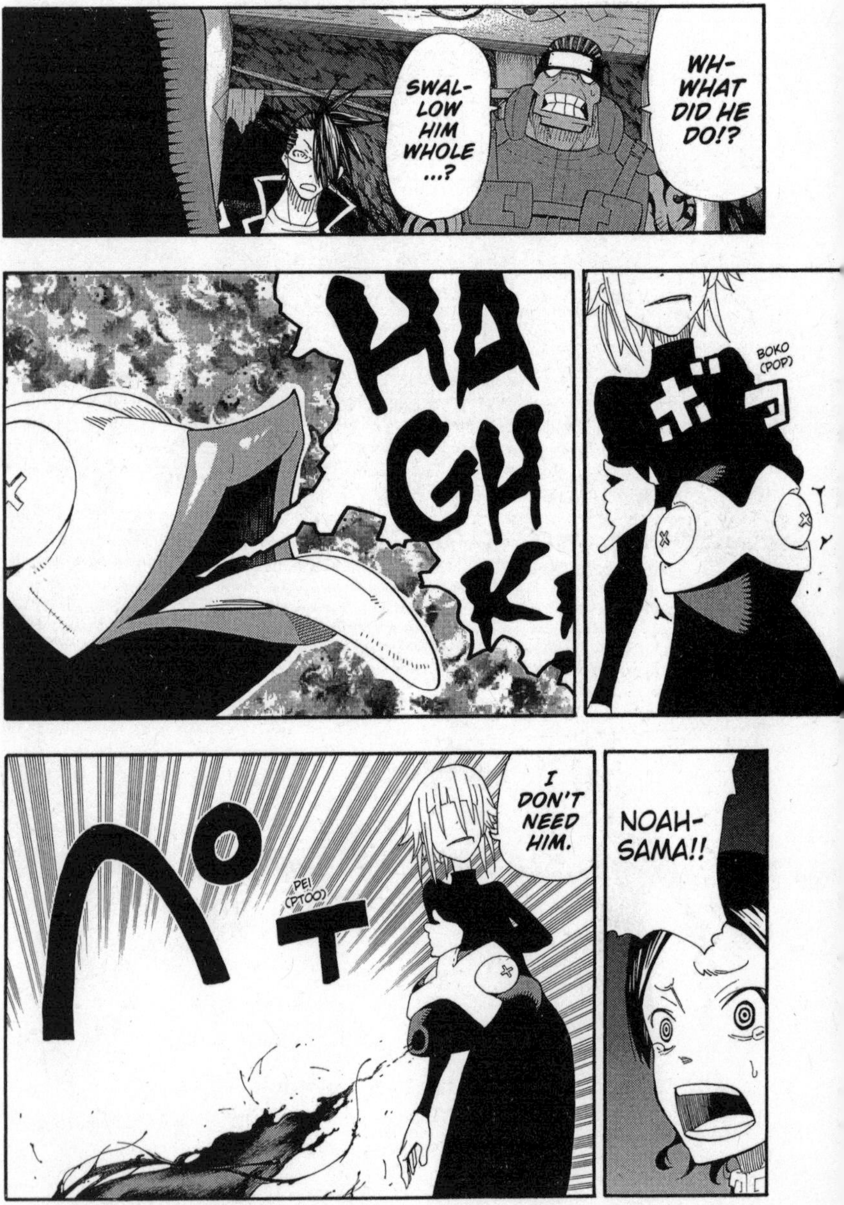
WH-WHAT DID HE DO!?
SWAL-LOW HIM WHOLE ...?
BOKO (POP)
HAGHK
NOAH-SAMA!!
I DON'T NEED HIM.
PEI (PTOO)

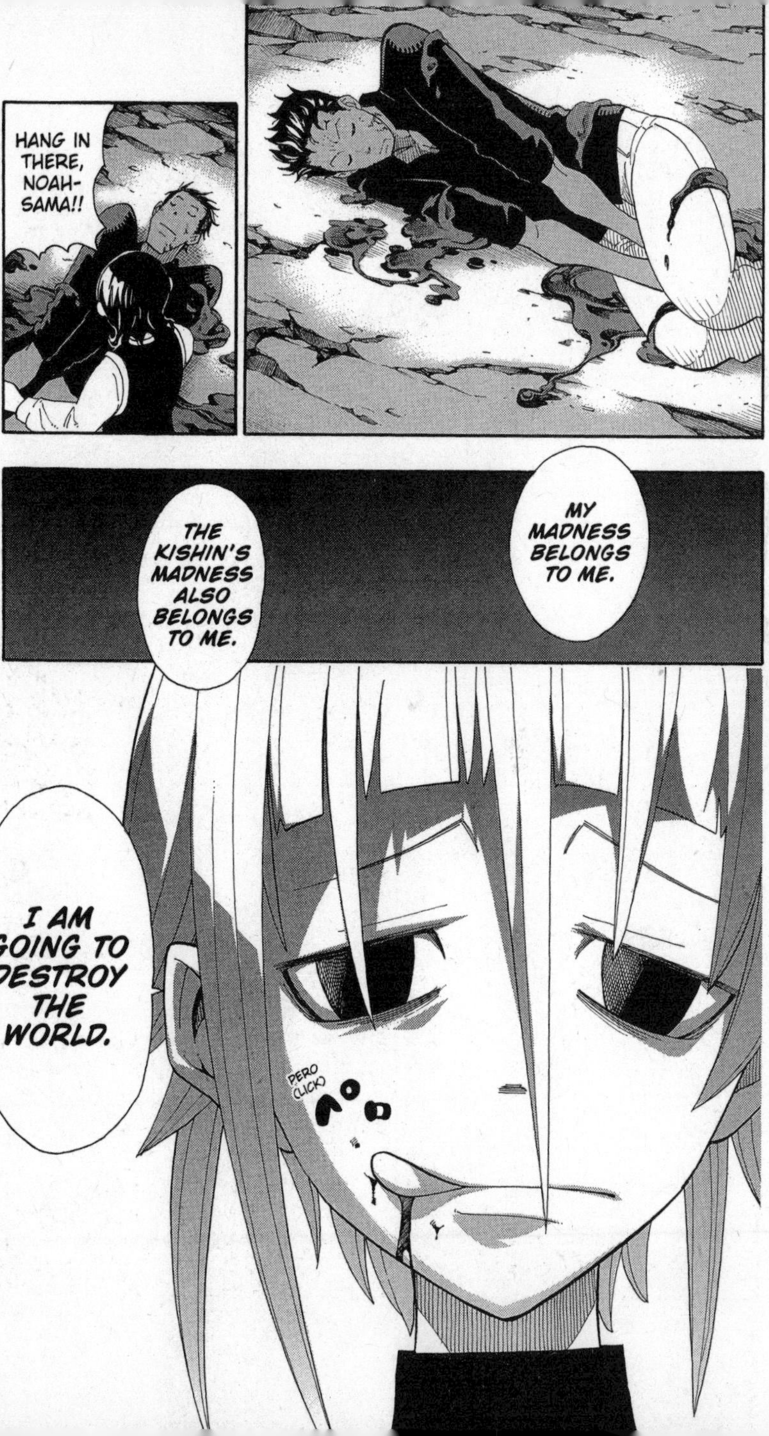
HANG IN THERE, NOAH-SAMA!!
MY MADNESS BELONGS TO ME.
THE KISHIN'S MADNESS ALSO BELONGS TO ME.
I AM GOING TO DESTROY THE WORLD.
PERO (LICK)

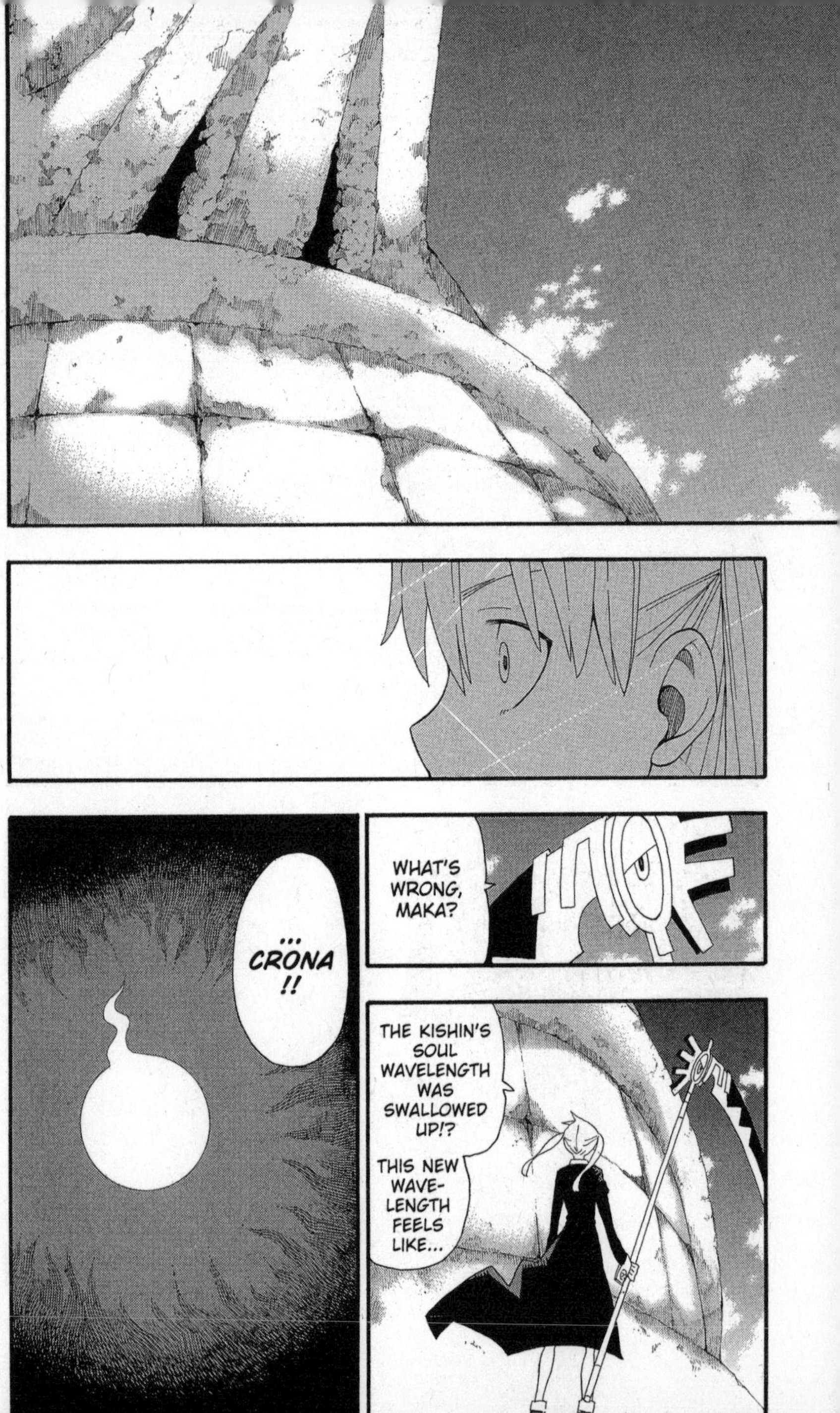
WHAT'S WRONG, MAKA?
THE KISHIN'S SOUL WAVELENGTH WAS SWALLOWED UP!?
THIS NEW WAVE-LENGTH FEELS LIKE...
...CRONA!!

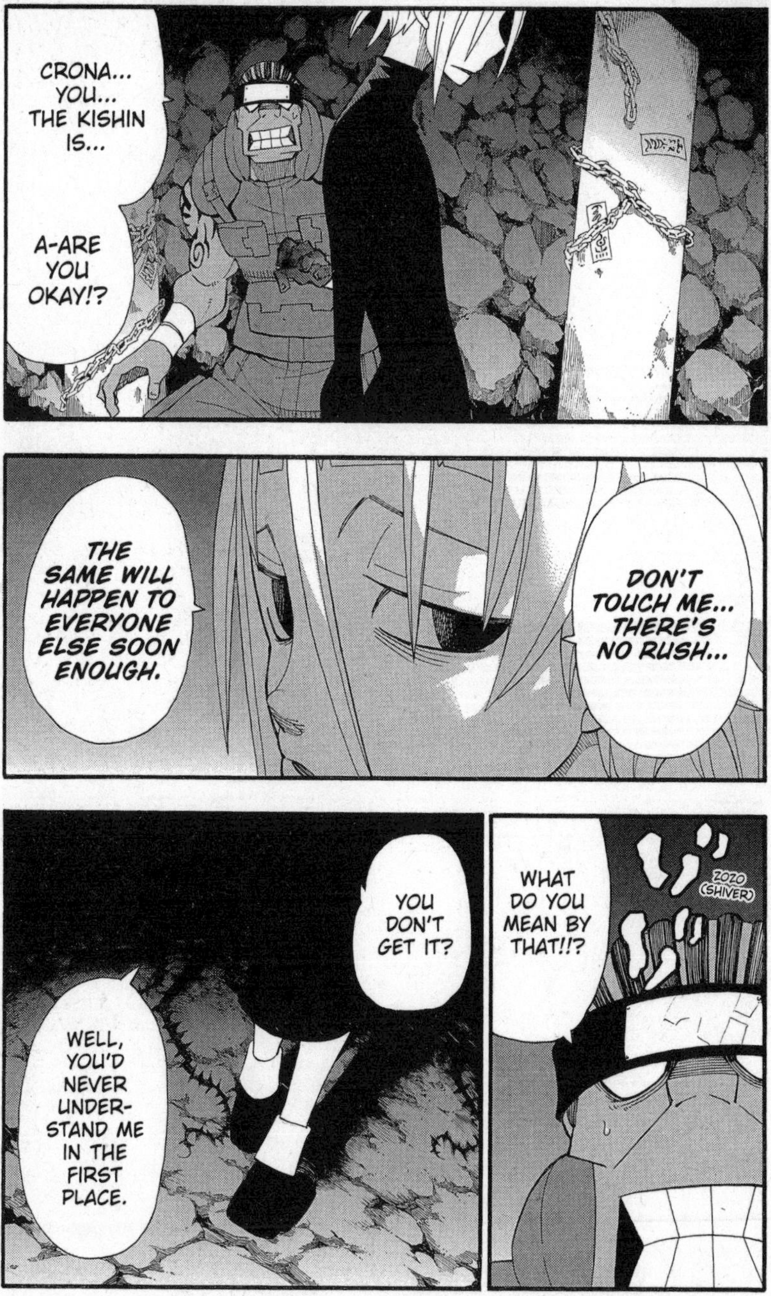
CRONA... YOU... THE KISHIN IS...
A-ARE YOU OKAY!?
DON'T TOUCH ME... THERE'S NO RUSH...
THE SAME WILL HAPPEN TO EVERYONE ELSE SOON ENOUGH.
ZOZO (SHIVER)
WHAT DO YOU MEAN BY THAT!!?
YOU DON'T GET IT?
WELL, YOU'D NEVER UNDER-STAND ME IN THE FIRST PLACE.

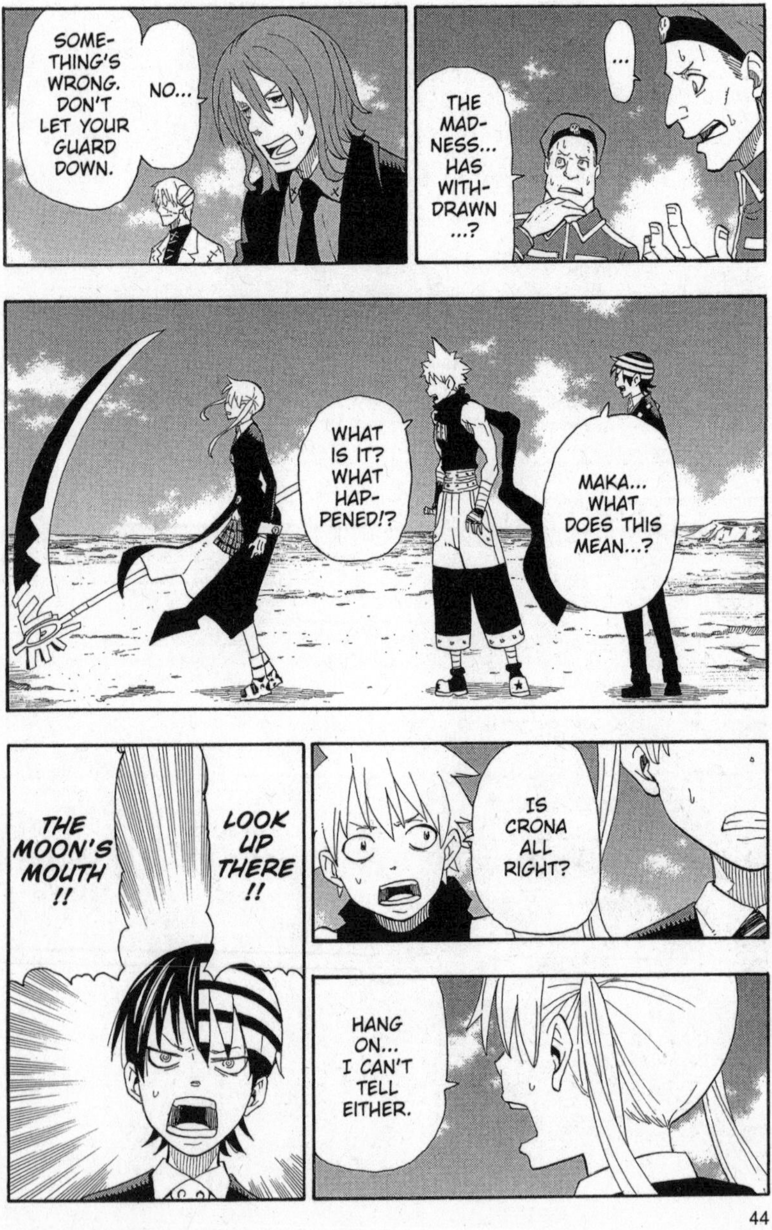
...
THE MADNESS... HAS WITHDRAWN...?
NO...
SOMETHING'S WRONG. DON'T LET YOUR GUARD DOWN.
MAKA... WHAT DOES THIS MEAN...?
WHAT IS IT? WHAT HAPPENED!?
IS CRONA ALL RIGHT?
HANG ON... I CAN'T TELL EITHER.
LOOK UP THERE!!
THE MOON'S MOUTH!!

!!
SHURURU (SLITHER)
WHAT IS THAT !!?
GOGOGOGO (RRRUMBLE)

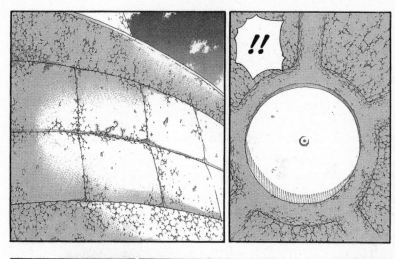

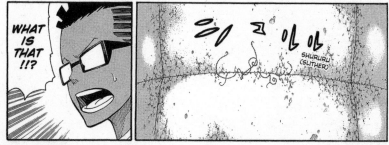

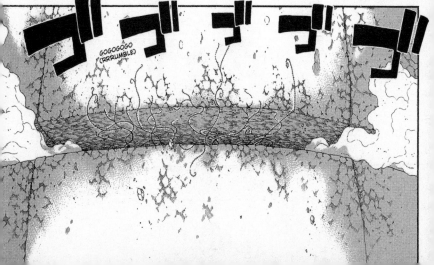

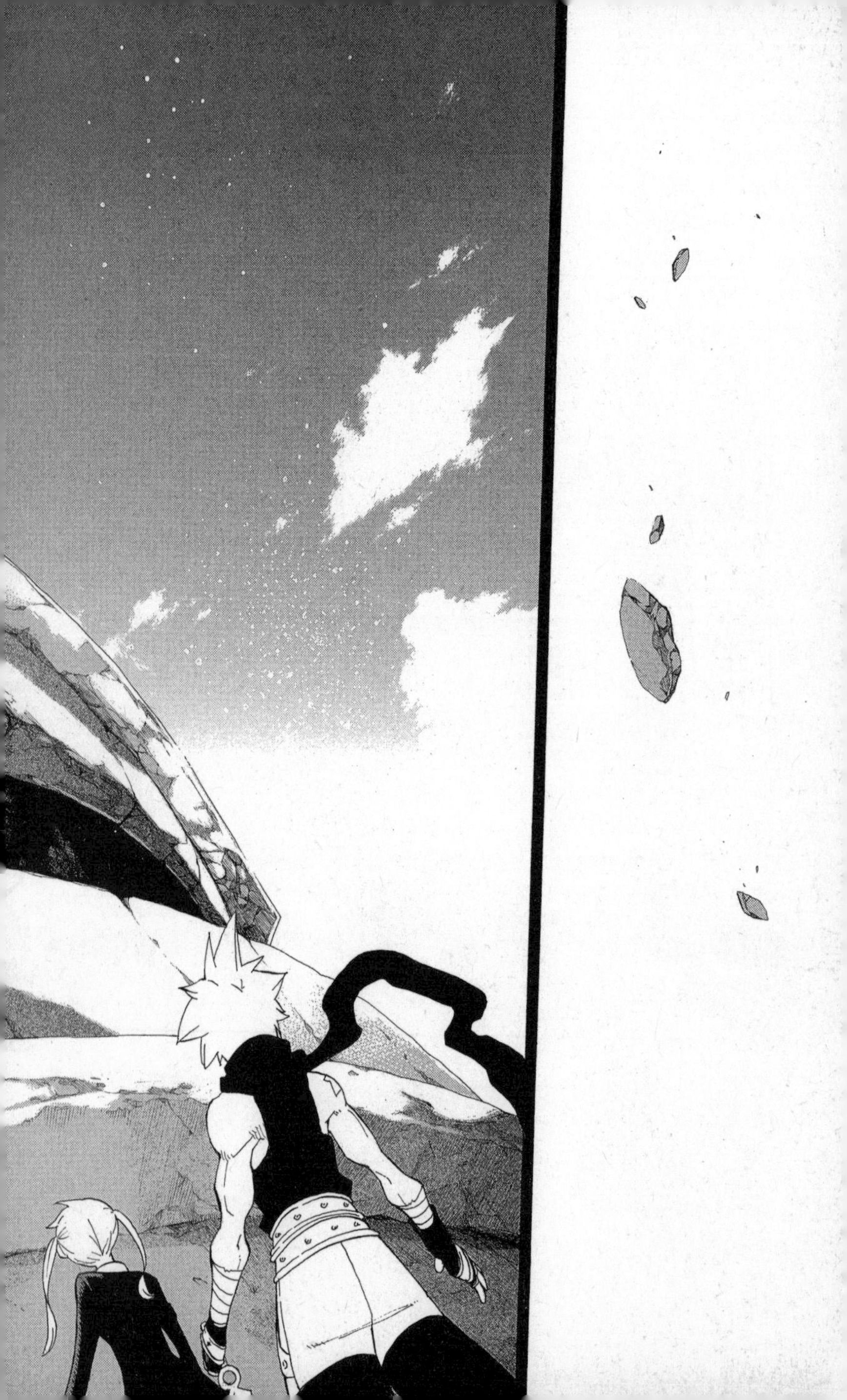

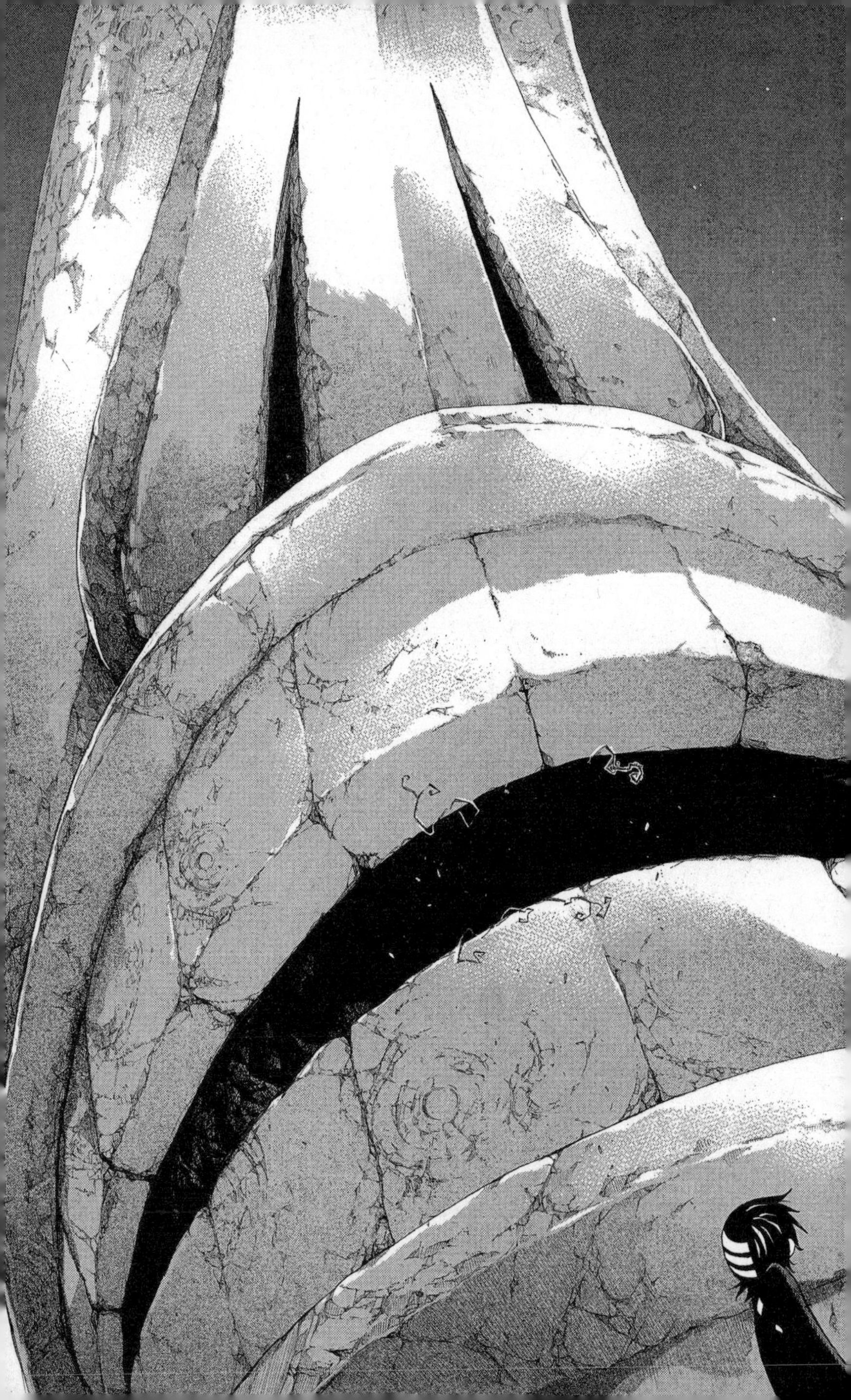

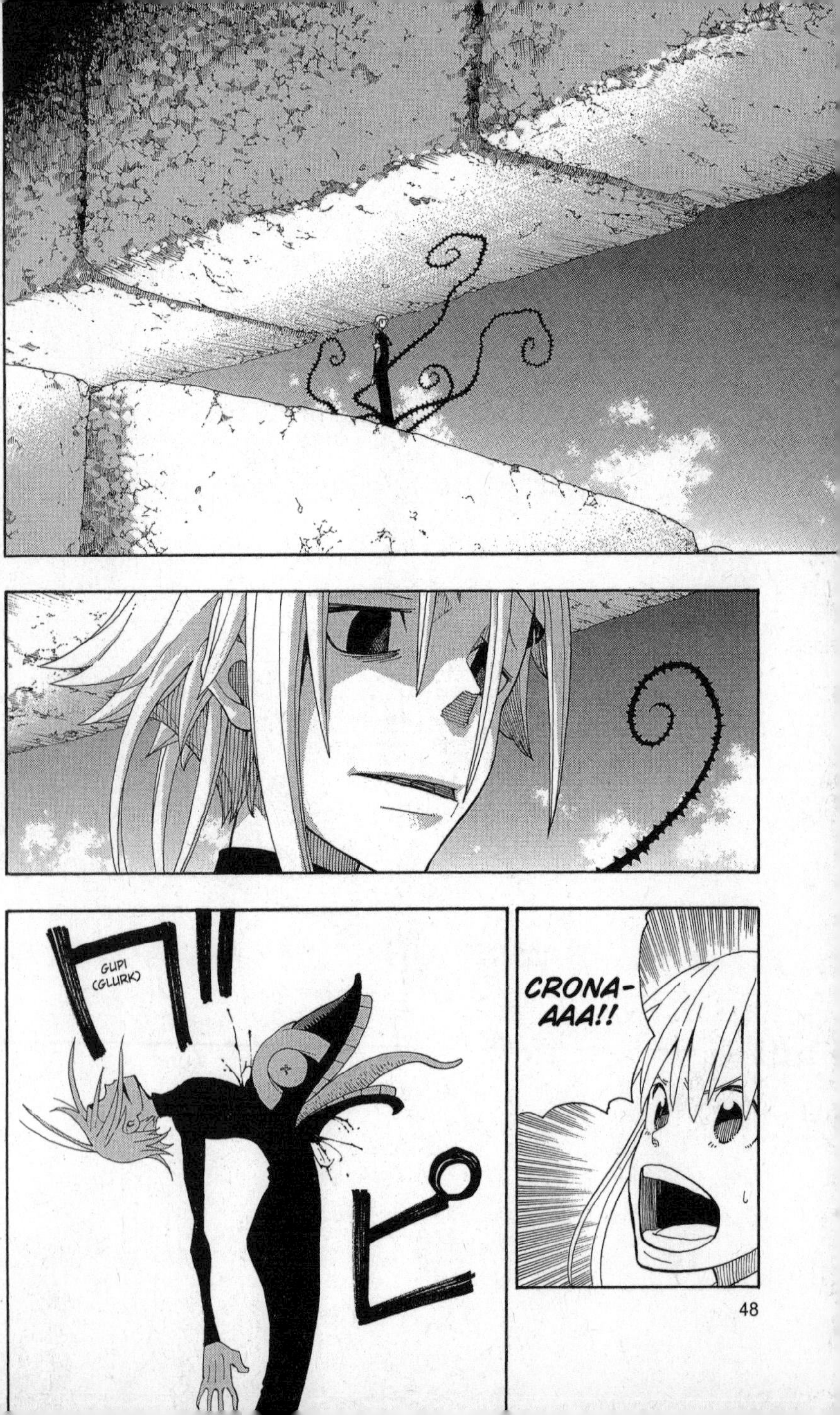
CRONA-AAA!!
GUPI (GLURK)

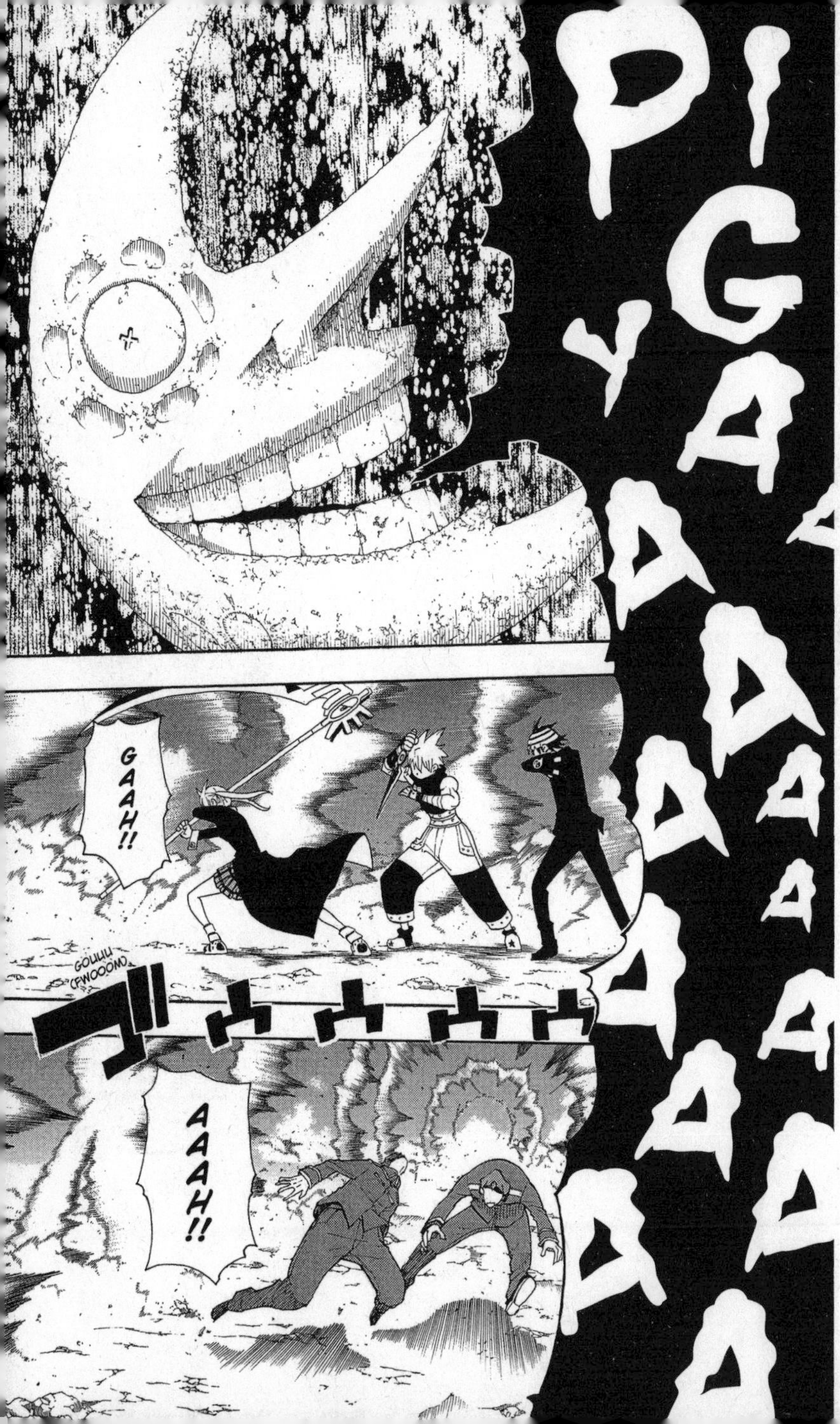
PIGYAAAAAAAAAAAAAAAAAAA
GAAH!!
GOUUU (FWOOOM)
AAAAH!!

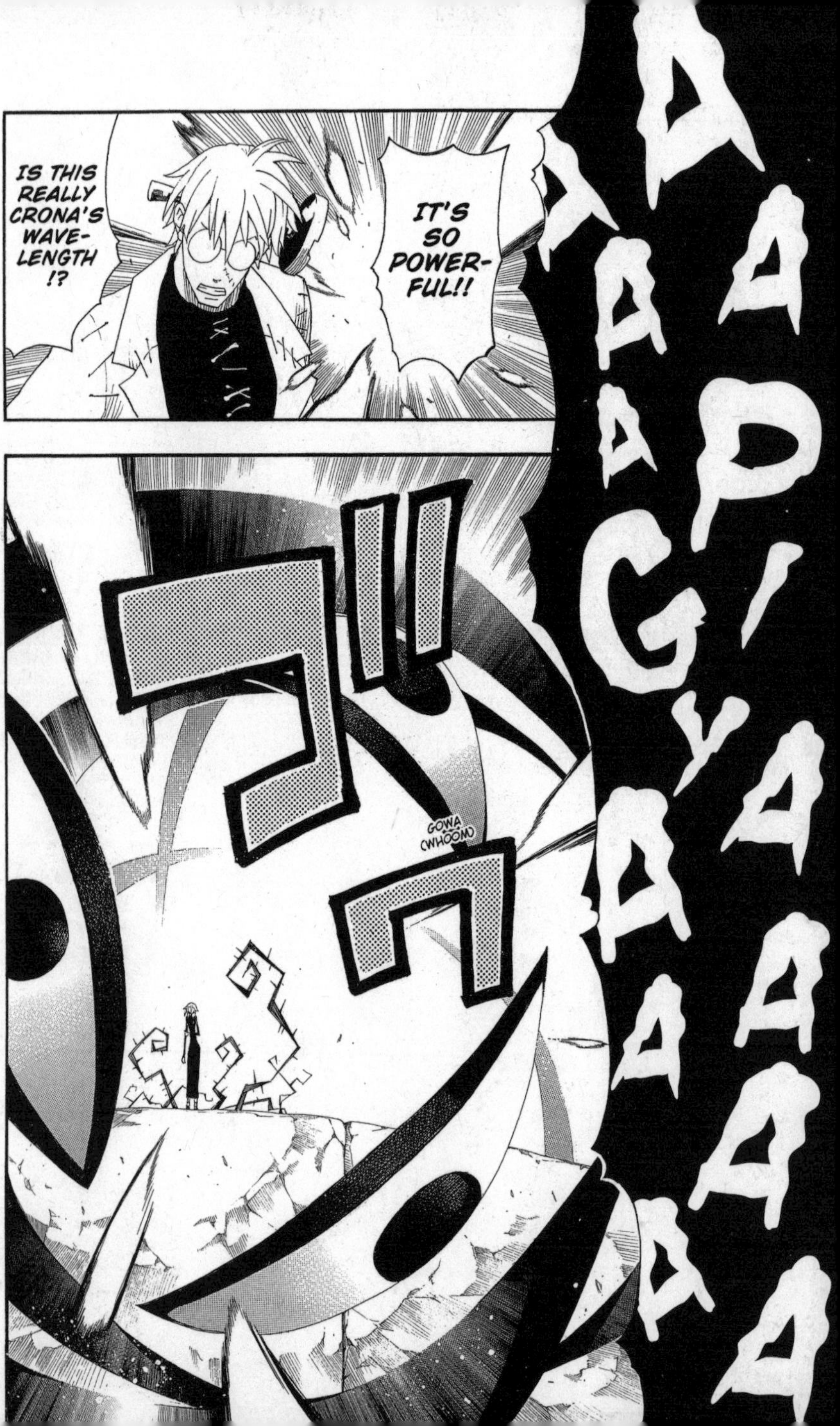
IT'S SO POWERFUL!!
IS THIS REALLY CRONA'S WAVELENGTH!?
GOWA (WHOOM)

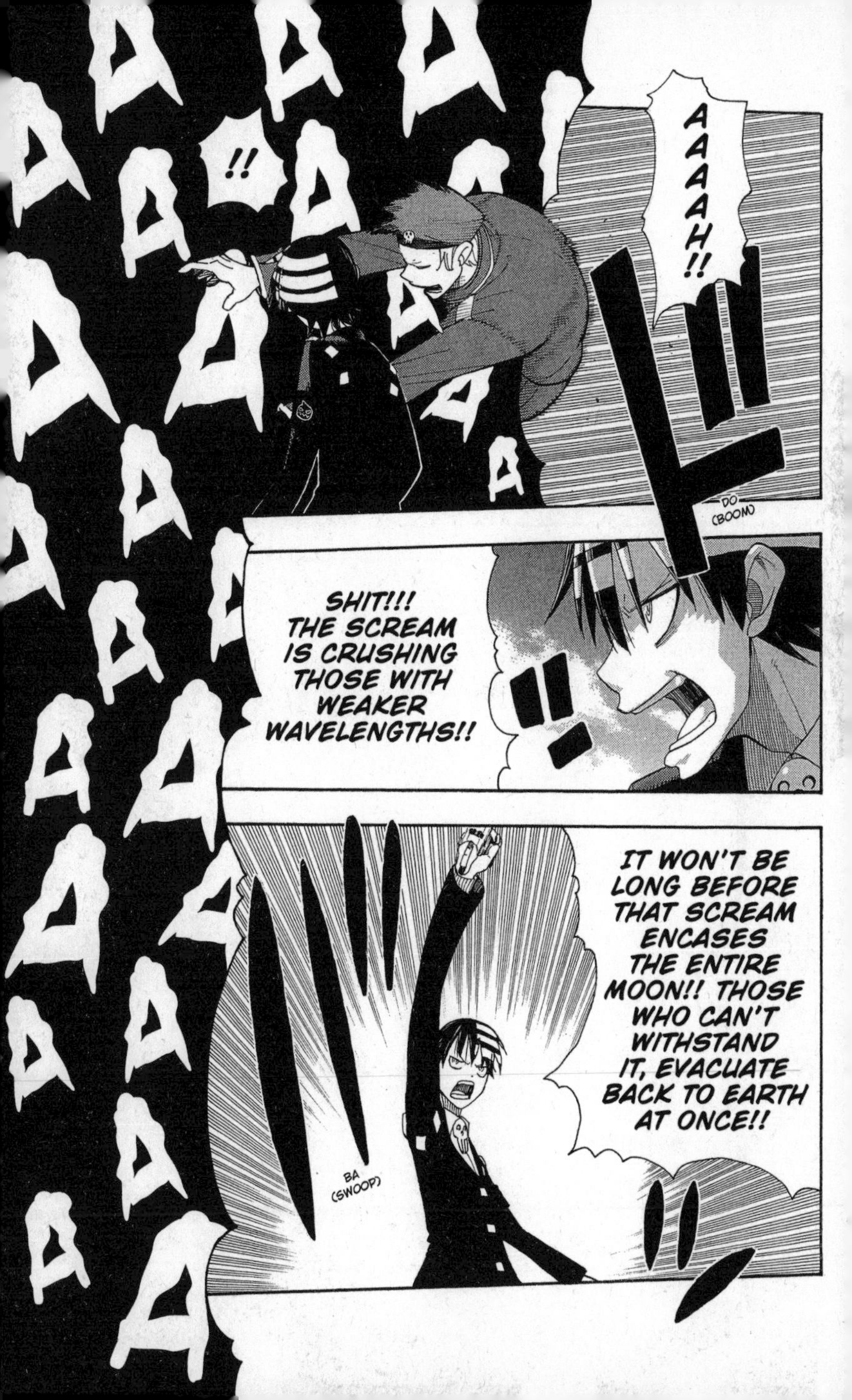
AAAAAH!!
!!
AAAAAAAAAAAAAAAAAAAAAAAAAAAAAAAAAAA
DO (BOOM)
SHIT!!! THE SCREAM IS CRUSHING THOSE WITH WEAKER WAVELENGTHS!!
IT WON'T BE LONG BEFORE THAT SCREAM ENCASES THE ENTIRE MOON!! THOSE WHO CAN'T WITHSTAND IT, EVACUATE BACK TO EARTH AT ONCE!!
BA (SWOOP)

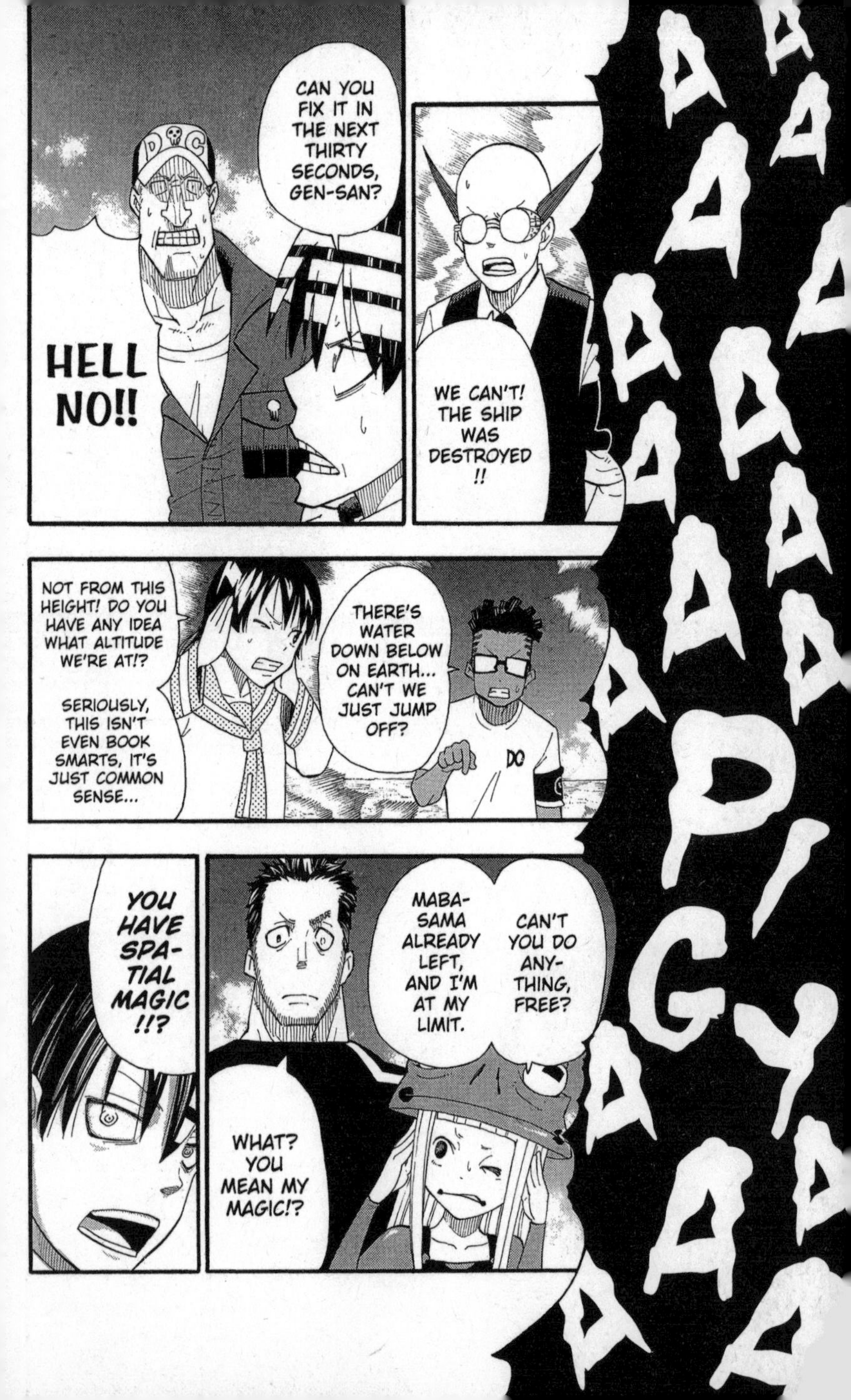
WE CAN'T! THE SHIP WAS DESTROYED!!
CAN YOU FIX IT IN THE NEXT THIRTY SECONDS, GEN-SAN?
HELL NO!!
THERE'S WATER DOWN BELOW ON EARTH... CAN'T WE JUST JUMP OFF?
NOT FROM THIS HEIGHT! DO YOU HAVE ANY IDEA WHAT ALTITUDE WE'RE AT!?
SERIOUSLY, THIS ISN'T EVEN BOOK SMARTS, IT'S JUST COMMON SENSE...
CAN'T YOU DO ANY-THING, FREE?
MABA-SAMA ALREADY LEFT, AND I'M AT MY LIMIT.
WHAT? YOU MEAN MY MAGIC!?
YOU HAVE SPA-TIAL MAGIC!!?

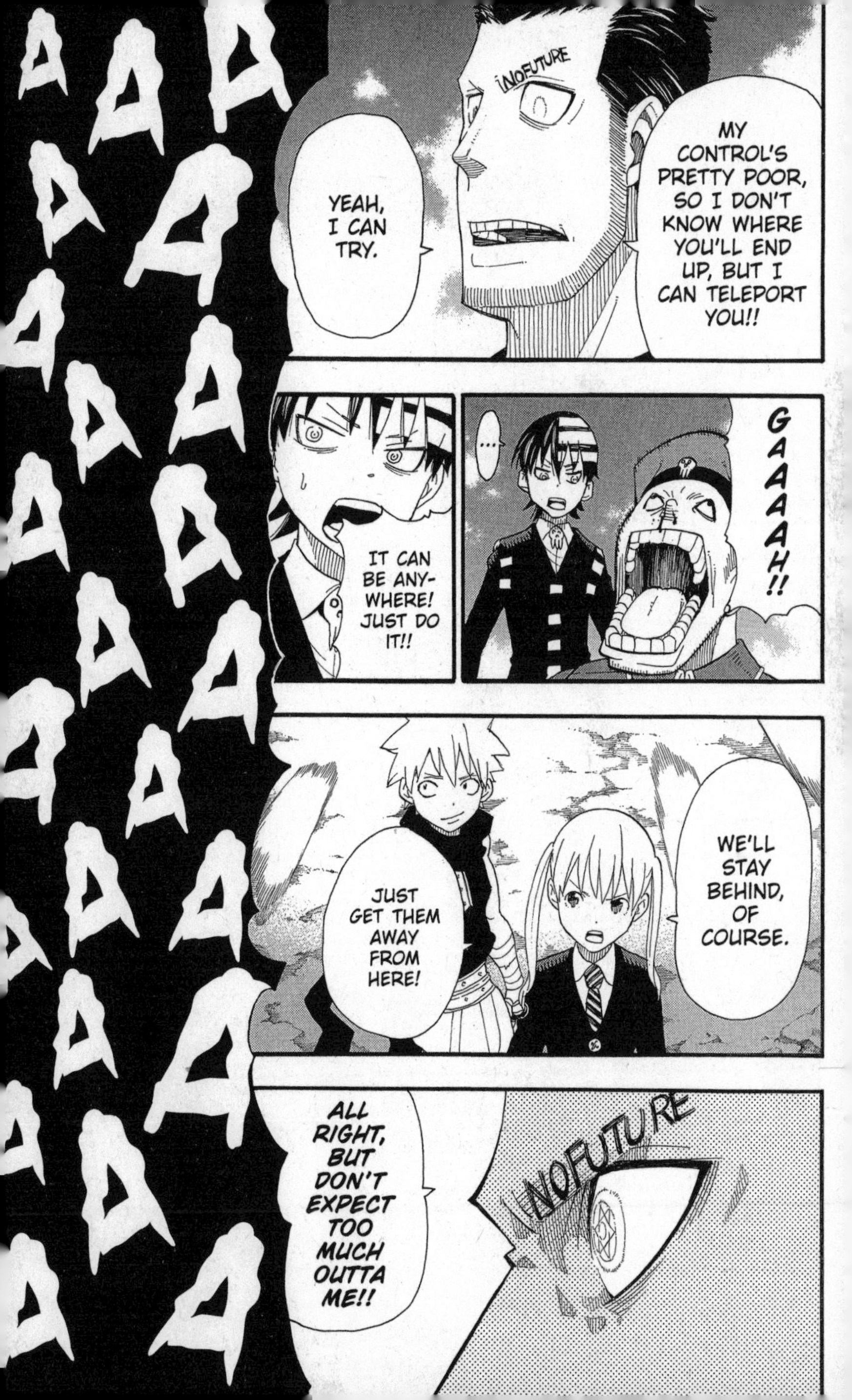
NOFUTURE
MY CONTROL'S PRETTY POOR, SO I DON'T KNOW WHERE YOU'LL END UP, BUT I CAN TELEPORT YOU!!
YEAH, I CAN TRY.
GAAAAAH!!
...
IT CAN BE ANY-WHERE! JUST DO IT!!
WE'LL STAY BEHIND, OF COURSE.
JUST GET THEM AWAY FROM HERE!
NOFUTURE
ALL RIGHT, BUT DON'T EXPECT TOO MUCH OUTTA ME!!

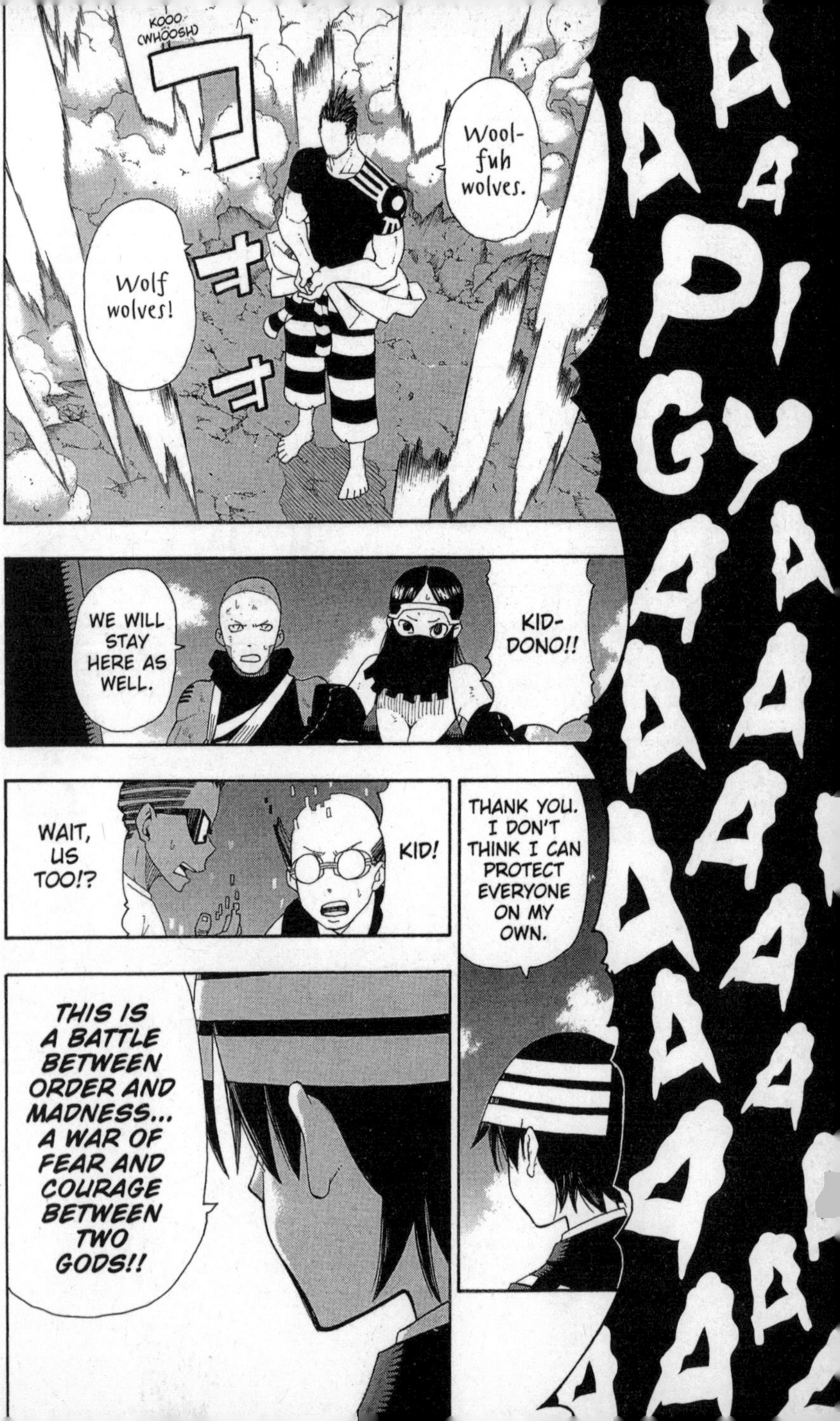
AAPIGYAAAAAAAAAAAAAAAAAA
KOOO (WHOOSH)
Wool-fuh wolves.
Wolf wolves!
KID-DONO!!
WE WILL STAY HERE AS WELL.
THANK YOU. I DON'T THINK I CAN PROTECT EVERYONE ON MY OWN.
KID!
WAIT, US TOO!?
THIS IS A BATTLE BETWEEN ORDER AND MADNESS... A WAR OF FEAR AND COURAGE BETWEEN TWO GODS!!

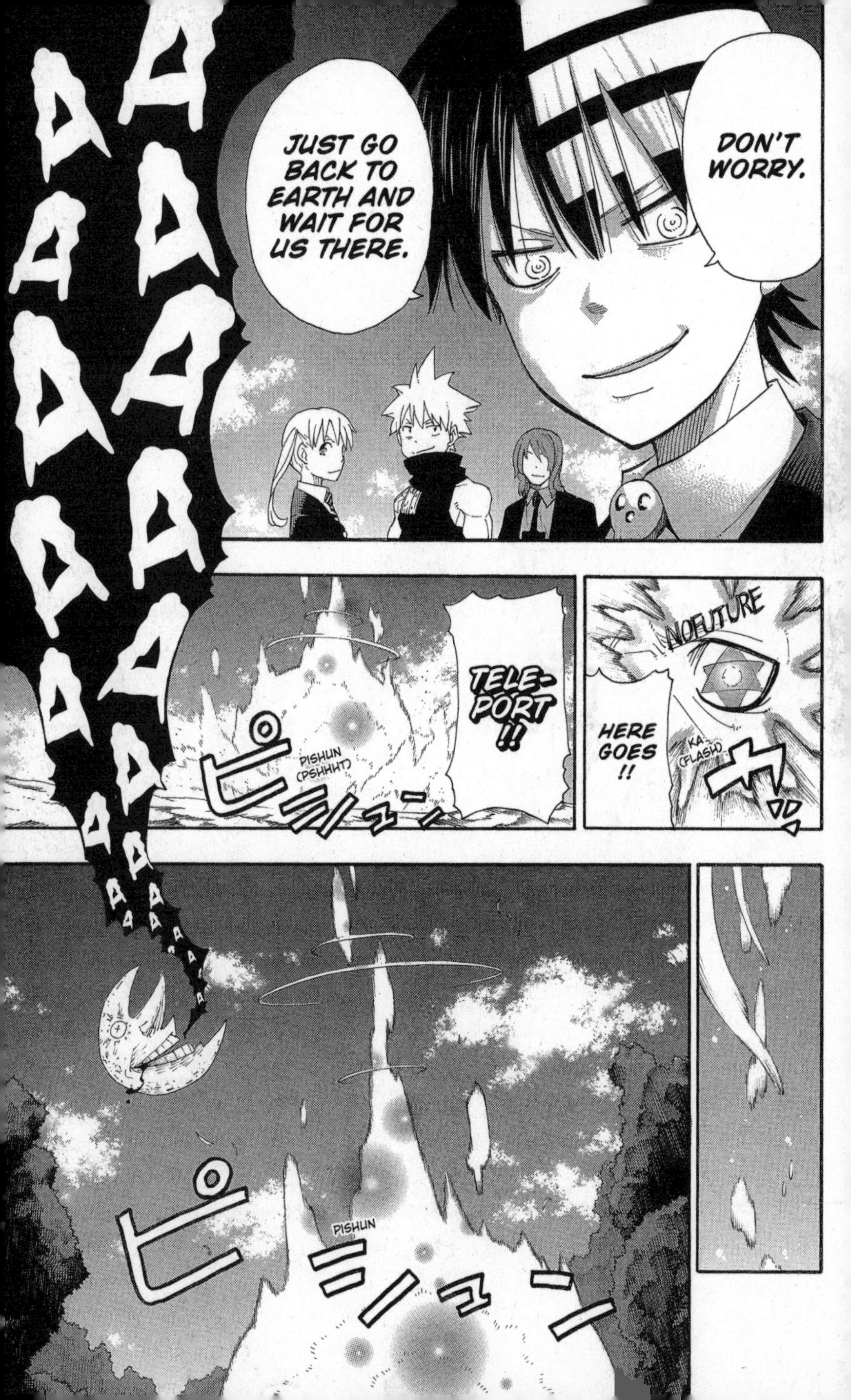
DON'T WORRY.
JUST GO BACK TO EARTH AND WAIT FOR US THERE.
NOFUTURE
HERE GOES!!
KA (FLASH)
TELE-PORT!!
PISHUN (PSHHHT)
PISHUN

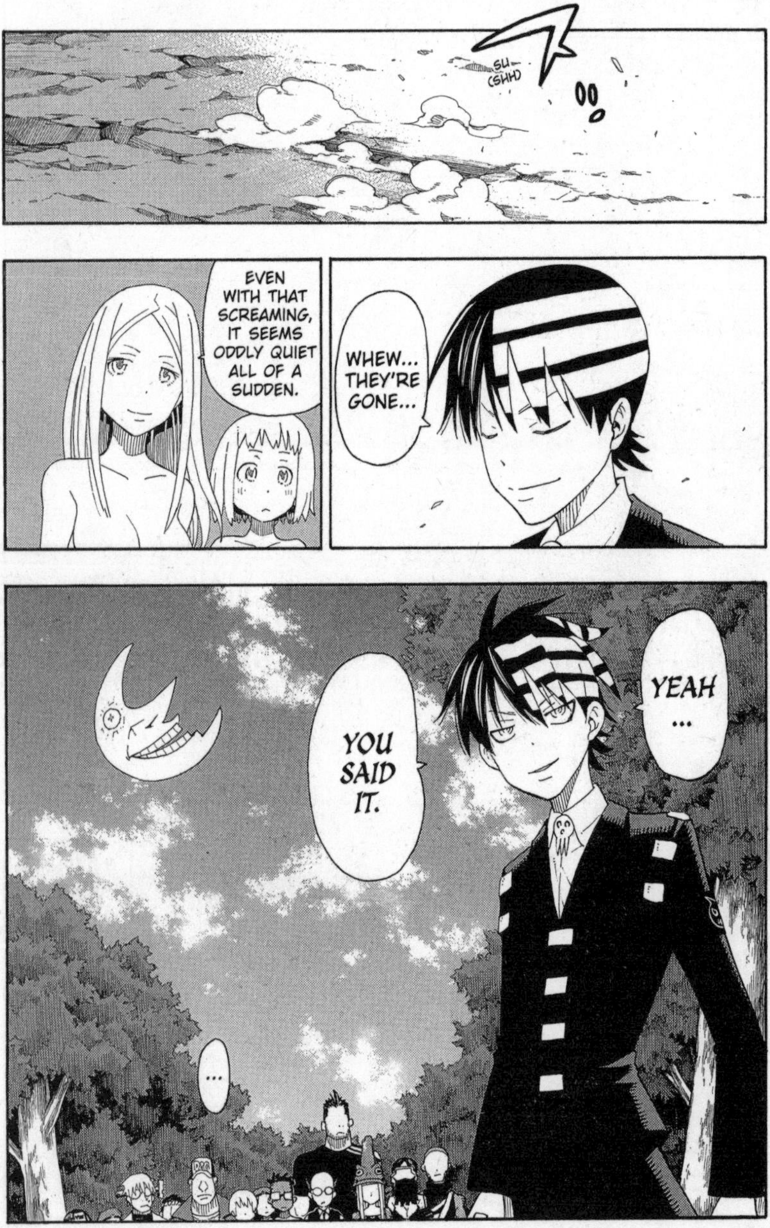
SU (SHH)
WHEW... THEY'RE GONE...
EVEN WITH THAT SCREAMING, IT SEEMS ODDLY QUIET ALL OF A SUDDEN.
YEAH ...
YOU SAID IT.
...

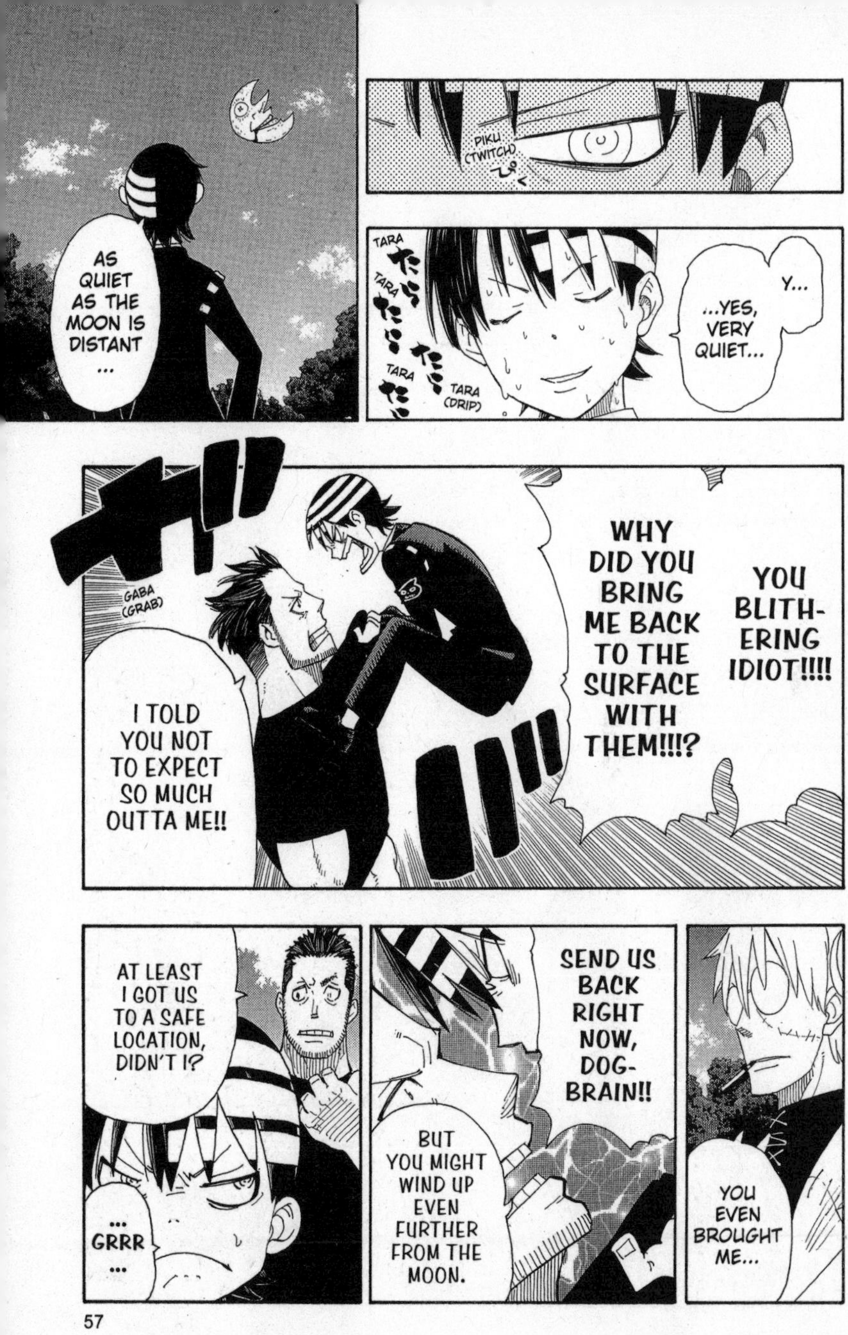
PIKU (TWITCH)
TARA TARA TARA TARA (DRIP)
Y...
...YES, VERY QUIET...
AS QUIET AS THE MOON IS DISTANT ...
YOU BLITHERING IDIOT!!!!
WHY DID YOU BRING ME BACK TO THE SURFACE WITH THEM!!!?
GABA (GRAB)
I TOLD YOU NOT TO EXPECT SO MUCH OUTTA ME!!
YOU EVEN BROUGHT ME...
SEND US BACK RIGHT NOW, DOG-BRAIN!!
BUT YOU MIGHT WIND UP EVEN FURTHER FROM THE MOON.
AT LEAST I GOT US TO A SAFE LOCATION, DIDN'T I?
... GRRR ...

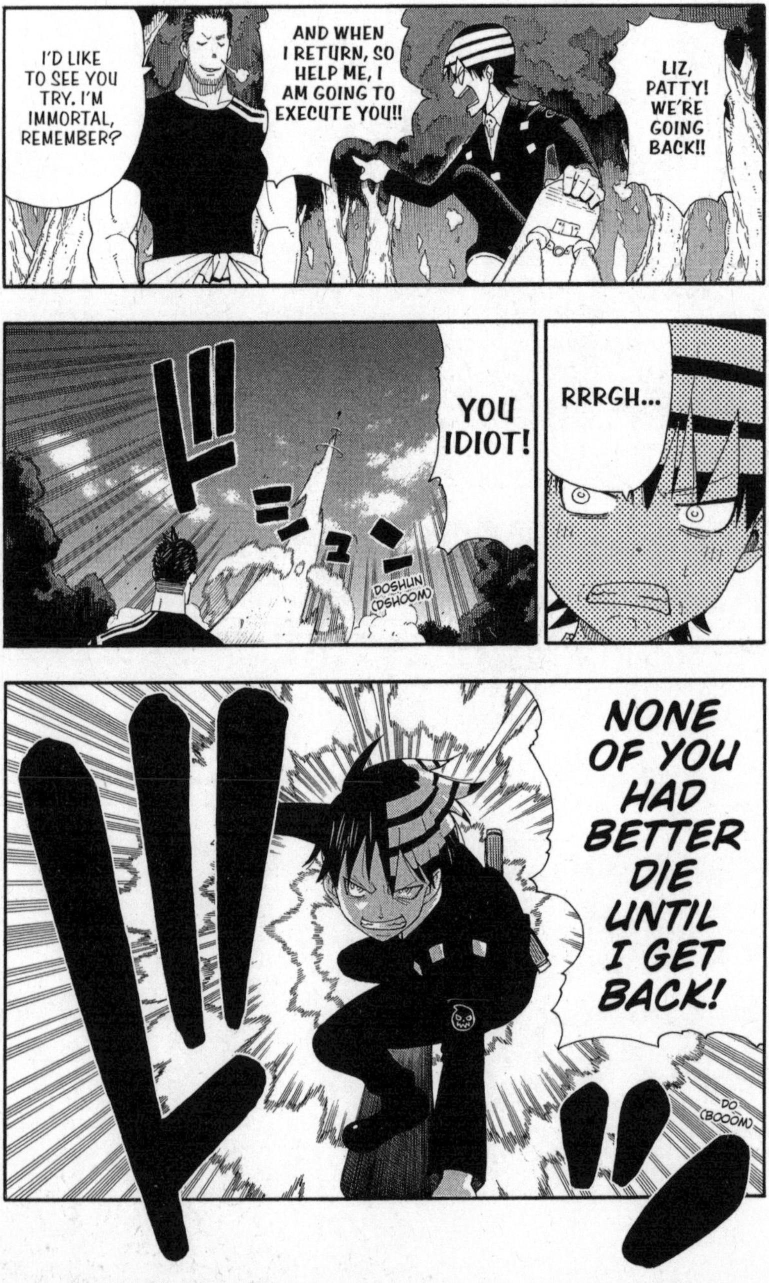
LIZ, PATTY! WE'RE GOING BACK!!
AND WHEN I RETURN, SO HELP ME, I AM GOING TO EXECUTE YOU!!
I'D LIKE TO SEE YOU TRY. I'M IMMORTAL, REMEMBER?
RRRGH...
YOU IDIOT!
DOSHUN (DSHOOM)
NONE OF YOU HAD BETTER DIE UNTIL I GET BACK!
DO (BOOOM)

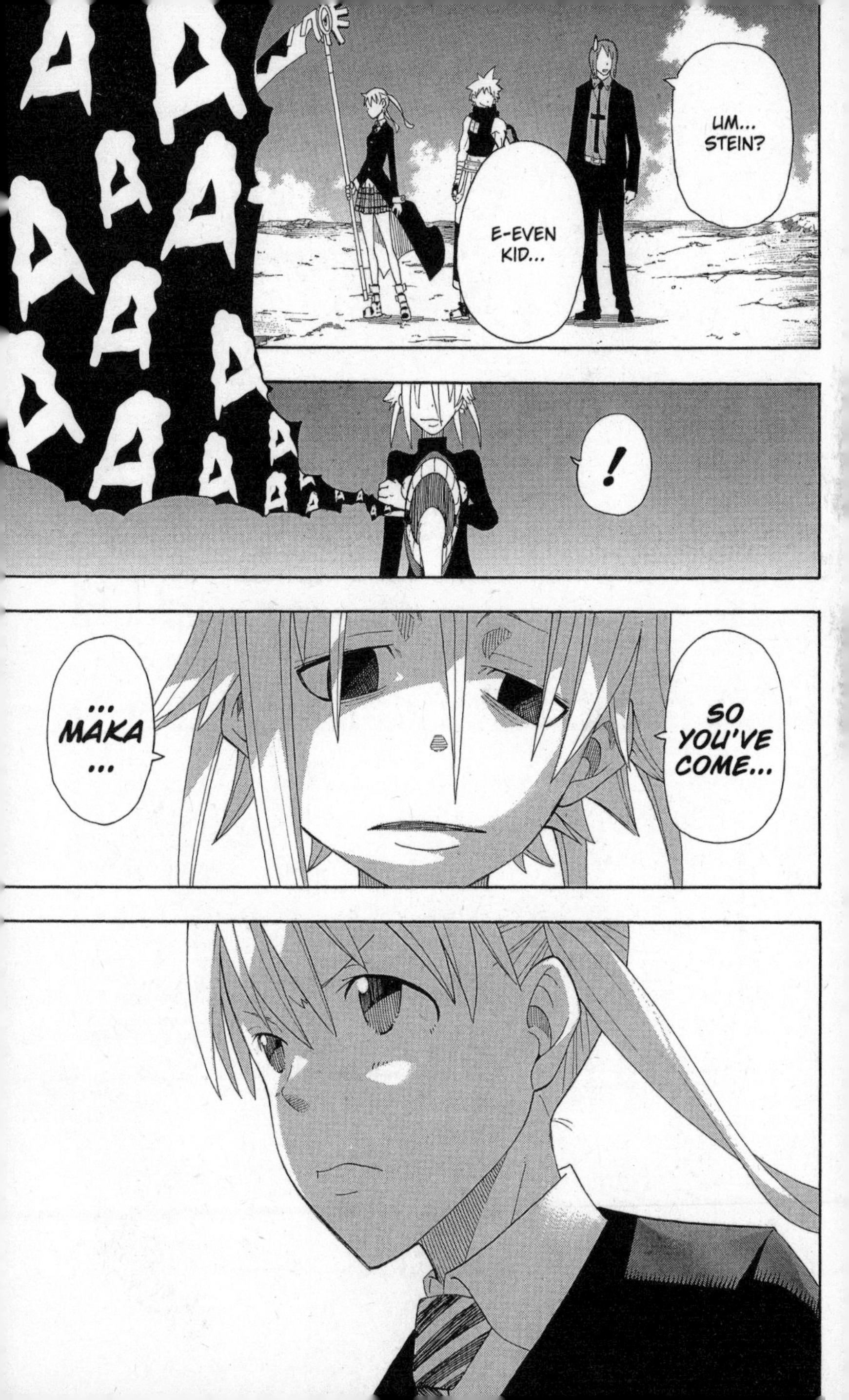
UM... STEIN?
E-EVEN KID...
!
SO YOU'VE COME...
... MAKA ...

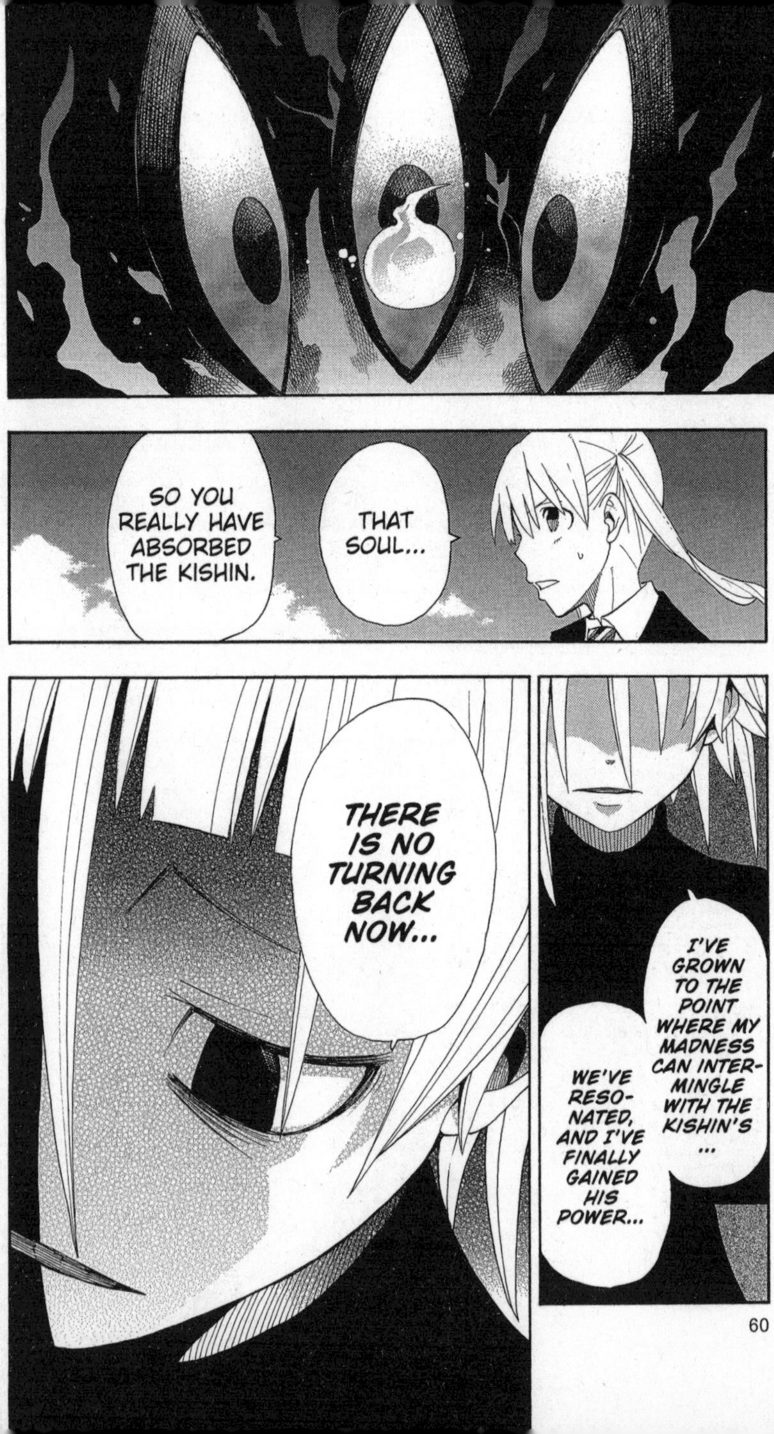
THAT SOUL...
SO YOU REALLY HAVE ABSORBED THE KISHIN.
I'VE GROWN TO THE POINT WHERE MY MADNESS CAN INTER-MINGLE WITH THE KISHIN'S...
WE'VE RESO-NATED, AND I'VE FINALLY GAINED HIS POWER...
THERE IS NO TURNING BACK NOW...

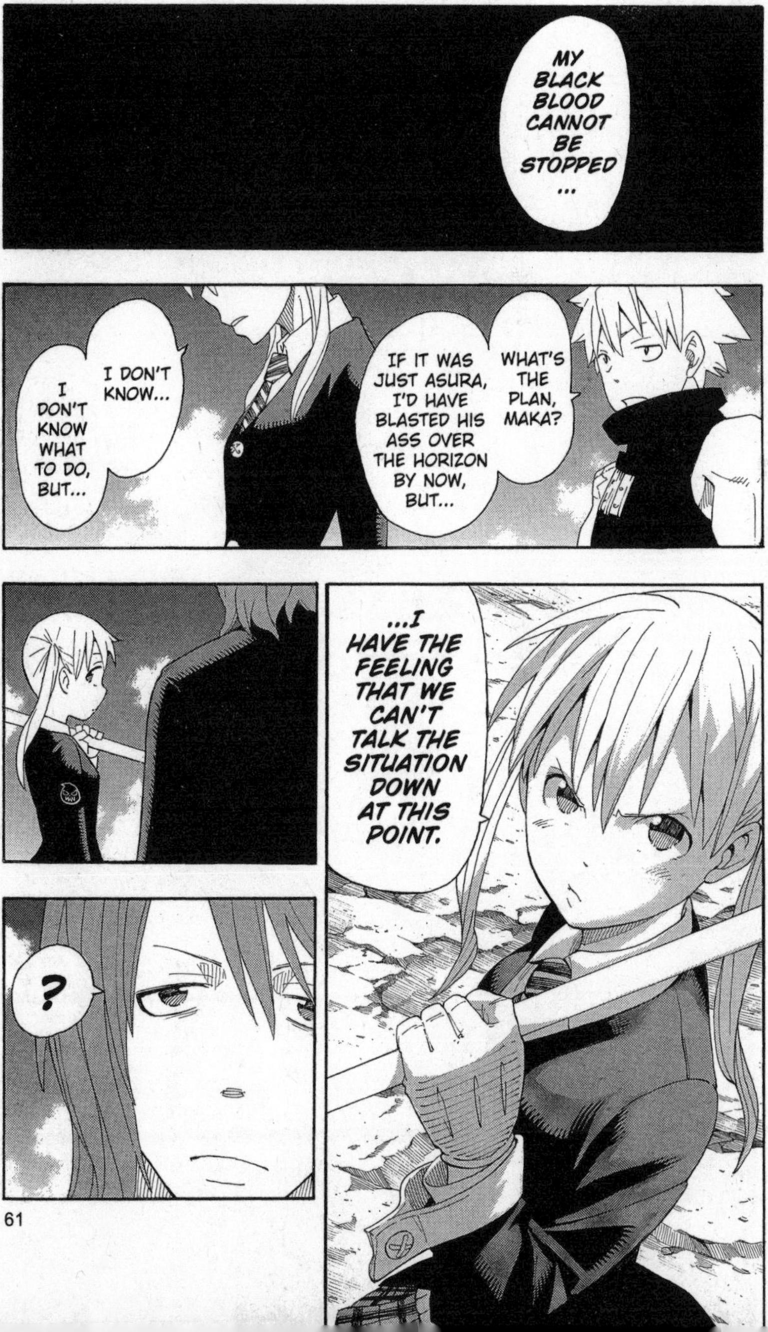
MY BLACK BLOOD CANNOT BE STOPPED...
WHAT'S THE PLAN, MAKA?
IF IT WAS JUST ASURA, I'D HAVE BLASTED HIS ASS OVER THE HORIZON BY NOW, BUT...
I DON'T KNOW...
I DON'T KNOW WHAT TO DO, BUT...
...I HAVE THE FEELING THAT WE CAN'T TALK THE SITUATION DOWN AT THIS POINT.
?

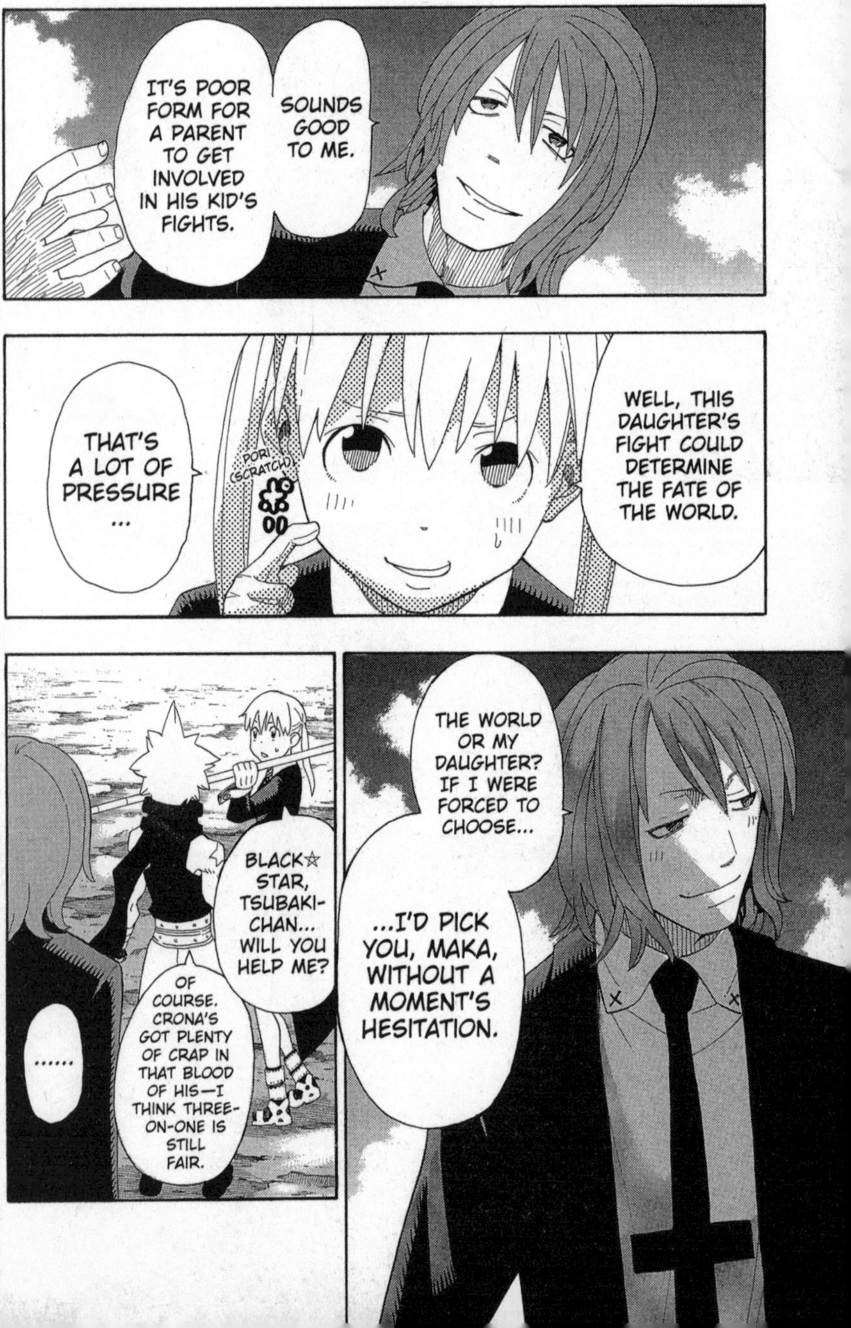
SOUNDS GOOD TO ME.
IT'S POOR FORM FOR A PARENT TO GET INVOLVED IN HIS KID'S FIGHTS.
WELL, THIS DAUGHTER'S FIGHT COULD DETERMINE THE FATE OF THE WORLD.
PORI (SCRATCH)
THAT'S A LOT OF PRESSURE ...
THE WORLD OR MY DAUGHTER? IF I WERE FORCED TO CHOOSE...
...I'D PICK YOU, MAKA, WITHOUT A MOMENT'S HESITATION.
BLACK☆STAR, TSUBAKI-CHAN... WILL YOU HELP ME?
OF COURSE. CRONA'S GOT PLENTY OF CRAP IN THAT BLOOD OF HIS—I THINK THREE-ON-ONE IS STILL FAIR.
......

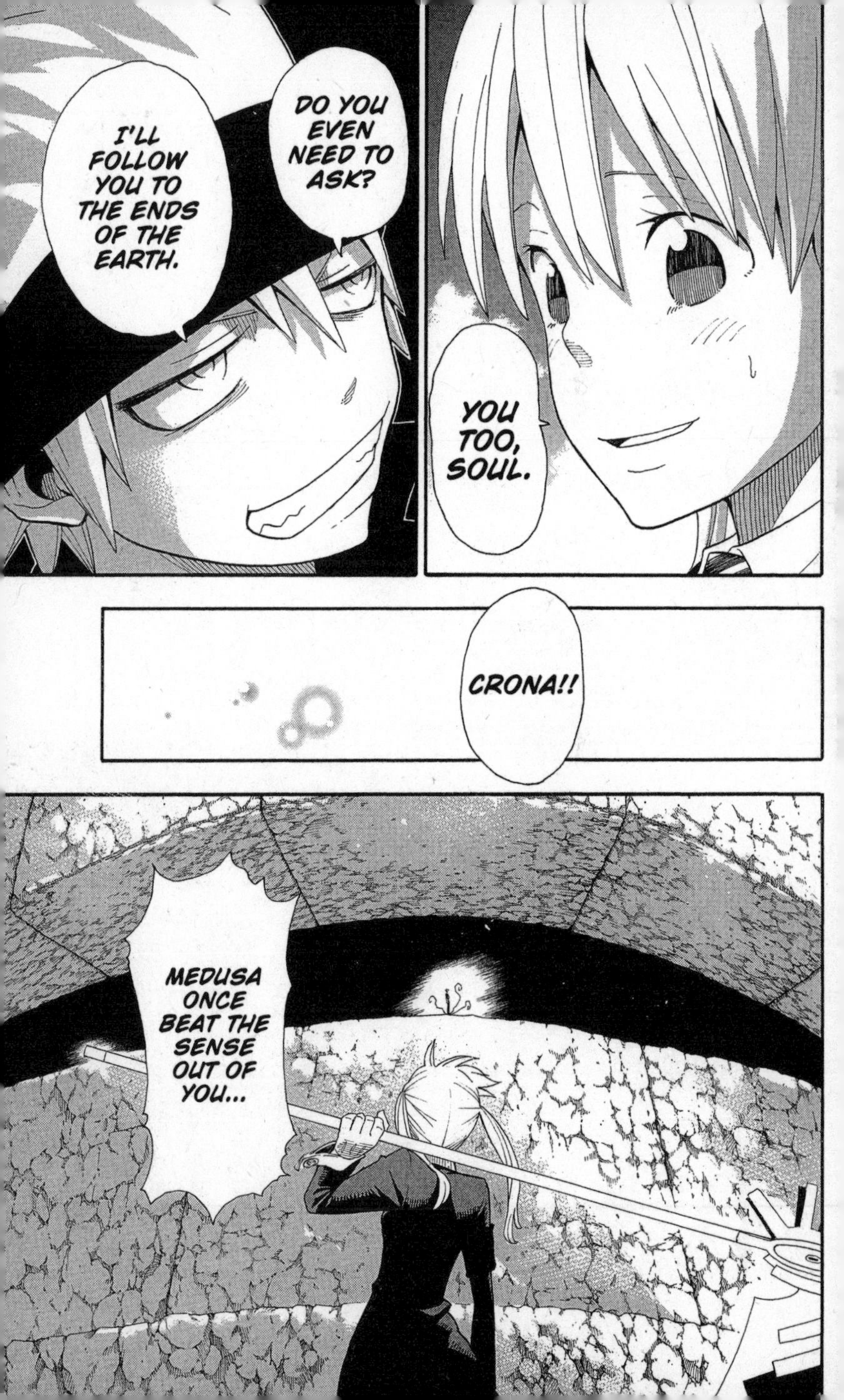
YOU TOO, SOUL.
DO YOU EVEN NEED TO ASK?
I'LL FOLLOW YOU TO THE ENDS OF THE EARTH.
CRONA!!
MEDUSA ONCE BEAT THE SENSE OUT OF YOU...

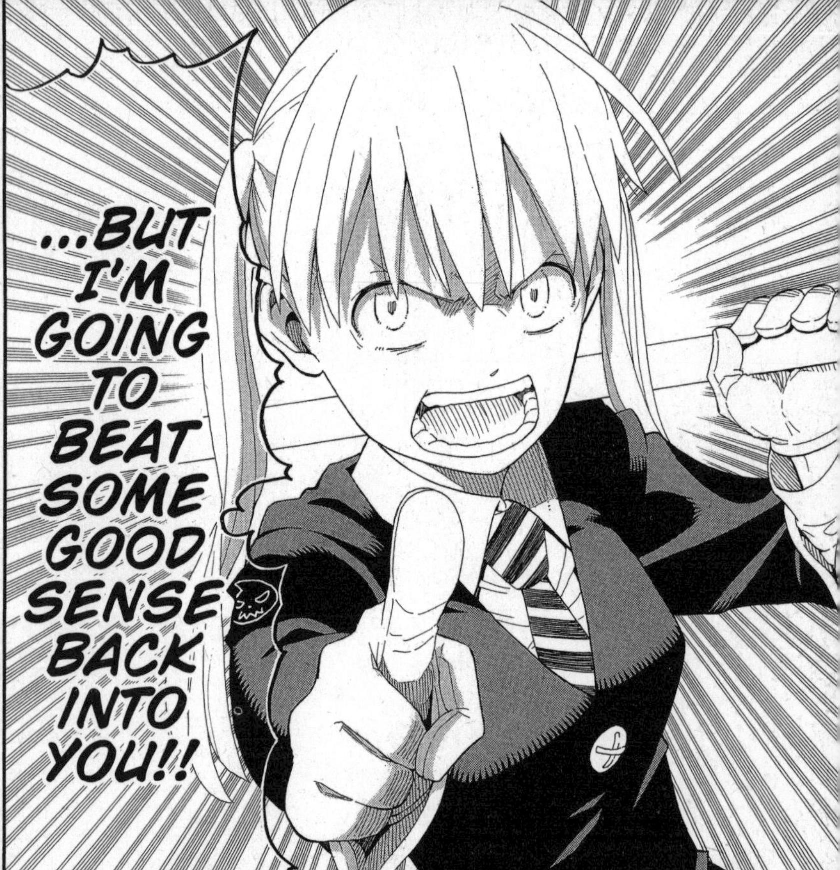
...BUT I'M GOING TO BEAT SOME GOOD SENSE BACK INTO YOU!!
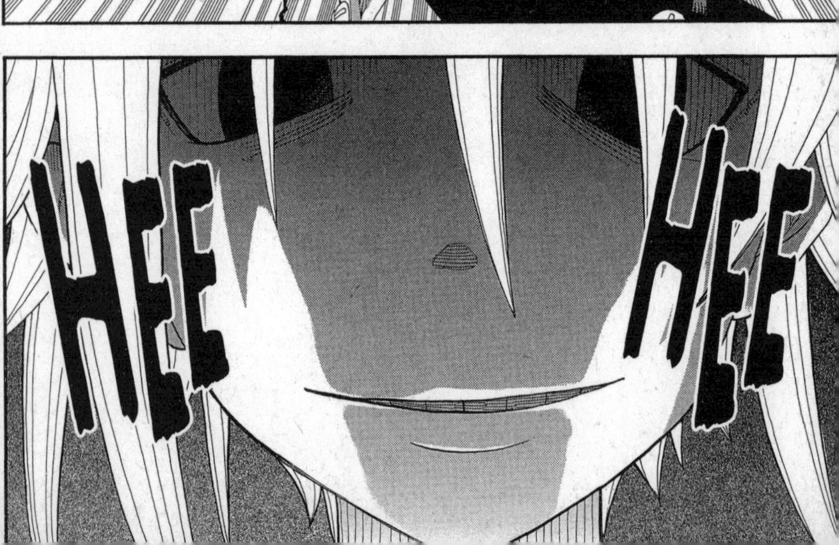
HEE
HEE

SOUL EATER

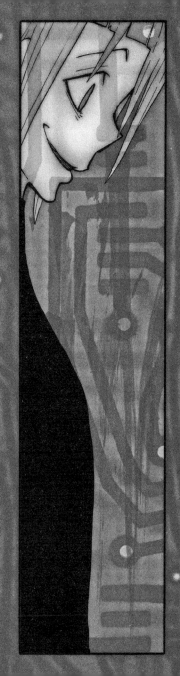

SOUL ☆ EATER

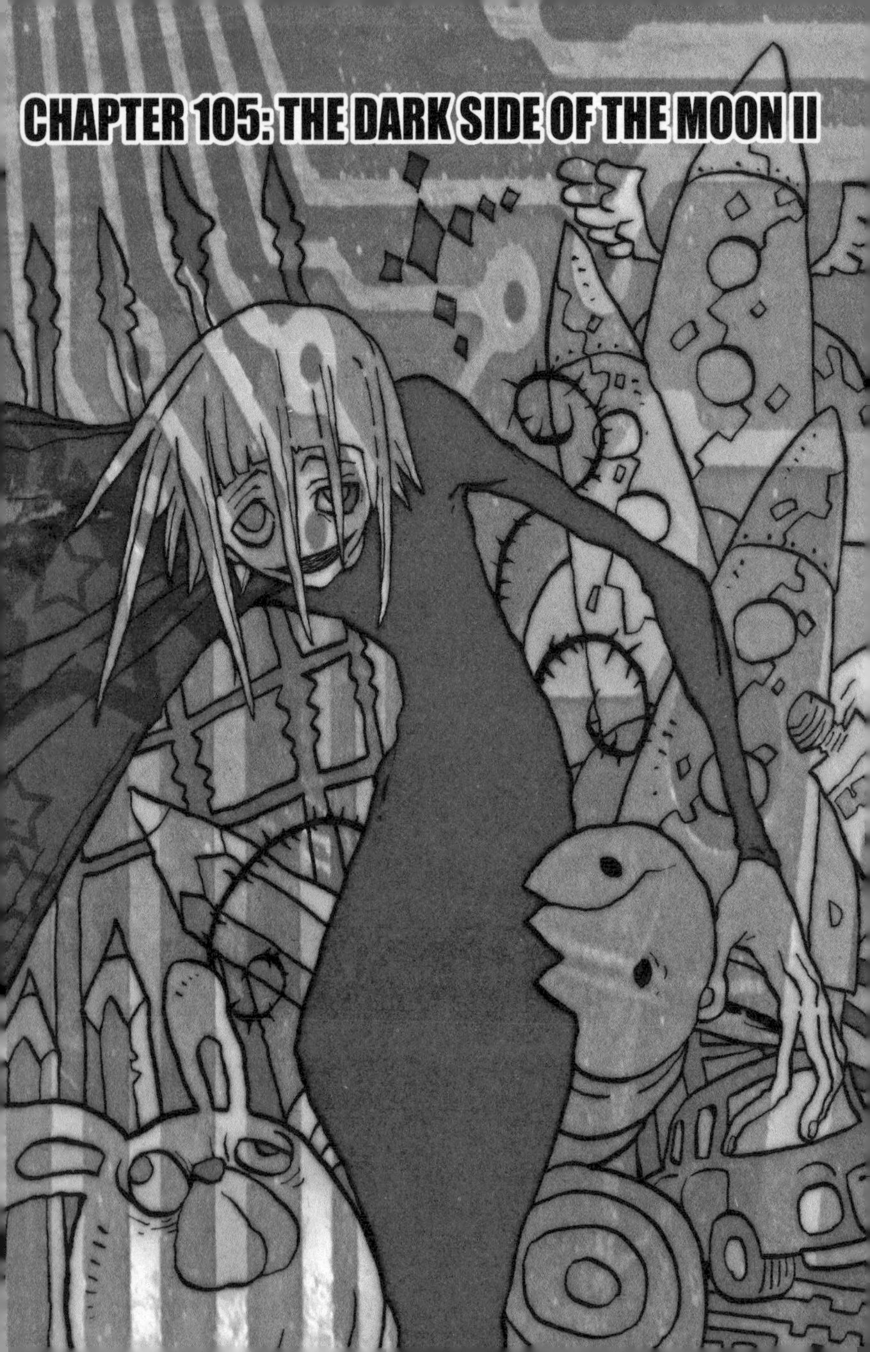
CHAPTER 105: THE DARK SIDE OF THE MOON II

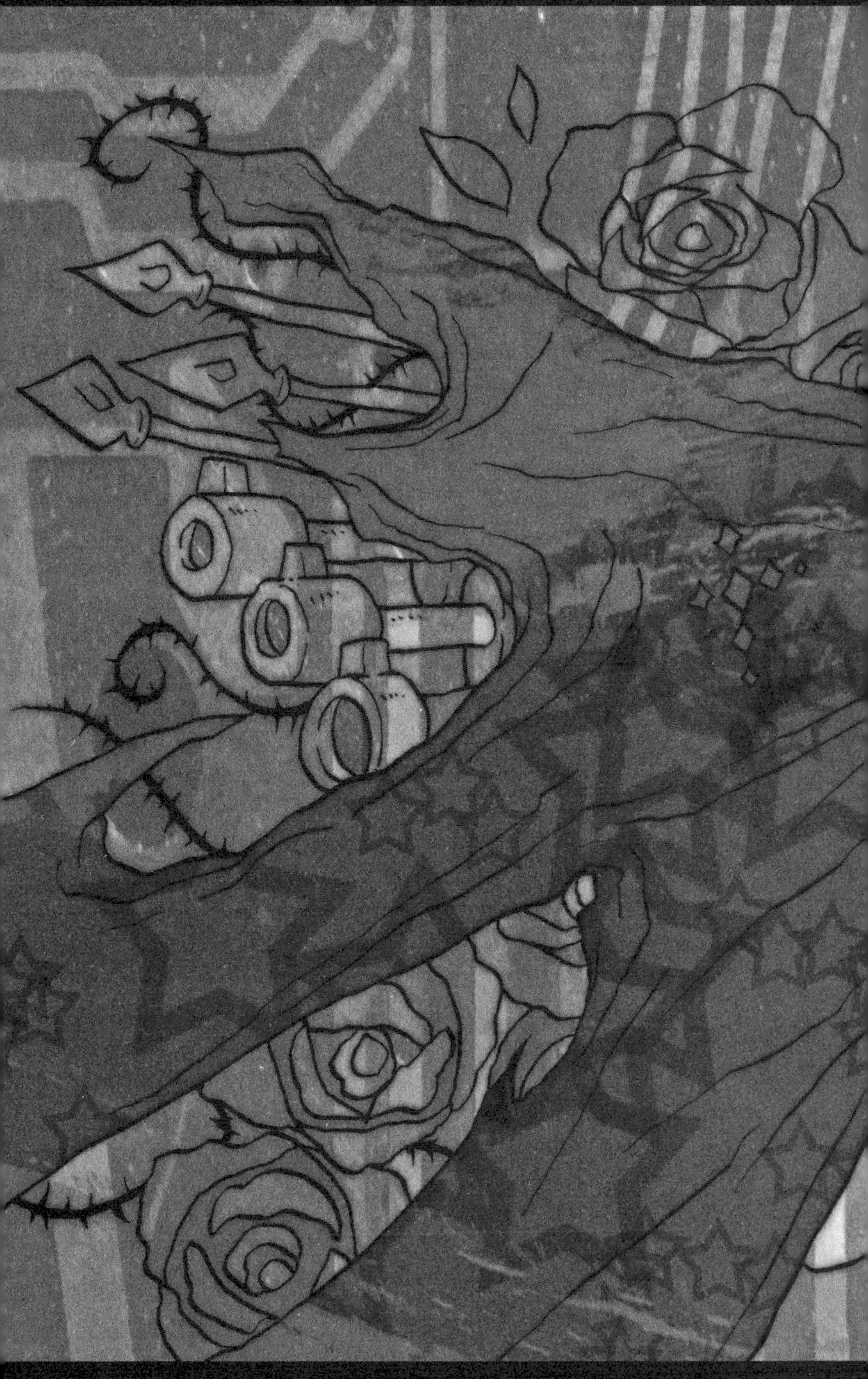

SOUL EATER

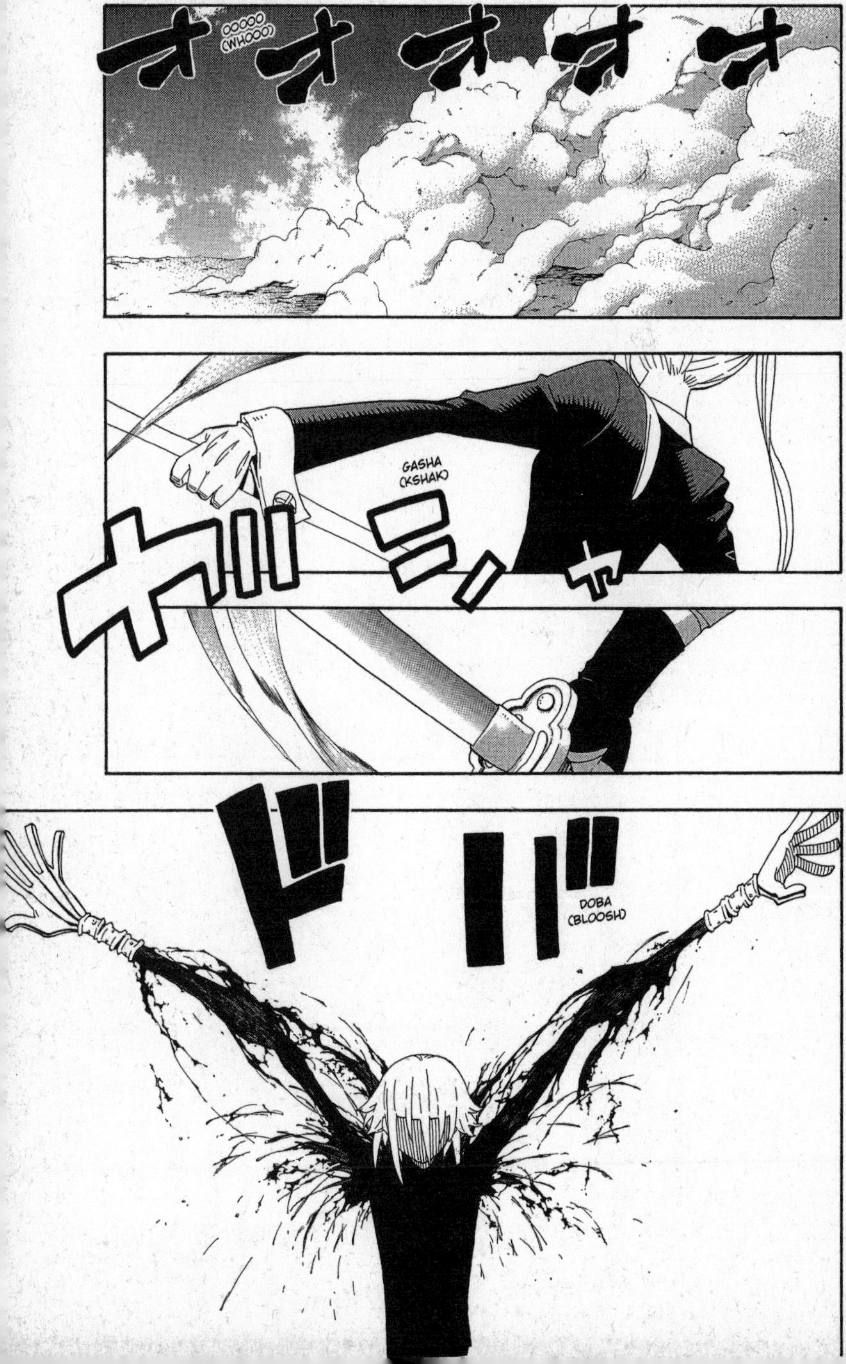
OOOOO (WHOOO)
GASHA (KSHAK)
DOBA (BLOOSH)

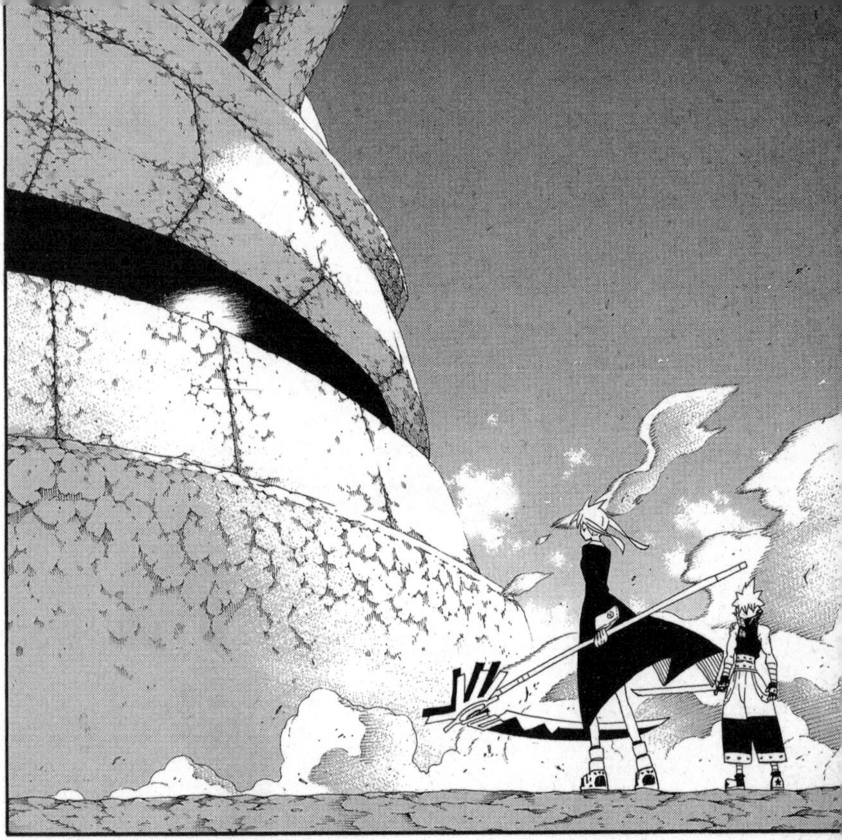

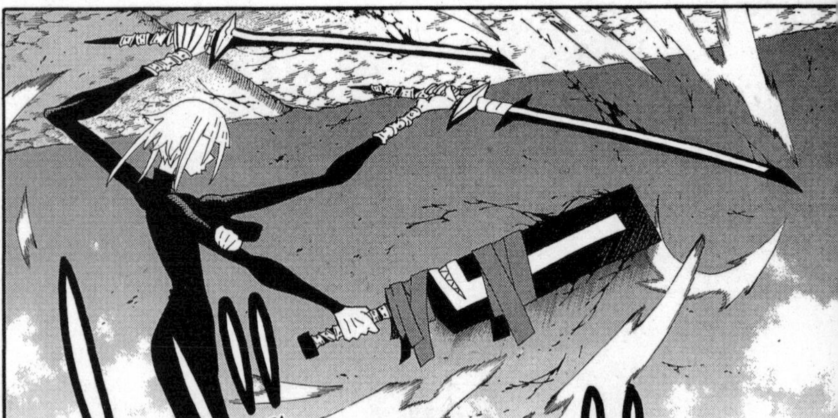
BA
(WHOOSH)

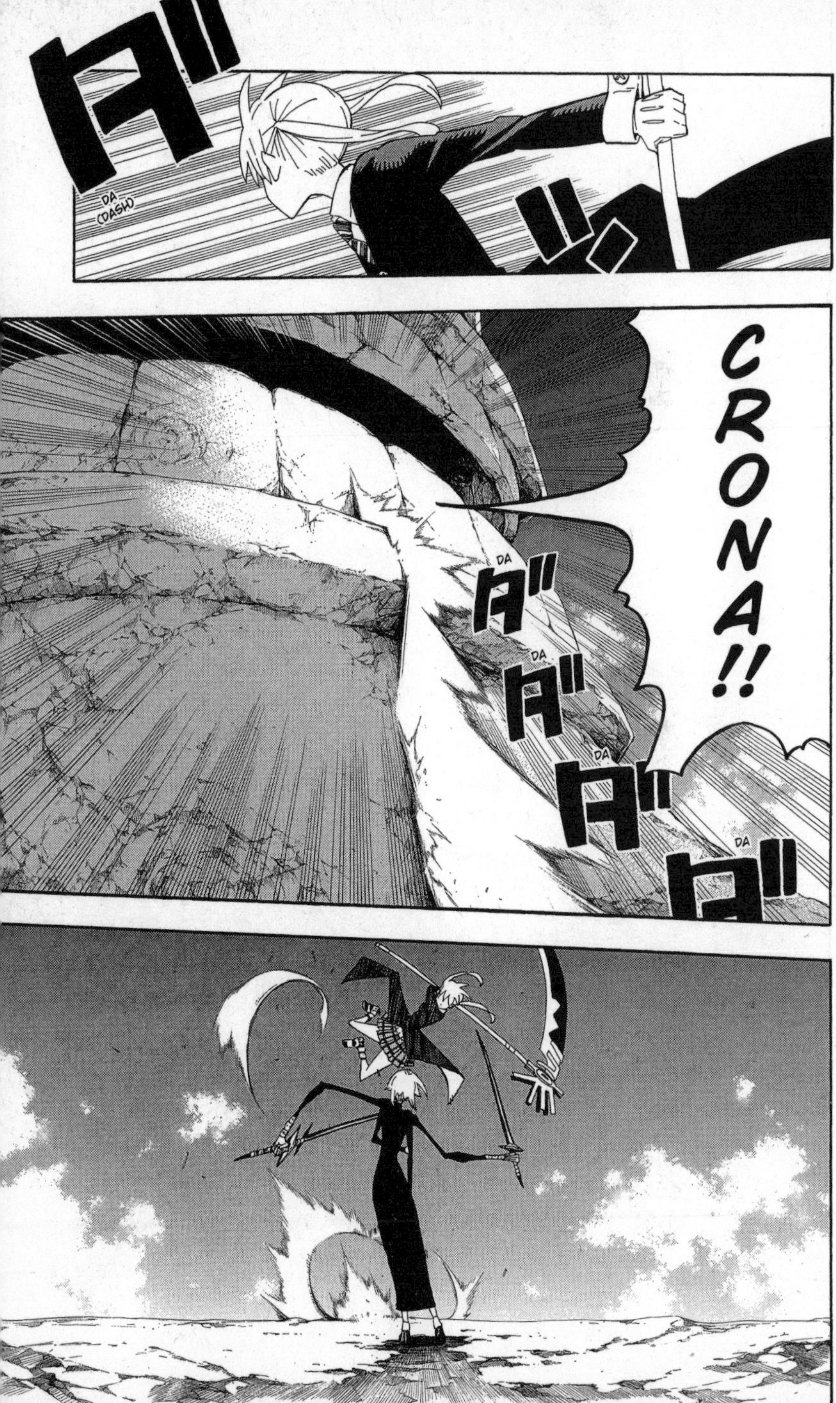
ダ
DA (DASH)
CRONA!!
ダ DA
ダ DA
ダ DA
ダ DA

YOU BIG, STUBBORN DUMMY!!

GIN (CLANG)

HOW COULD YOU ACTUALLY SWALLOW THE KISHIN!?

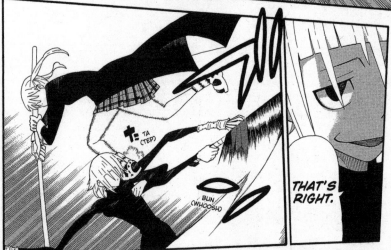

TA (TEP)

BUN (WHOOSH)

THAT'S RIGHT.

GA (WHAK)

I'VE GAINED THE POWER OF THE KISHIN'S MADNESS— AND I'LL USE IT TO DESTROY THE WORLD!!

!?

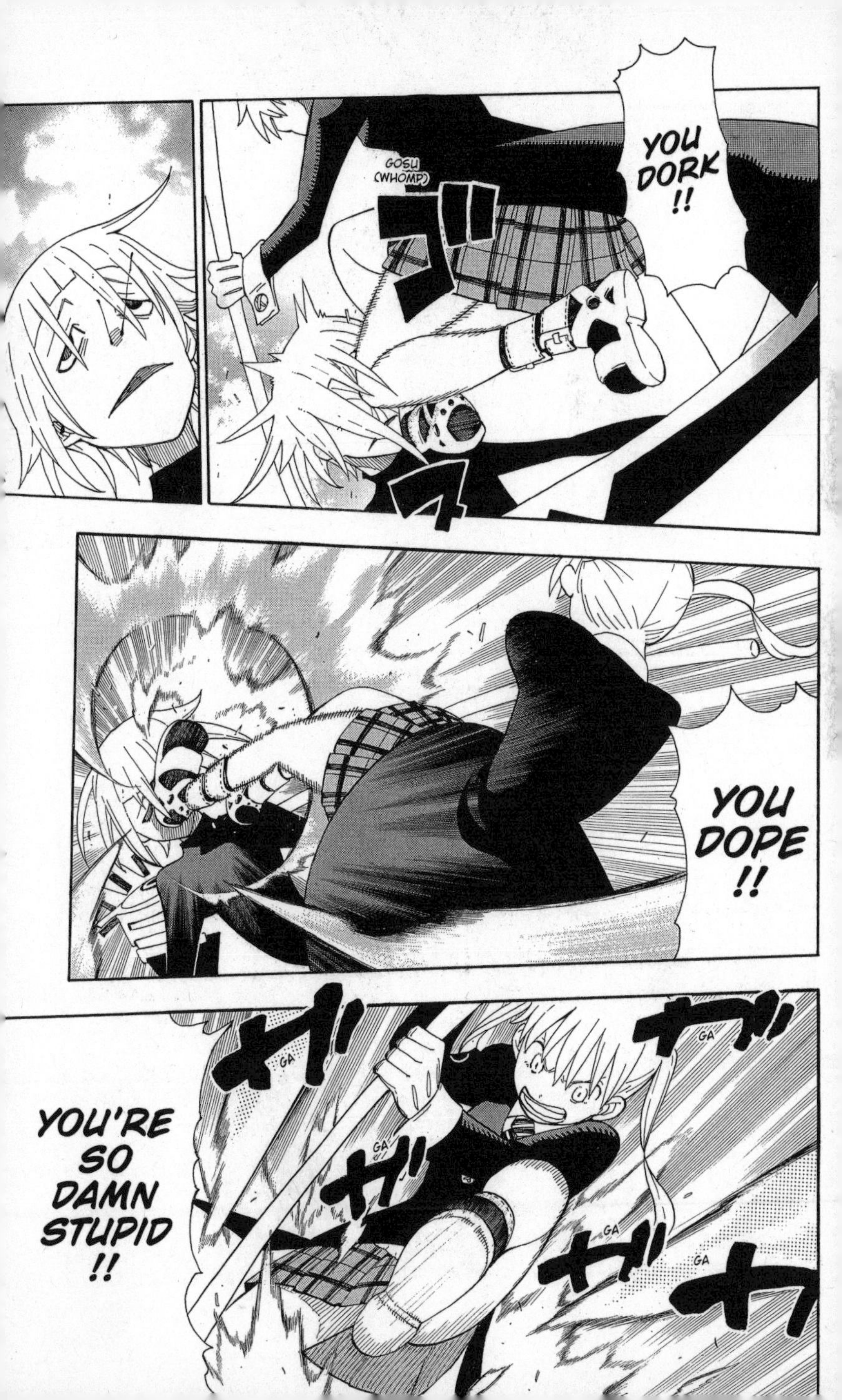
YOU DORK !!
GOSU (WHOMP)
YOU DOPE !!
GA
GA
YOU'RE SO DAMN STUPID !!
GA
GA

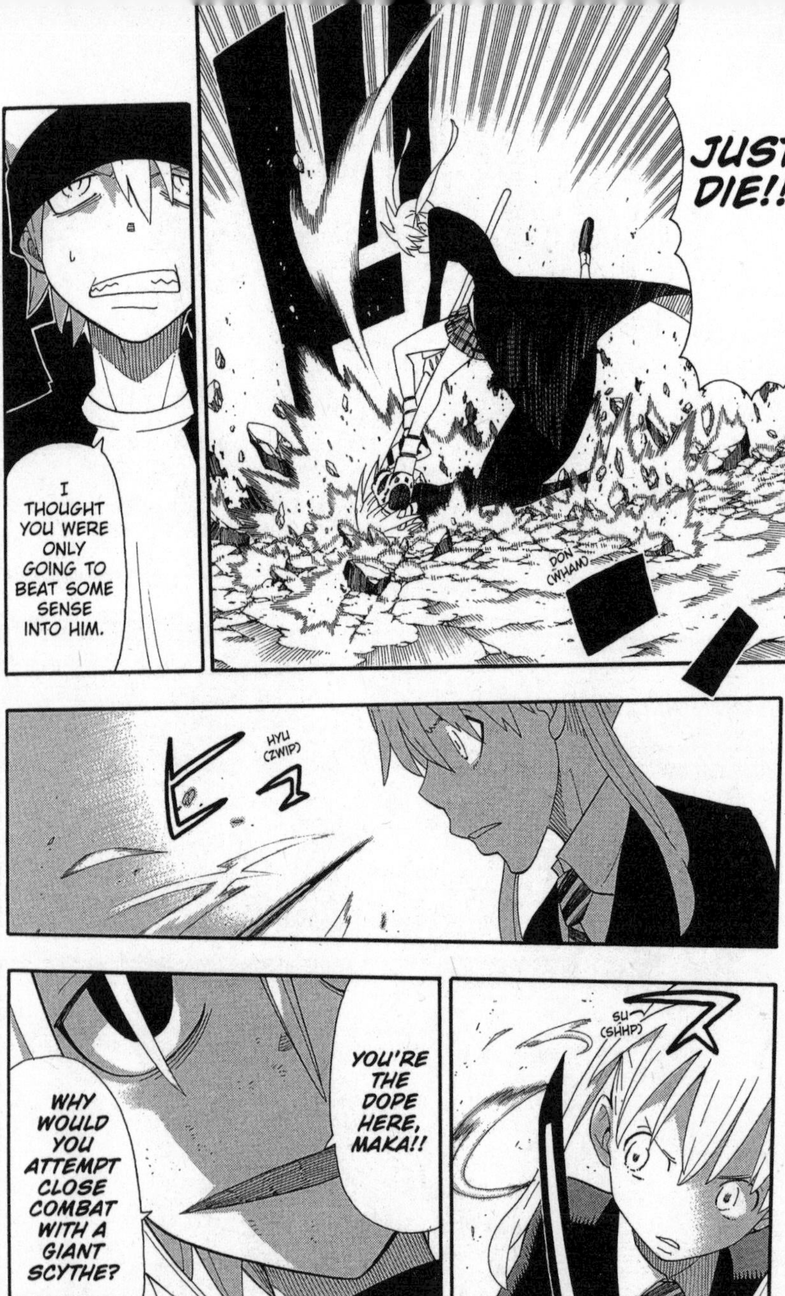
JUST DIE!!
DON (WHAM)
I THOUGHT YOU WERE ONLY GOING TO BEAT SOME SENSE INTO HIM.
HYU (ZWIP)
SU (SHHP)
YOU'RE THE DOPE HERE, MAKA!!
WHY WOULD YOU ATTEMPT CLOSE COMBAT WITH A GIANT SCYTHE?

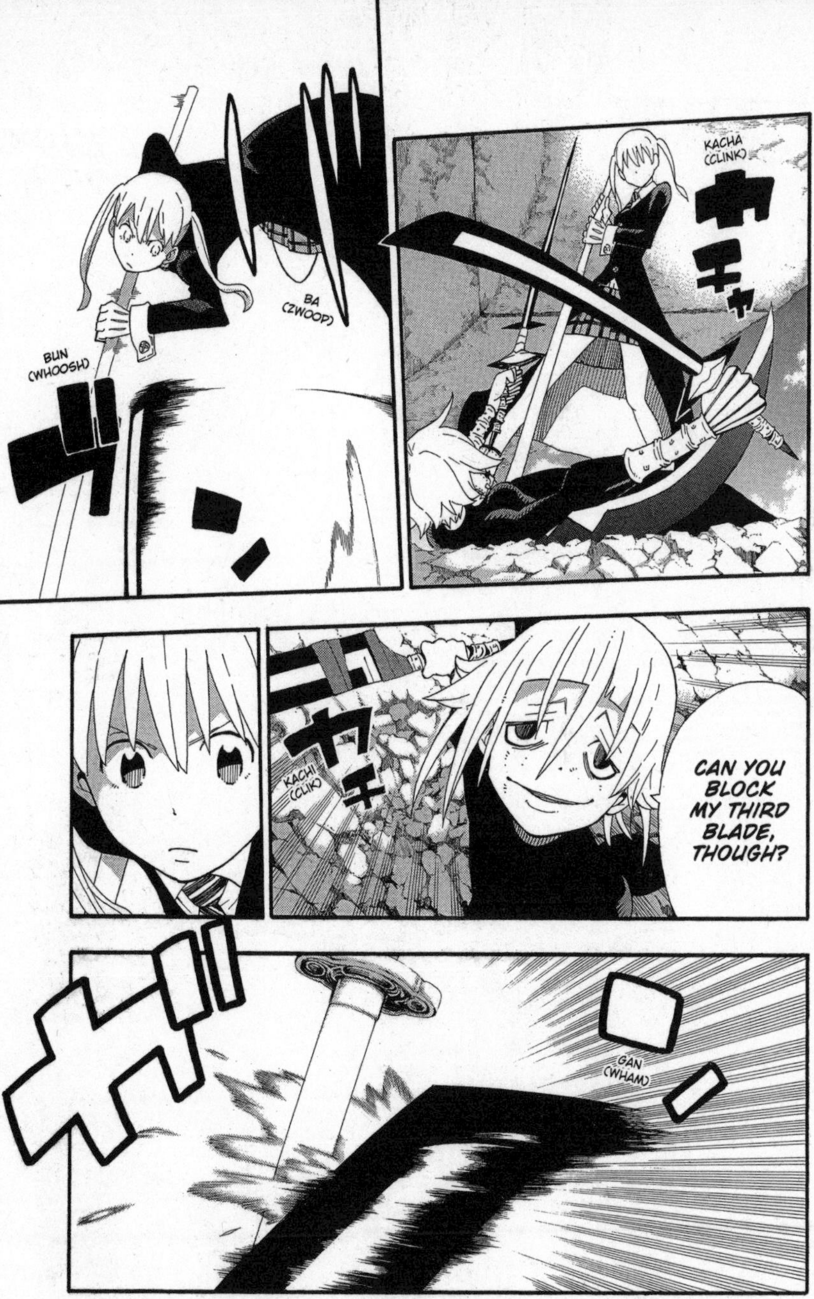
KACHA (CLINK)
BA (ZWOOP)
BUN (WHOOSH)
CAN YOU BLOCK MY THIRD BLADE, THOUGH?
KACHI (CLIK)
GAN (WHAM)

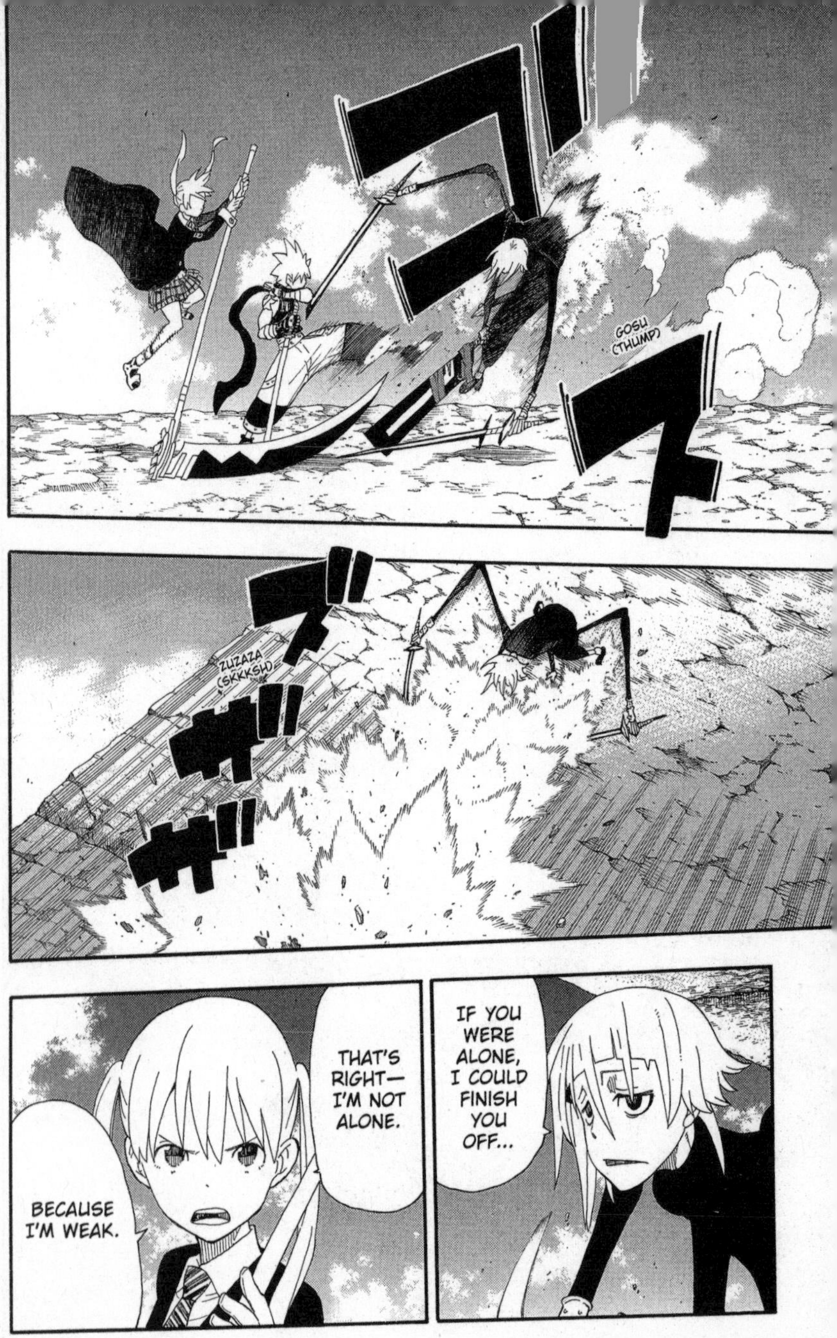
GOSU (THUMP)
ZUZAZA (SKKKSH)
IF YOU WERE ALONE, I COULD FINISH YOU OFF...
THAT'S RIGHT— I'M NOT ALONE.
BECAUSE I'M WEAK.

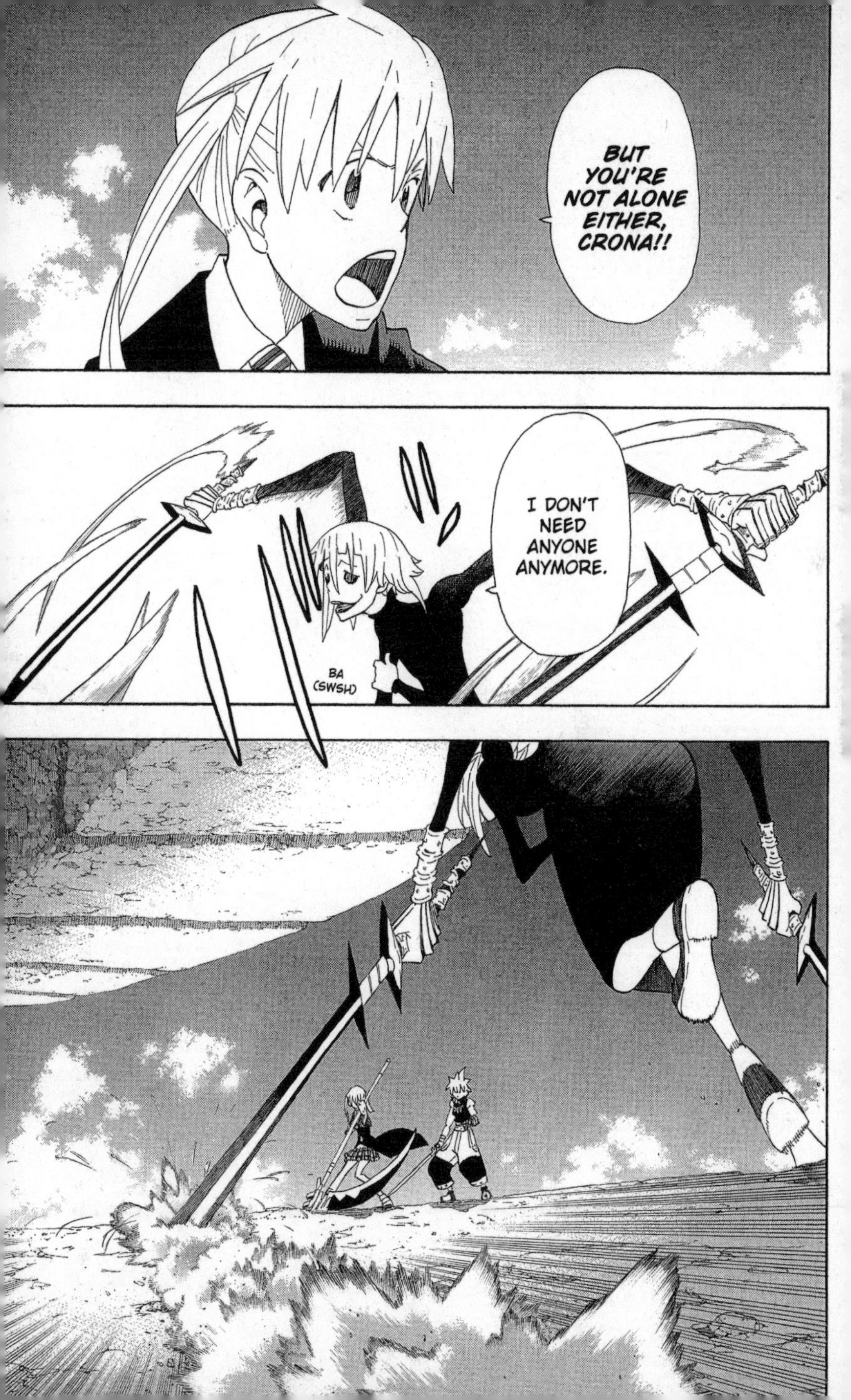
BUT YOU'RE NOT ALONE EITHER, CRONA!!
I DON'T NEED ANYONE ANYMORE.
BA (SWSH)

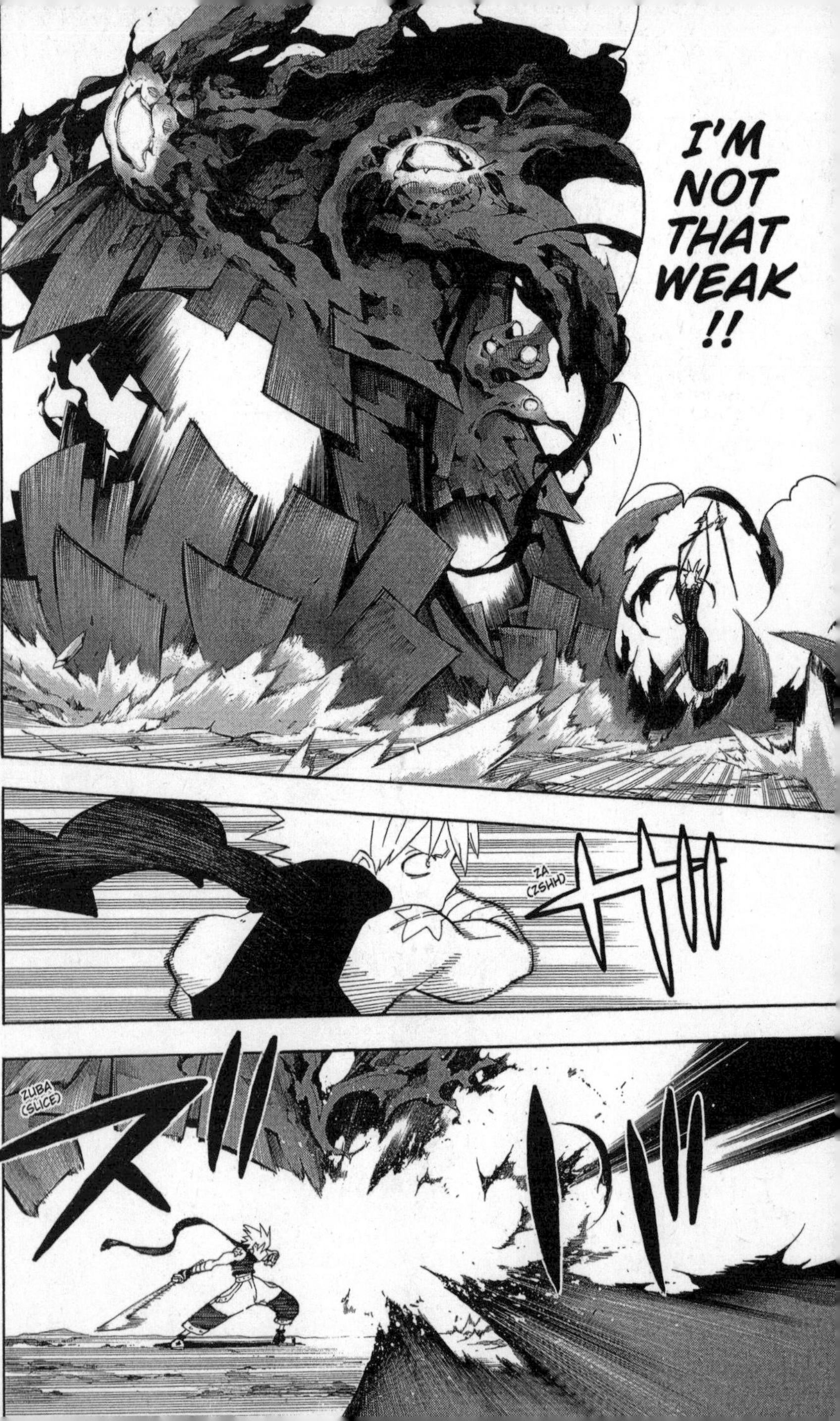
I'M NOT THAT WEAK !!
ZA (ZSHH)
ZUBA (SLICE)

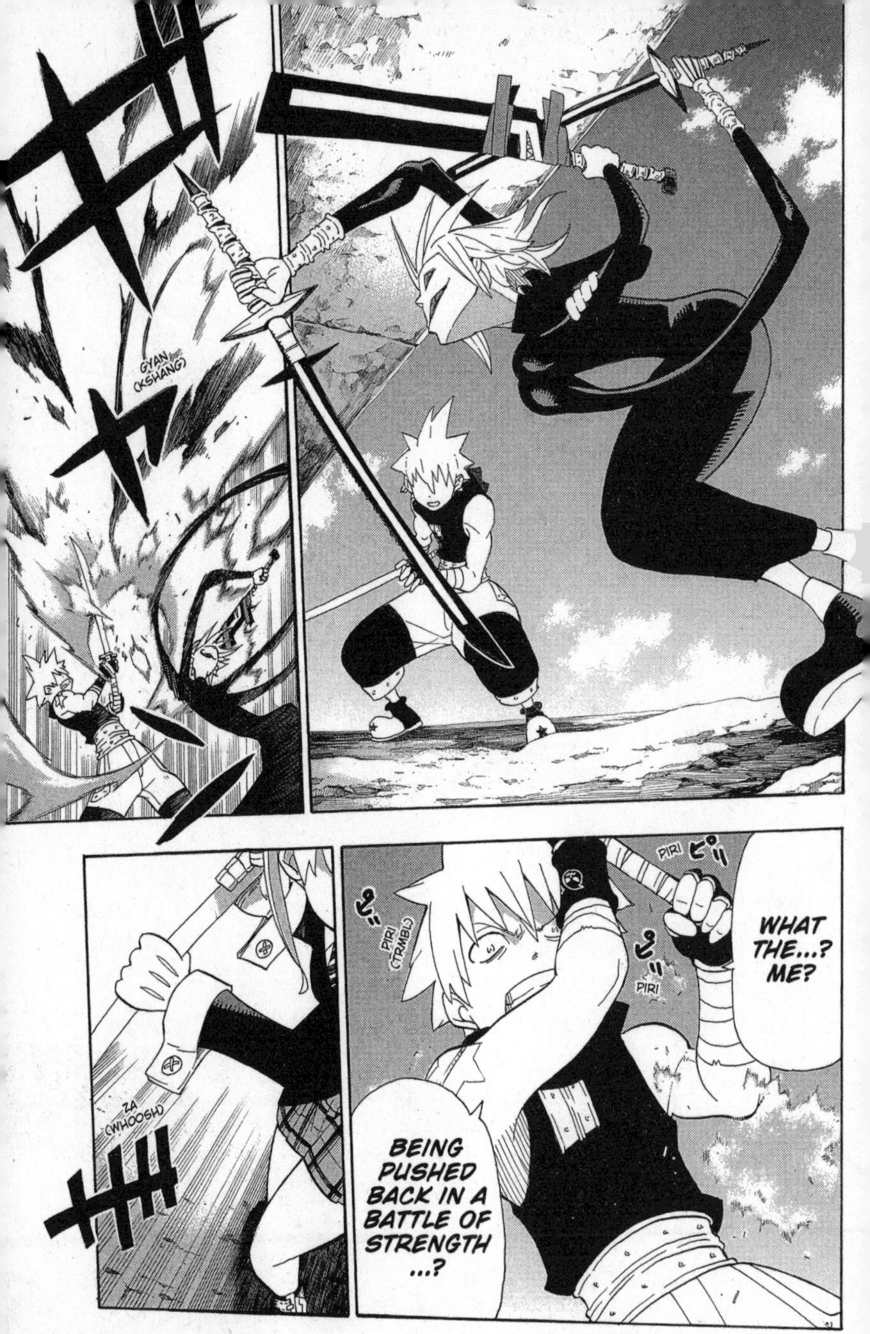
GYAN (KSHANG)
PIRI
WHAT THE...? ME?
PIRI
PIRI (TRMBL)
BEING PUSHED BACK IN A BATTLE OF STRENGTH ...?
ZA (WHOOSH)

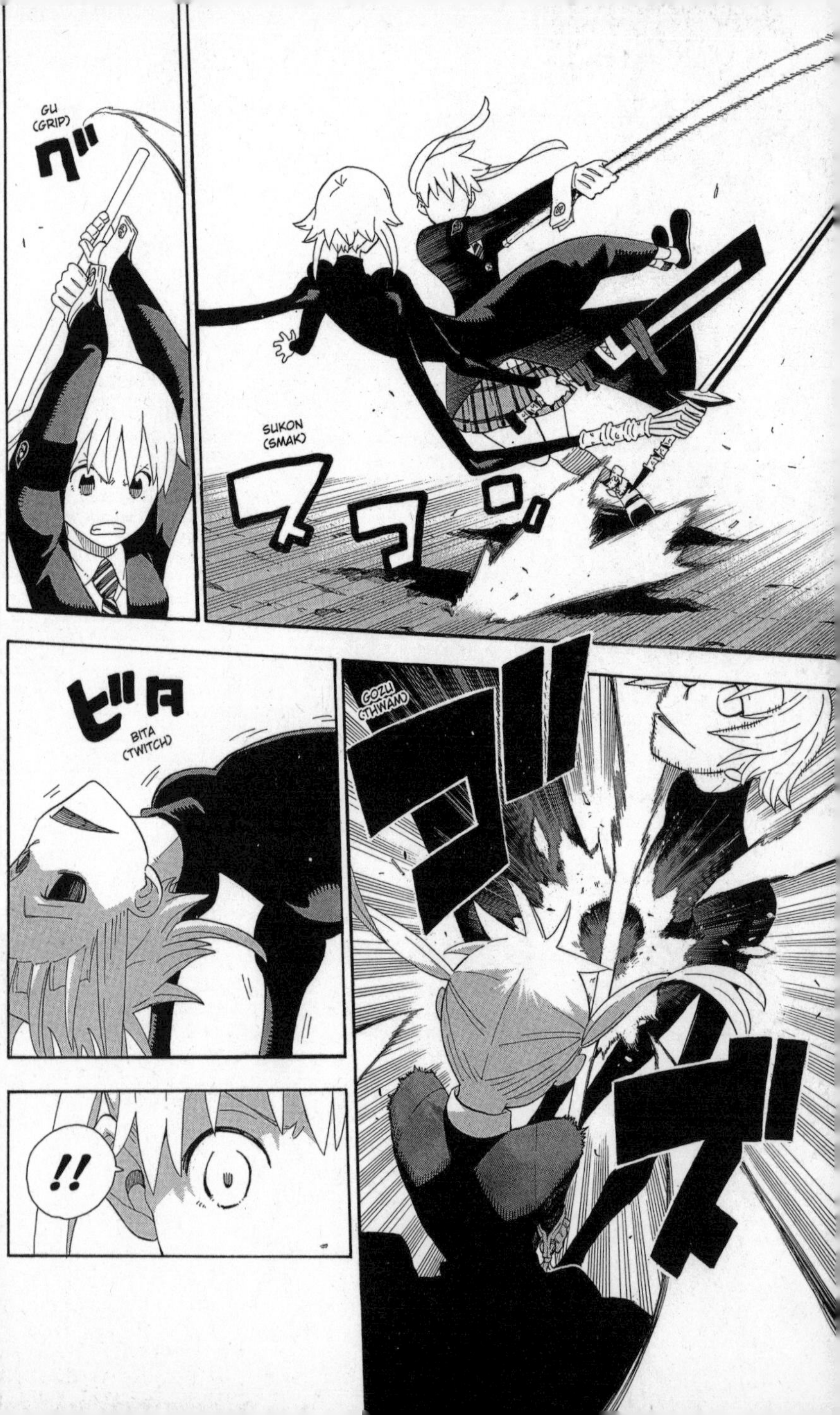
SUKON (SMAK)
GU (GRIP)
GOZU (THWAM)
BITA (TWITCH)
!!

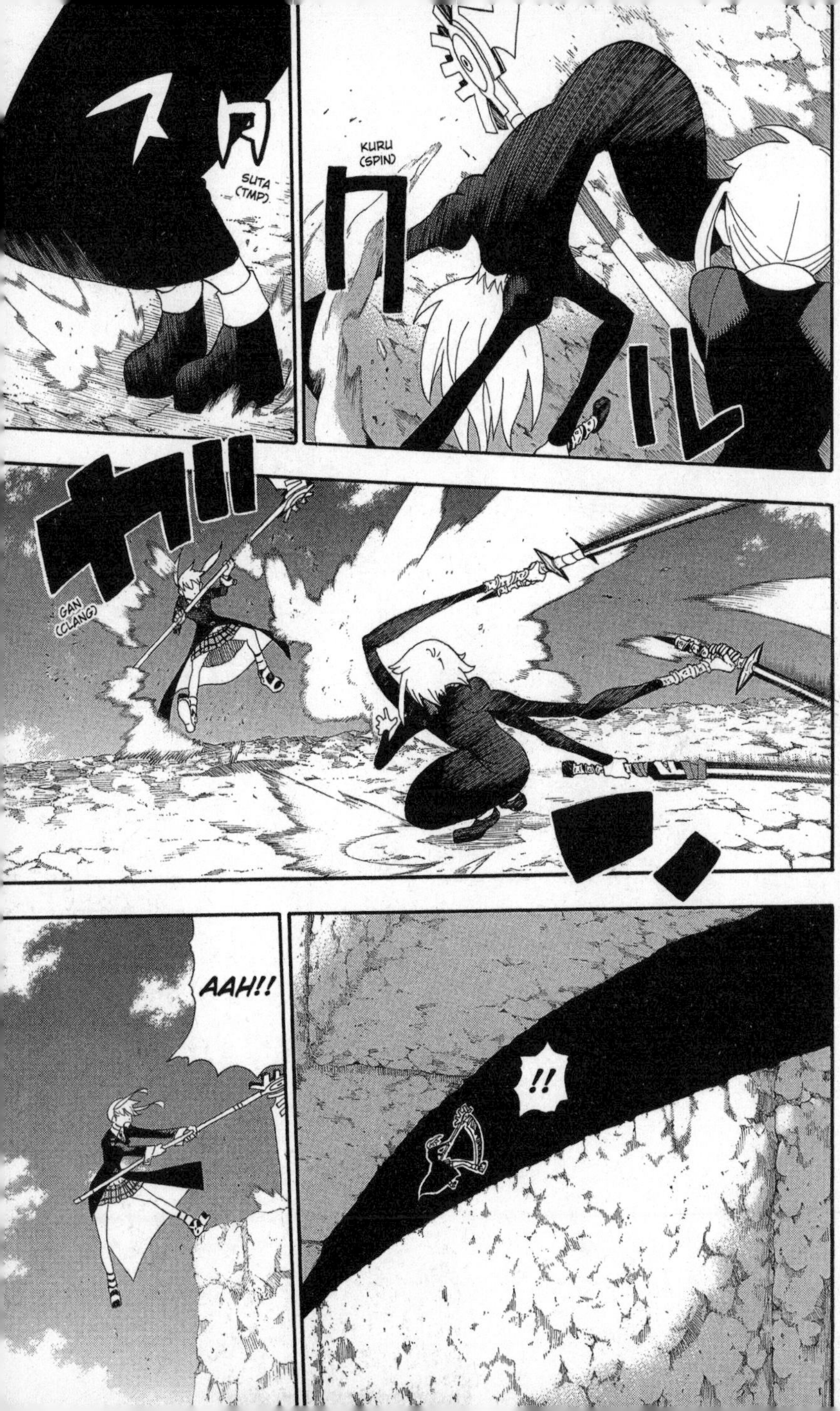
KURU (SPIN)
SUTA (TMP)
GAN (CLANG)
!!
AAH!!

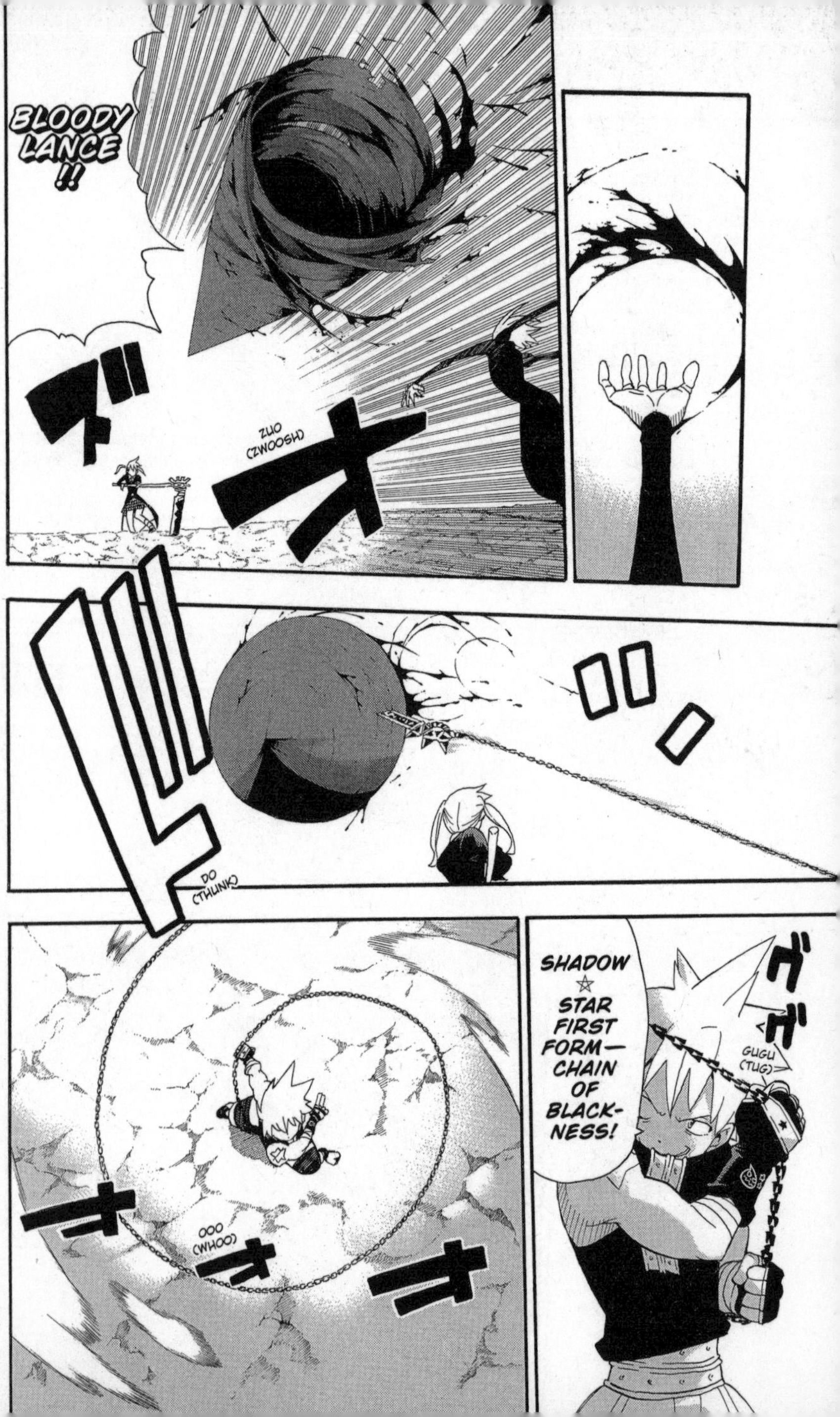
BLOODY LANCE !!
ZUO (ZWOOSH)
DO (THUNK)
SHADOW ☆ STAR FIRST FORM—CHAIN OF BLACKNESS!
GUGU (TUG)
OOO (WHOO)

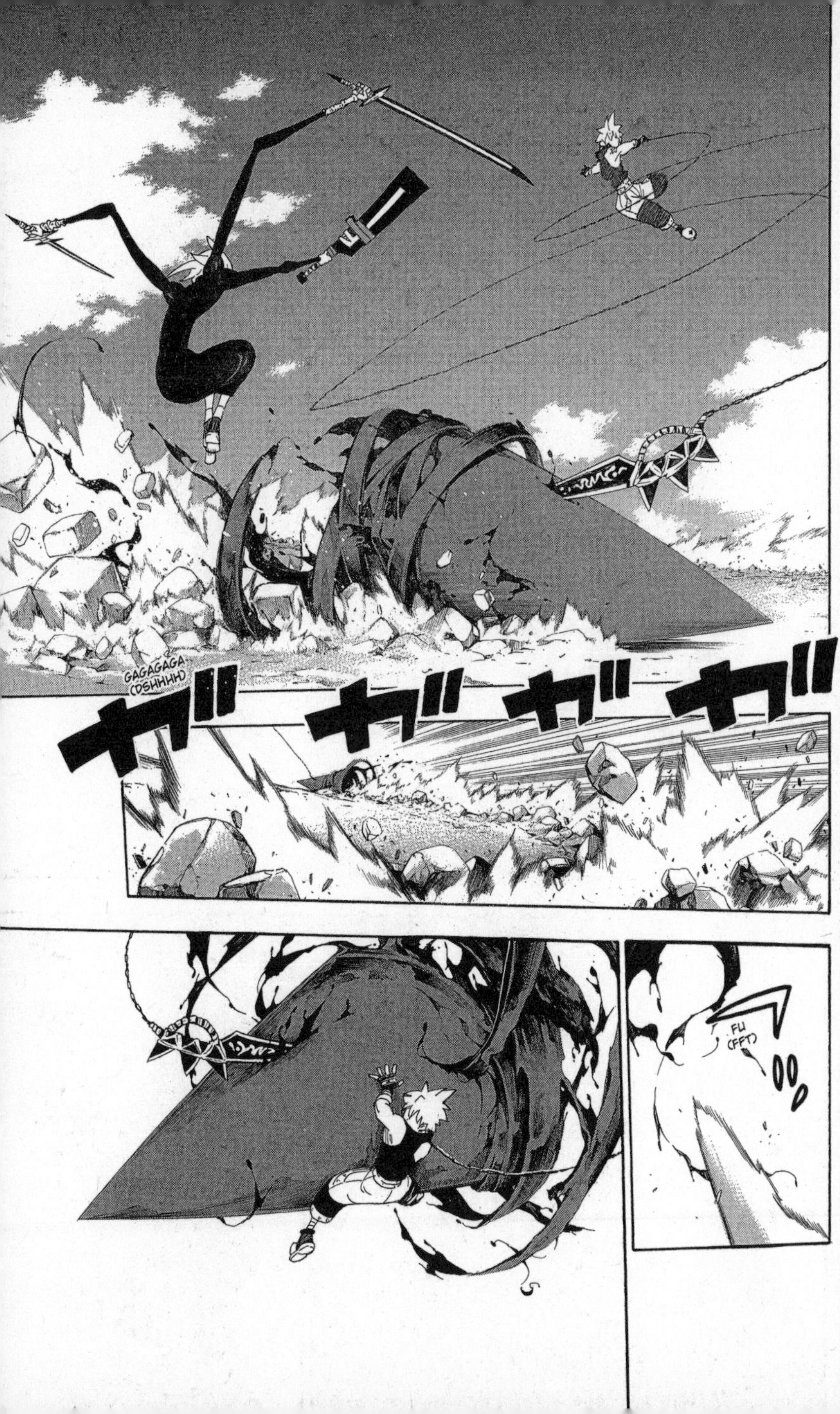
GAGAGAGA
(DSHHHH)
ガガガガ
FU
(FFT)

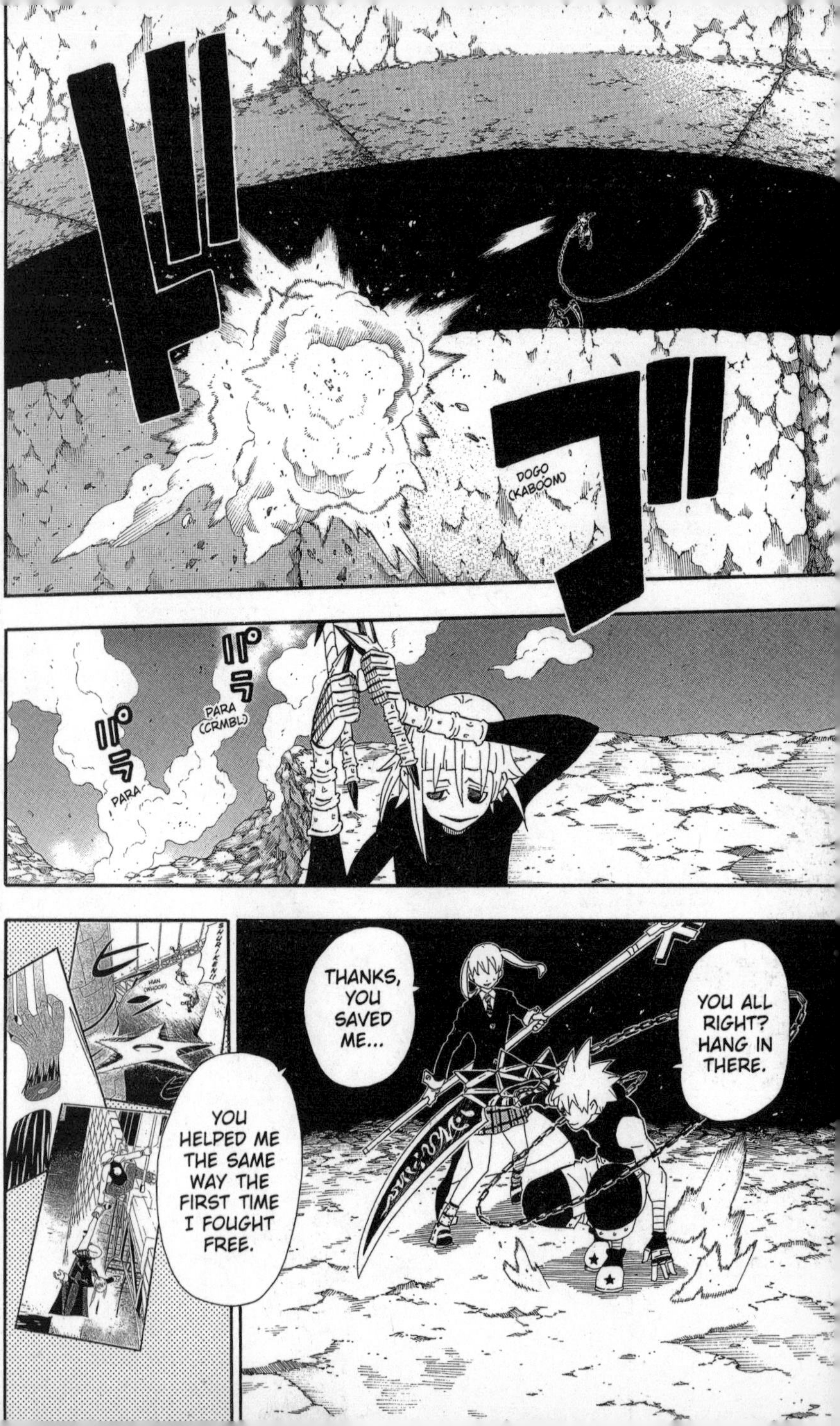
ドゴ
DOGO (KABOOM)
パラ
PARA (CRMBL)
パラ
PARA
YOU ALL RIGHT? HANG IN THERE.
THANKS, YOU SAVED ME...
YOU HELPED ME THE SAME WAY THE FIRST TIME I FOUGHT FREE.
SHURIKEN!!
HIAN (WHOOSH)

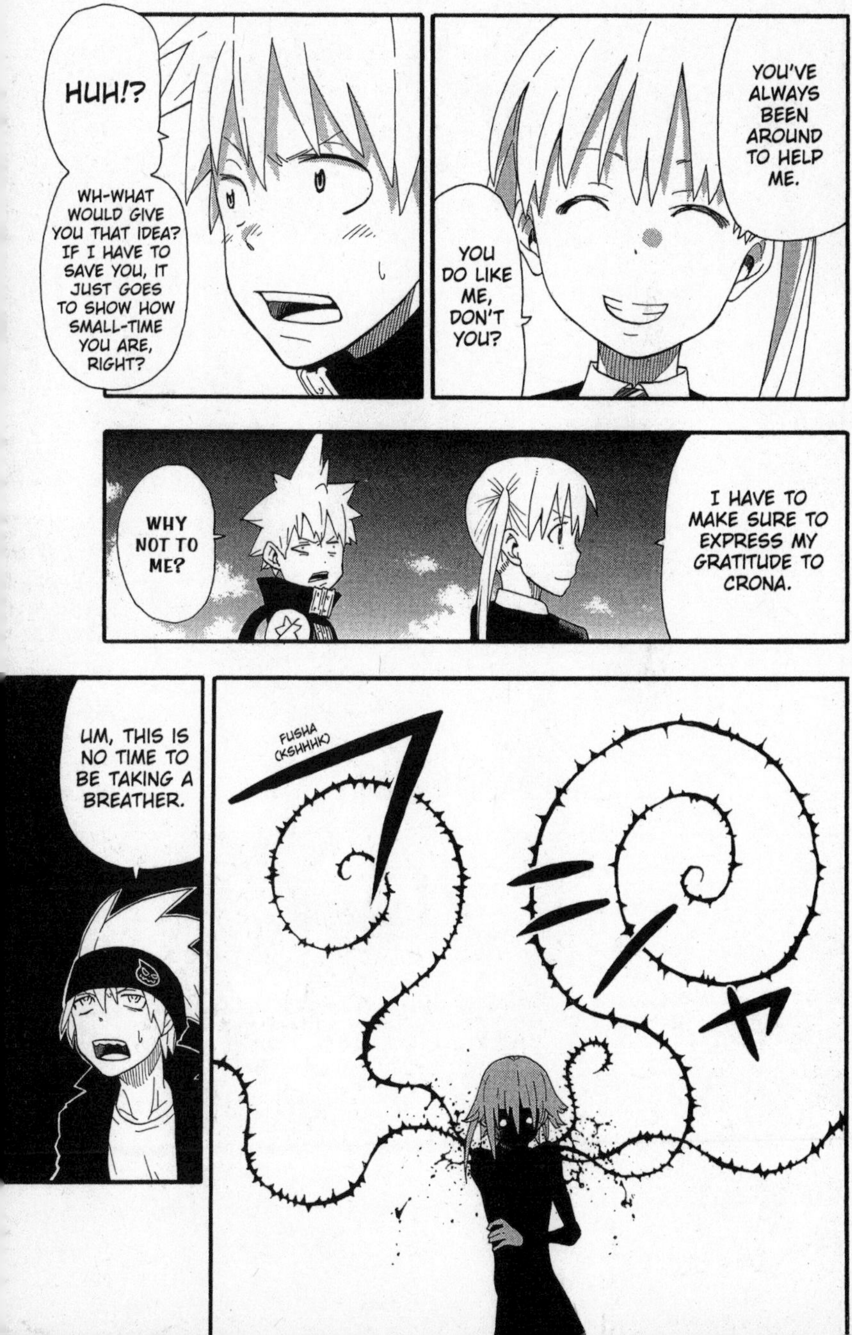
YOU'VE ALWAYS BEEN AROUND TO HELP ME.
YOU DO LIKE ME, DON'T YOU?
HUH!?
WH-WHAT WOULD GIVE YOU THAT IDEA? IF I HAVE TO SAVE YOU, IT JUST GOES TO SHOW HOW SMALL-TIME YOU ARE, RIGHT?
I HAVE TO MAKE SURE TO EXPRESS MY GRATITUDE TO CRONA.
WHY NOT TO ME?
FUSHA (KSHHHK)
UM, THIS IS NO TIME TO BE TAKING A BREATHER.

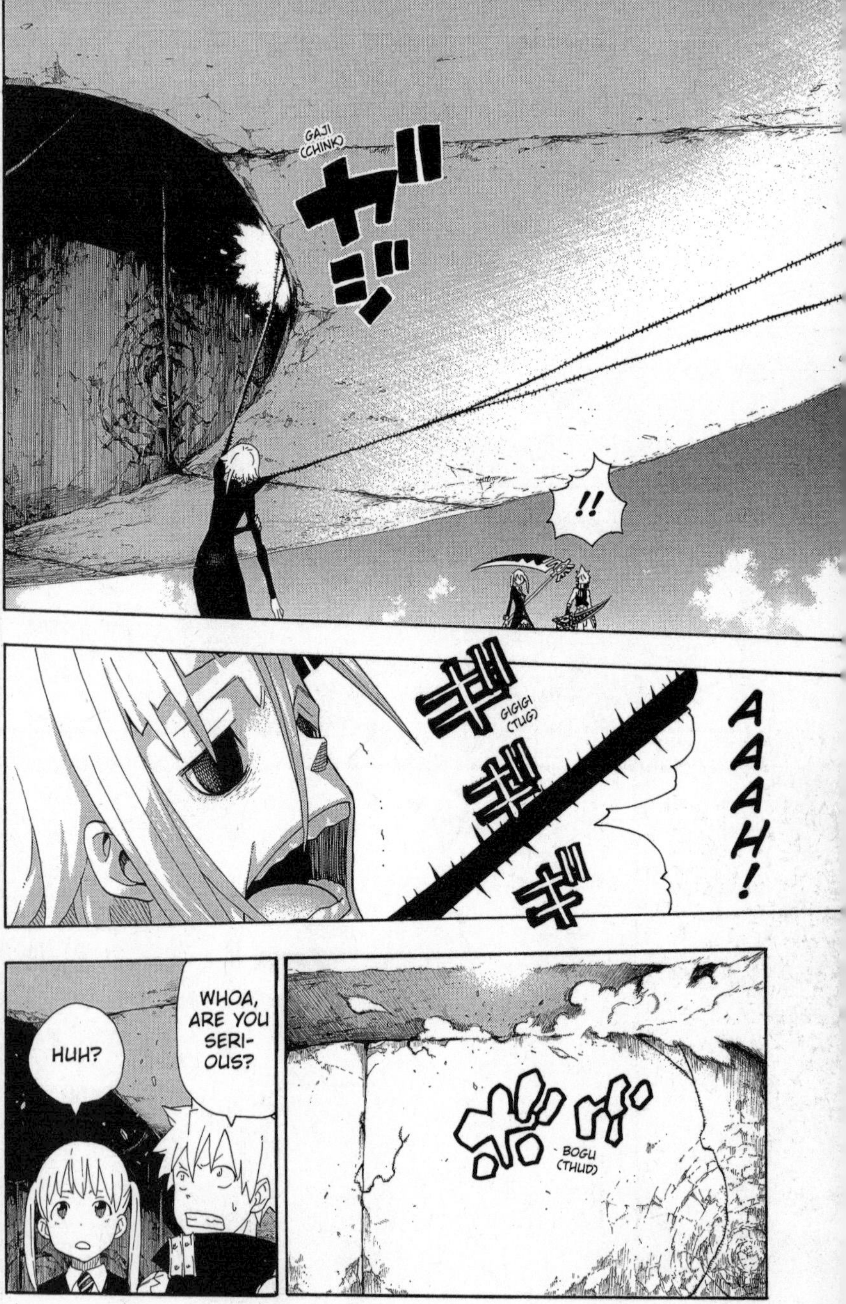
GAJI (CHINK)
!!
GIGIGI (TUG)
AAAH!
BOGU (THUD)
WHOA, ARE YOU SERI-OUS?
HUH?

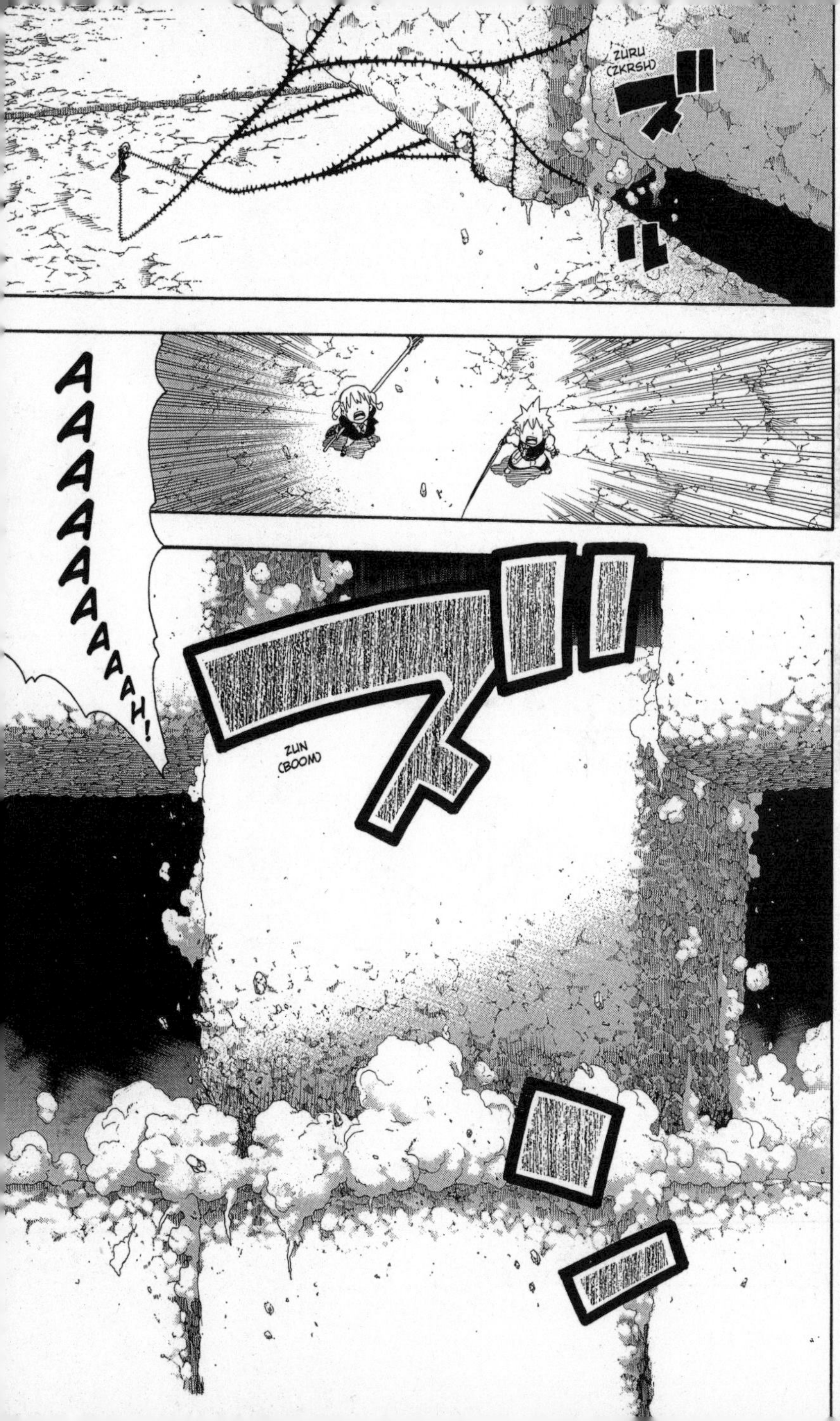
ZURU (ZKRSH)
AAAAAAAAAH!
ZUN (BOOM)

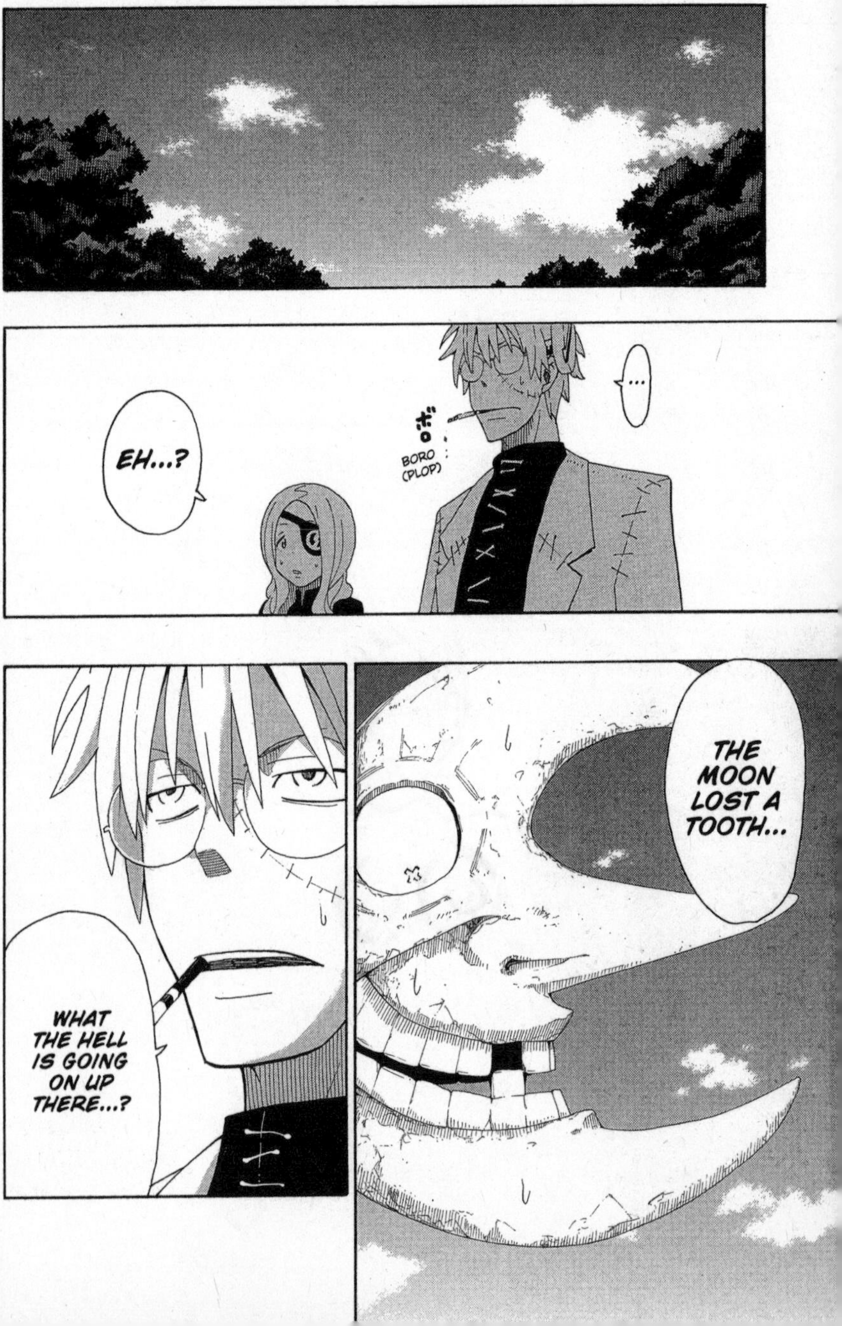
...
ボロ
BORO (PLOP)
EH...?
THE MOON LOST A TOOTH...
WHAT THE HELL IS GOING ON UP THERE...?

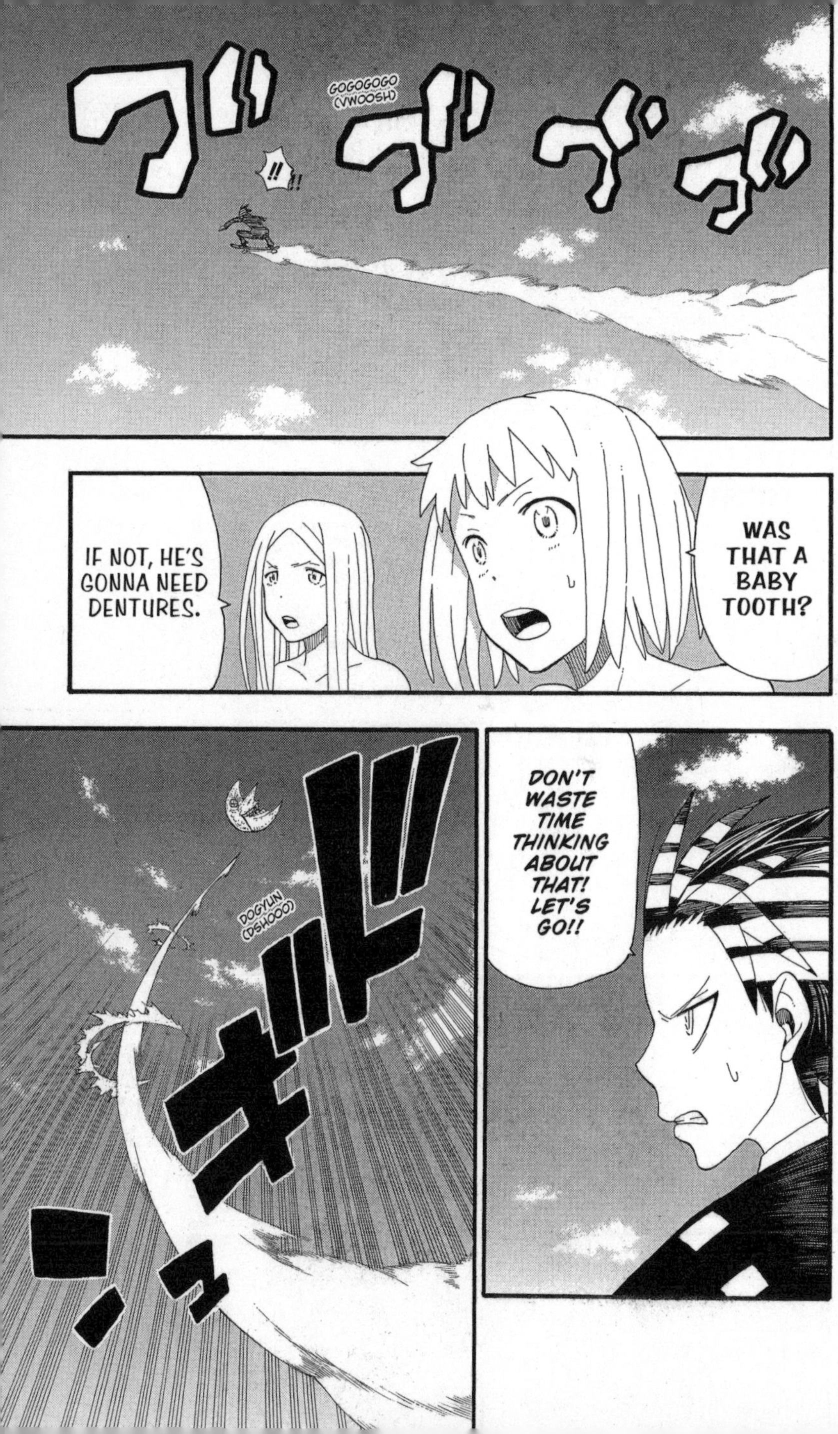
GOGOGOGO (VWOOSH)
!!
WAS THAT A BABY TOOTH?
IF NOT, HE'S GONNA NEED DENTURES.
DON'T WASTE TIME THINKING ABOUT THAT! LET'S GO!!
DOGYUN (DSHOOO)

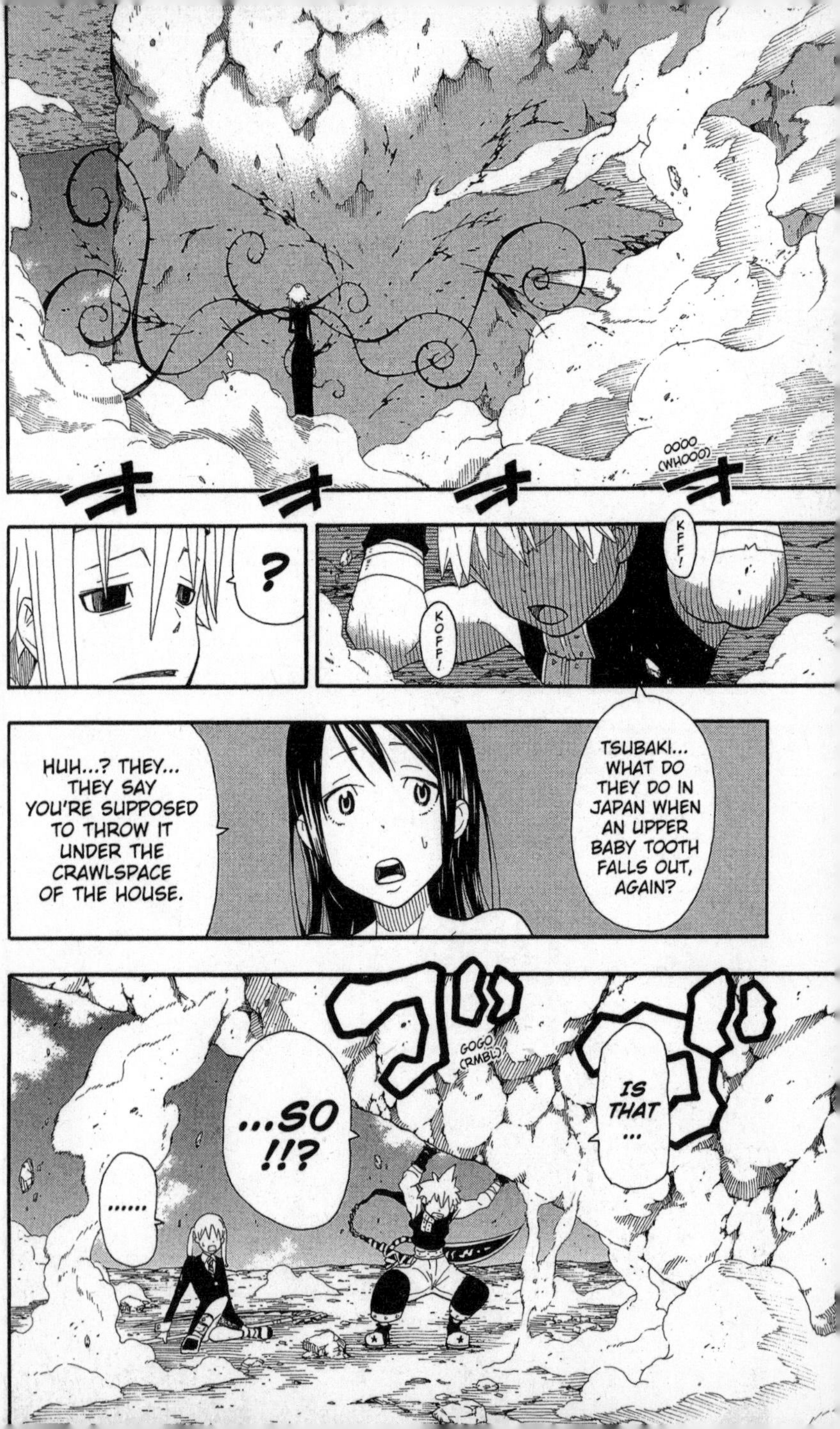
OOOO (WHOOO)
KFF!
KOFF!
?
TSUBAKI... WHAT DO THEY DO IN JAPAN WHEN AN UPPER BABY TOOTH FALLS OUT, AGAIN?
HUH...? THEY... THEY SAY YOU'RE SUPPOSED TO THROW IT UNDER THE CRAWLSPACE OF THE HOUSE.
IS THAT...
GOGO (RMBL)
...SO!!?
......

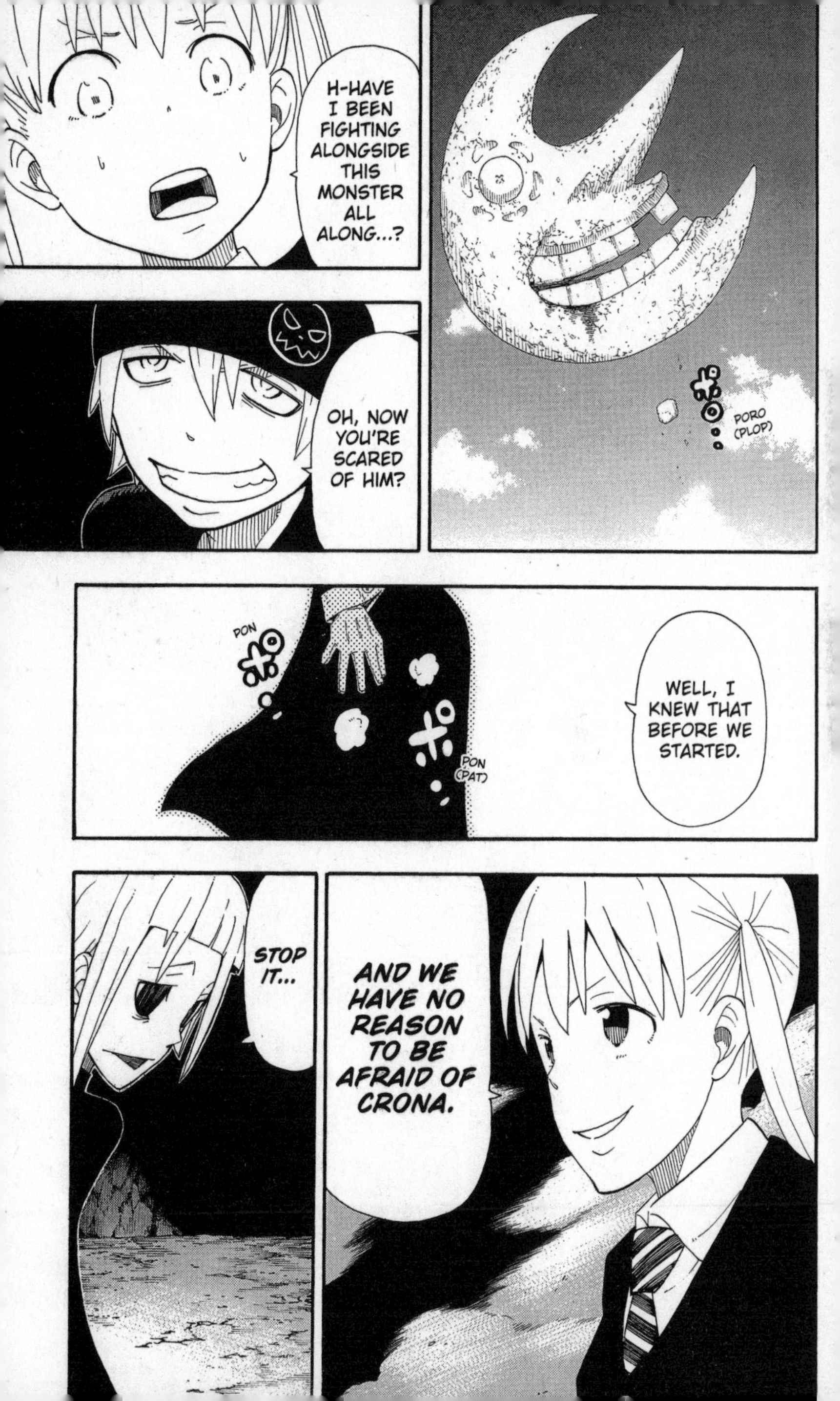
PORO (PLOP)
H-HAVE I BEEN FIGHTING ALONGSIDE THIS MONSTER ALL ALONG...?
OH, NOW YOU'RE SCARED OF HIM?
WELL, I KNEW THAT BEFORE WE STARTED.
PON
PON (PAT)
AND WE HAVE NO REASON TO BE AFRAID OF CRONA.
STOP IT...

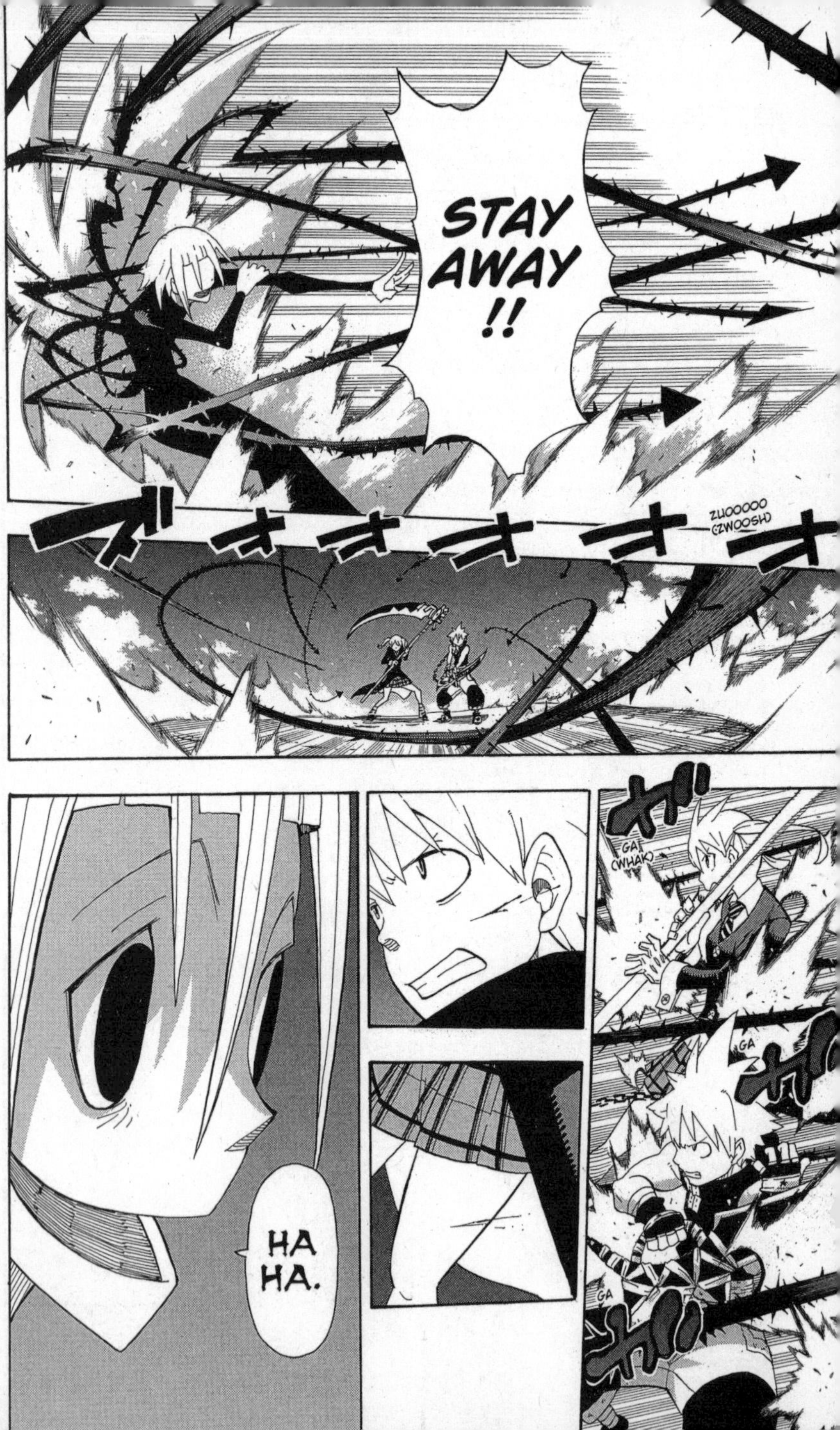
STAY AWAY!!
ZUOOOOO (ZWOOSH)
GA (WHAK)
GA
GA
HA HA.

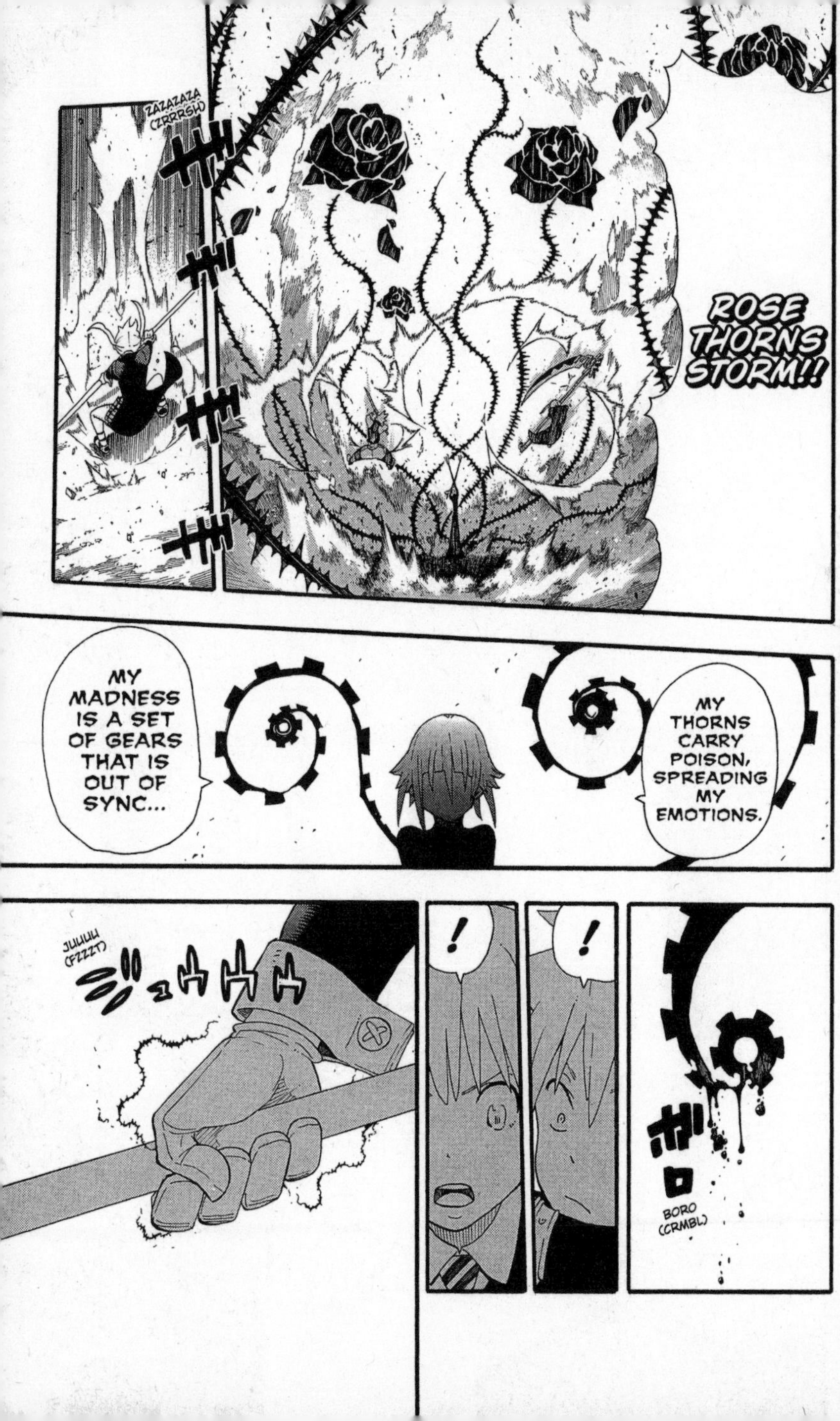
ROSE THORNS STORM!!
ZAZAZAZA (ZRRRSH)
MY THORNS CARRY POISON, SPREADING MY EMOTIONS.
MY MADNESS IS A SET OF GEARS THAT IS OUT OF SYNC...
BORO (CRMBL)
!
!
JUUUU (FZZZT)

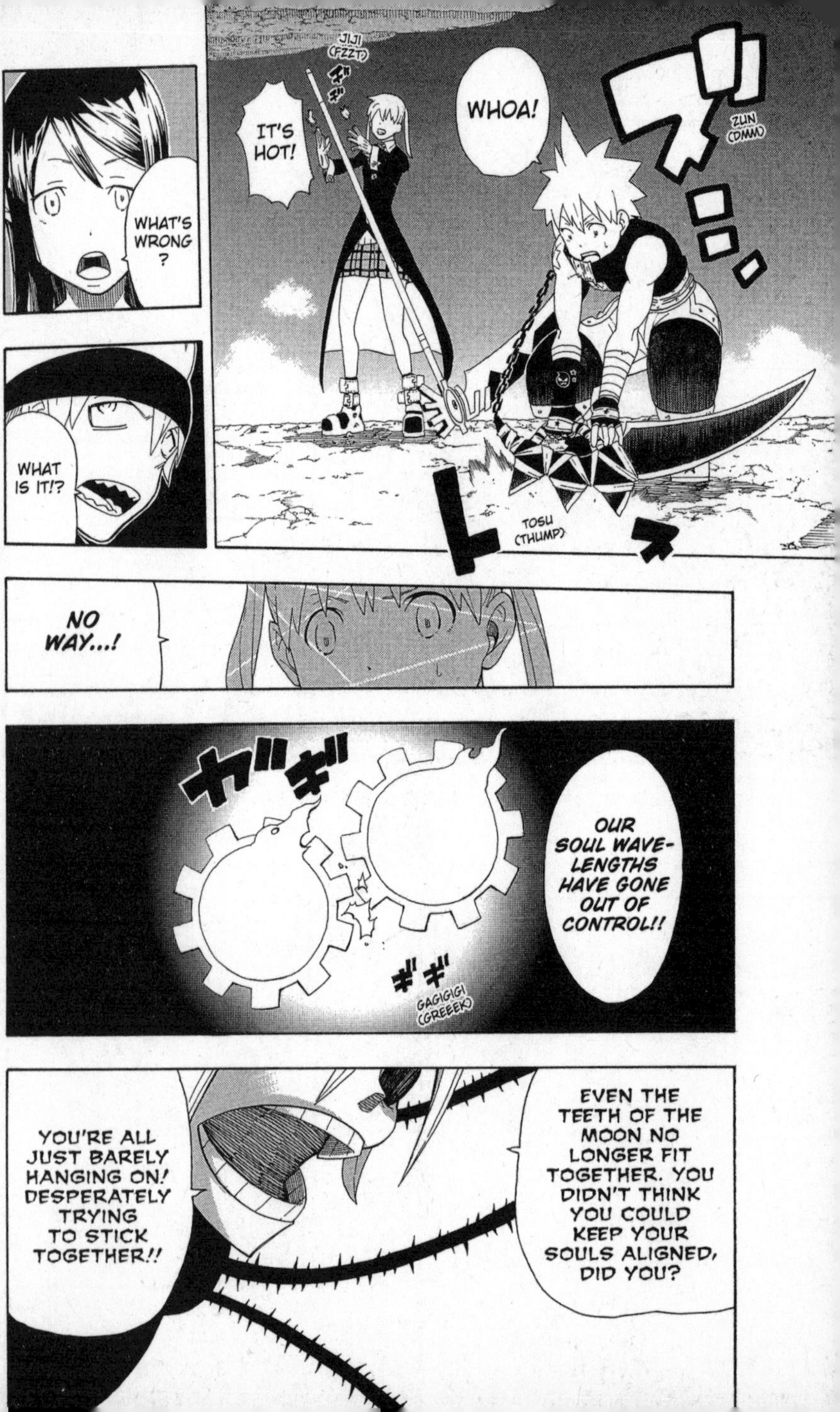
ZUN (DMM)
WHOA!
JIJI (FZZT)
IT'S HOT!
TOSU (THUMP)
WHAT'S WRONG?
WHAT IS IT!?
NO WAY...!
OUR SOUL WAVE-LENGTHS HAVE GONE OUT OF CONTROL!!
GAGIGIGI (GREEEK)
EVEN THE TEETH OF THE MOON NO LONGER FIT TOGETHER. YOU DIDN'T THINK YOU COULD KEEP YOUR SOULS ALIGNED, DID YOU?
YOU'RE ALL JUST BARELY HANGING ON! DESPERATELY TRYING TO STICK TOGETHER!!

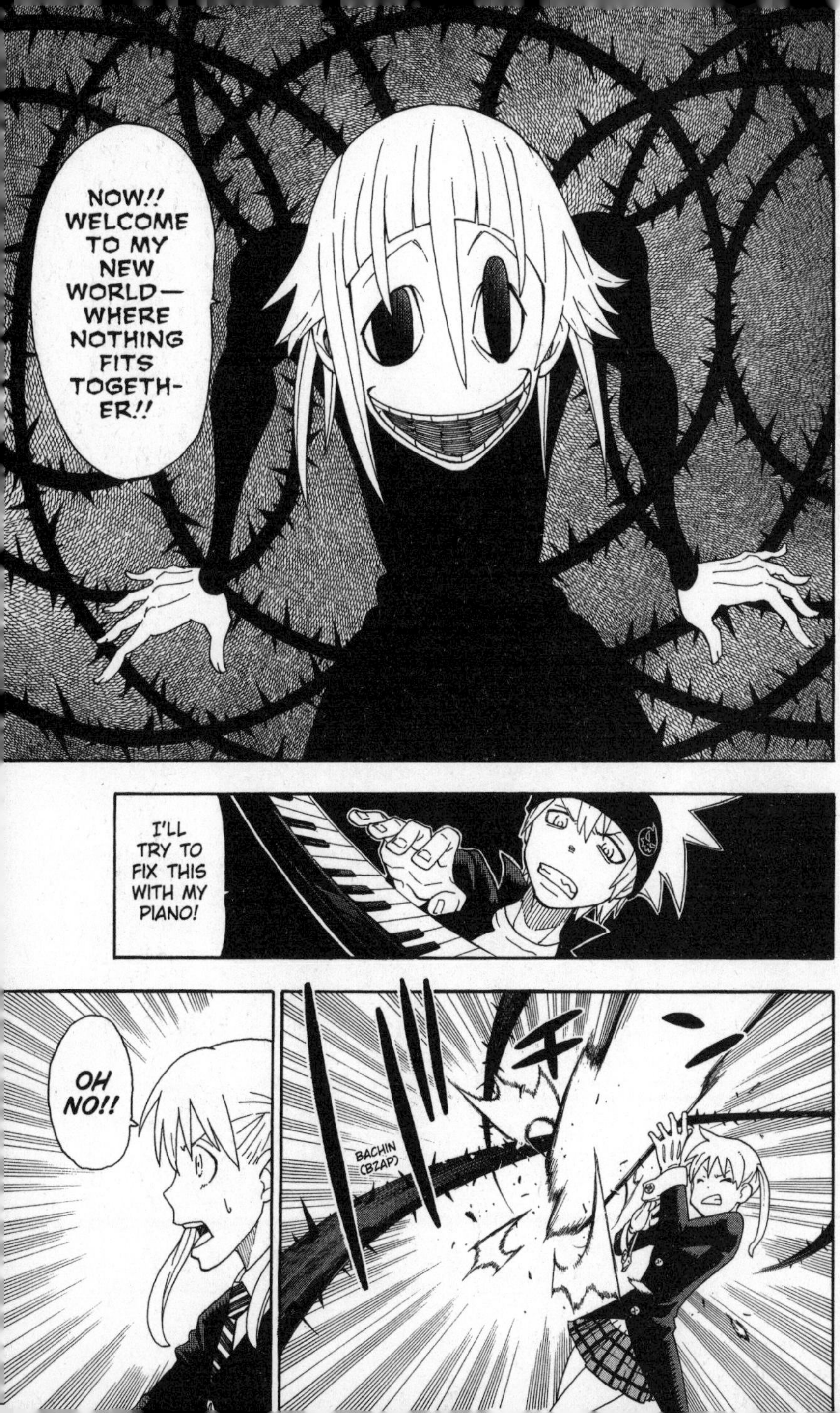
NOW!! WELCOME TO MY NEW WORLD—WHERE NOTHING FITS TOGETH-ER!!
I'LL TRY TO FIX THIS WITH MY PIANO!
BACHIN (BZAP)
OH NO!!

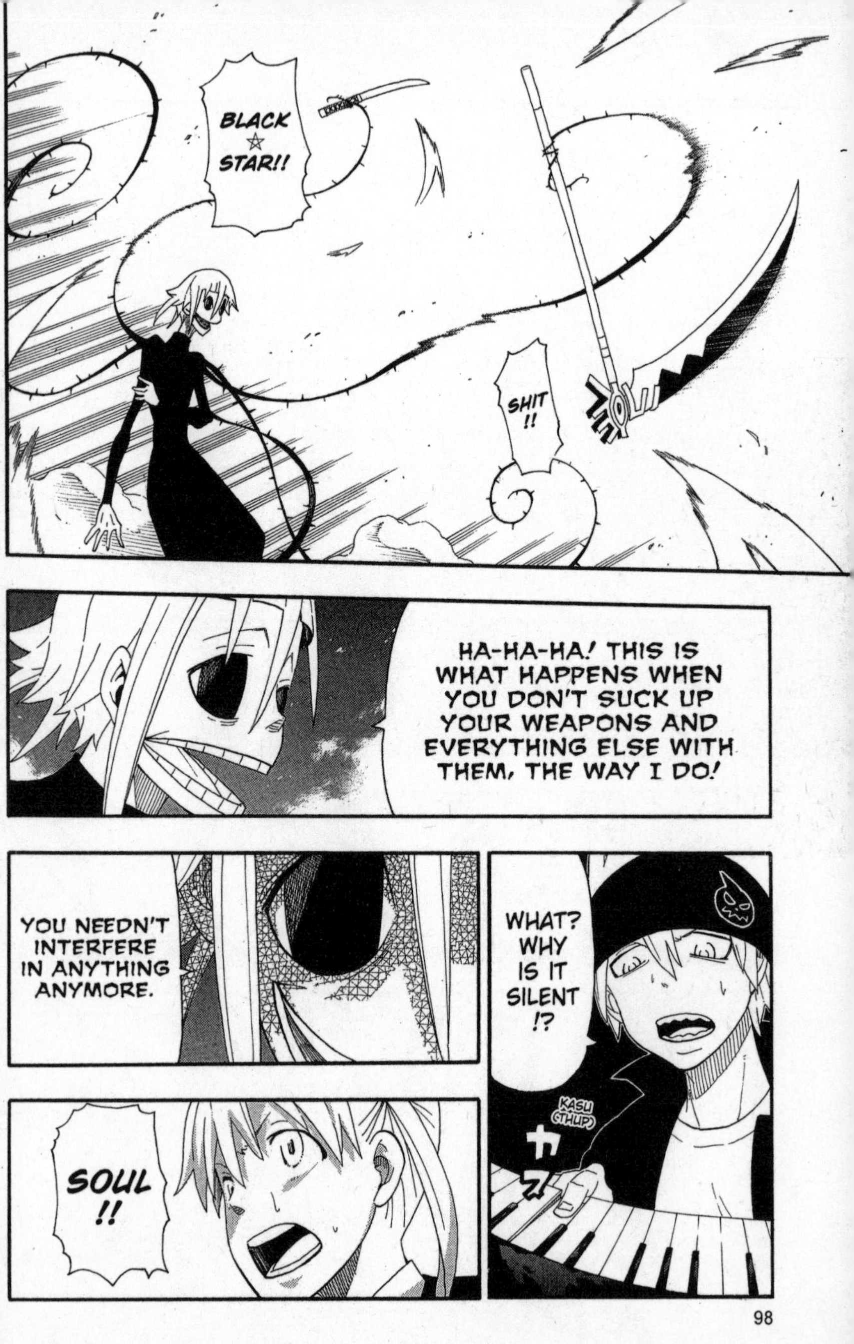
BLACK ☆ STAR!!
SHIT!!
HA-HA-HA! THIS IS WHAT HAPPENS WHEN YOU DON'T SUCK UP YOUR WEAPONS AND EVERYTHING ELSE WITH THEM, THE WAY I DO!
WHAT? WHY IS IT SILENT!?
KASU (THUP)
YOU NEEDN'T INTERFERE IN ANYTHING ANYMORE.
SOUL!!

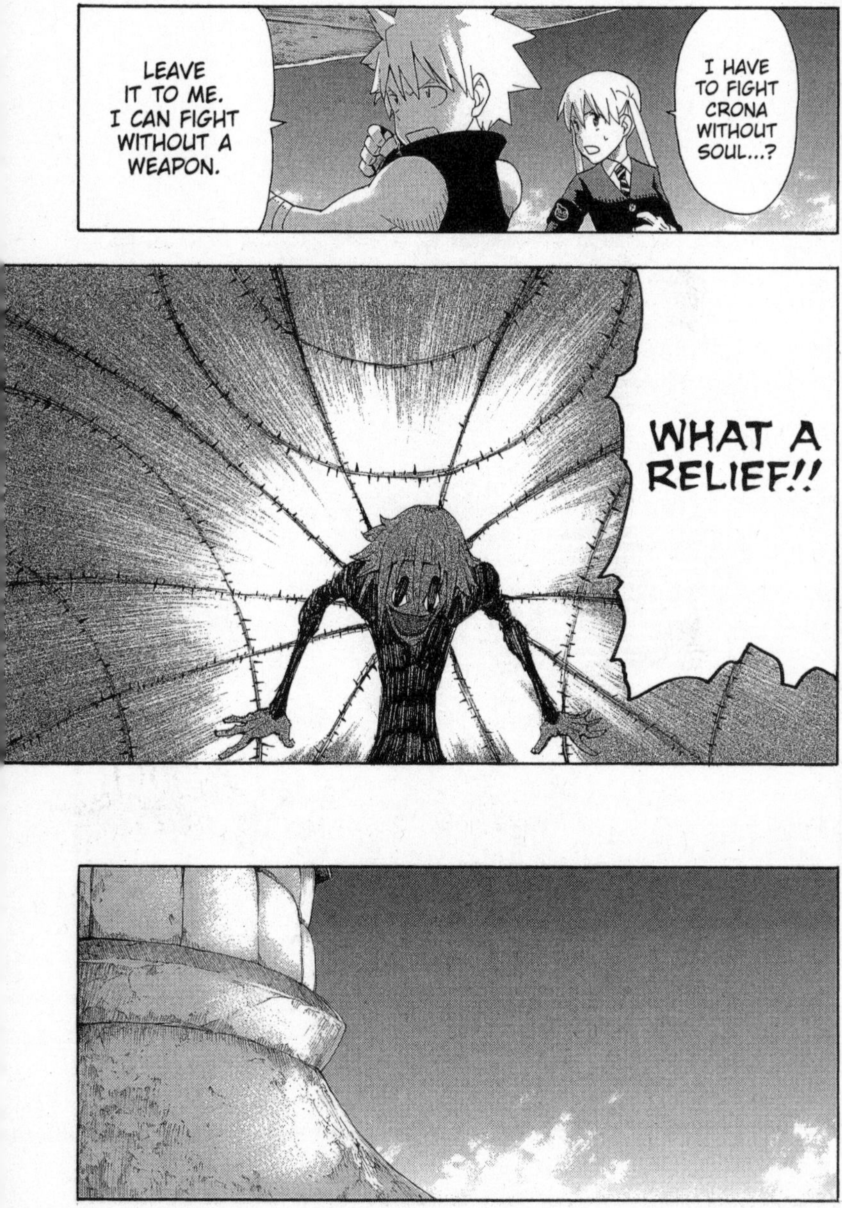

I HAVE TO FIGHT CRONA WITHOUT SOUL...?
LEAVE IT TO ME. I CAN FIGHT WITHOUT A WEAPON.
WHAT A RELIEF!!

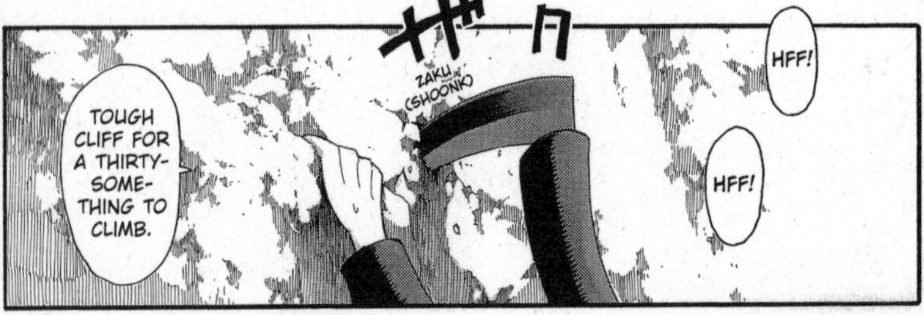
HFF!
HFF!
ZAKU (SHOONK)
TOUGH CLIFF FOR A THIRTY-SOMETHING TO CLIMB.

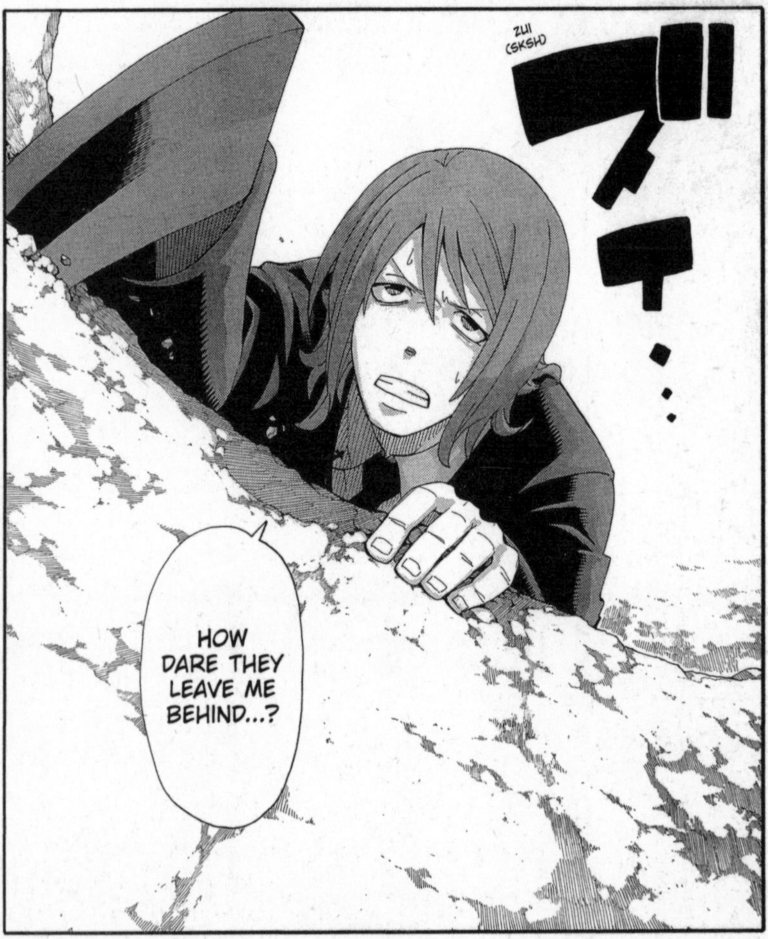
ZUI (SKSH)
HOW DARE THEY LEAVE ME BEHIND...?

SOUL EATER

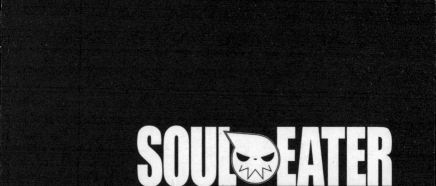

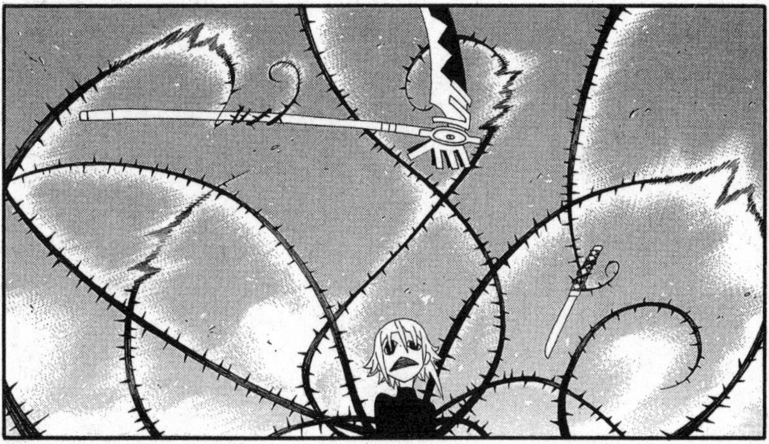

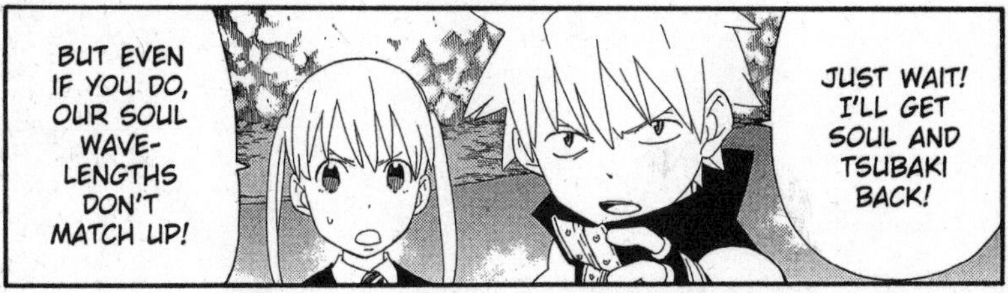
JUST WAIT! I'LL GET SOUL AND TSUBAKI BACK!
BUT EVEN IF YOU DO, OUR SOUL WAVE-LENGTHS DON'T MATCH UP!

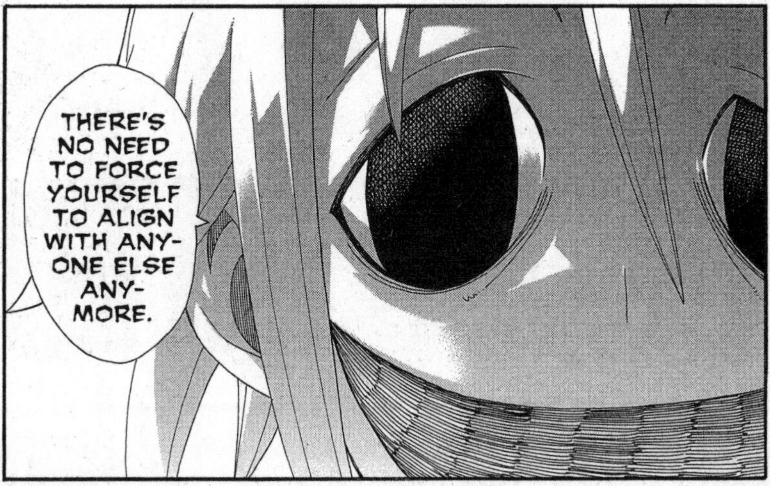
THERE'S NO NEED TO FORCE YOURSELF TO ALIGN WITH ANY-ONE ELSE ANY-MORE.

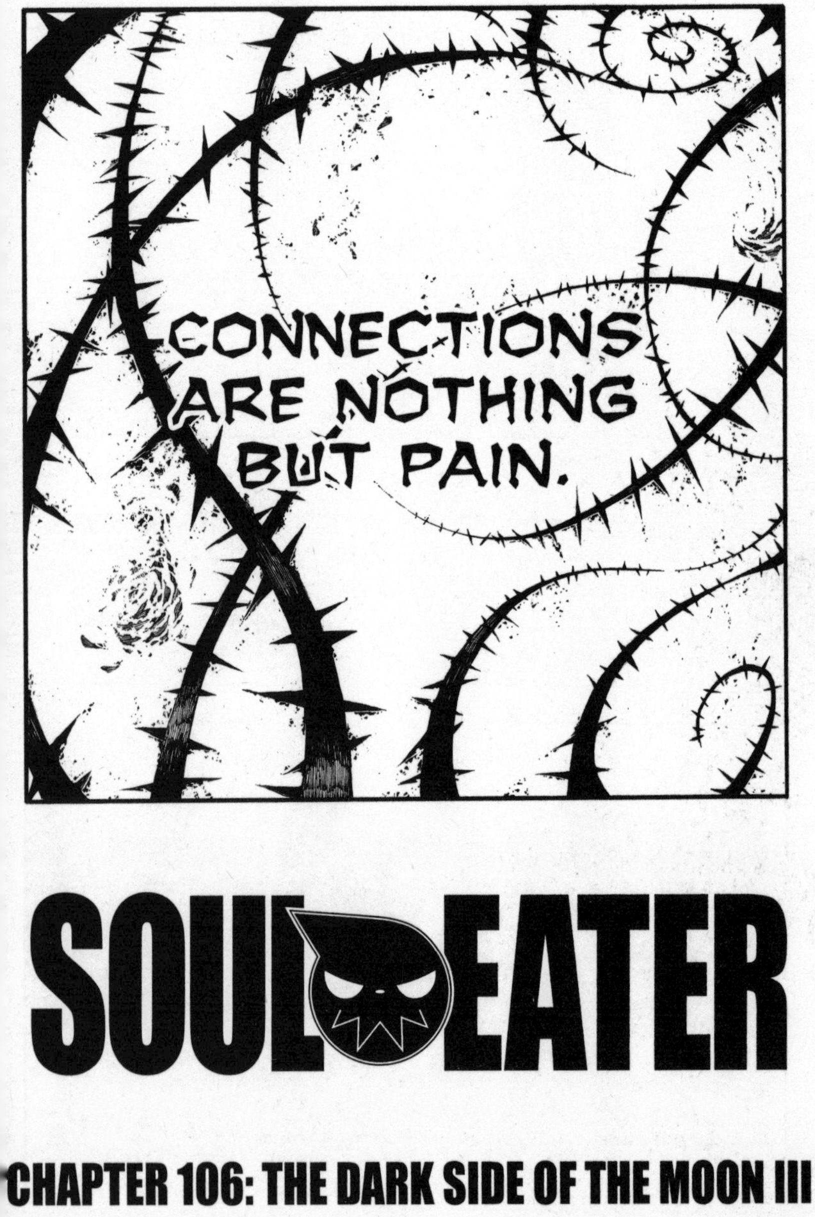
CONNECTIONS ARE NOTHING BUT PAIN.

SOUL EATER

CHAPTER 106: THE DARK SIDE OF THE MOON III

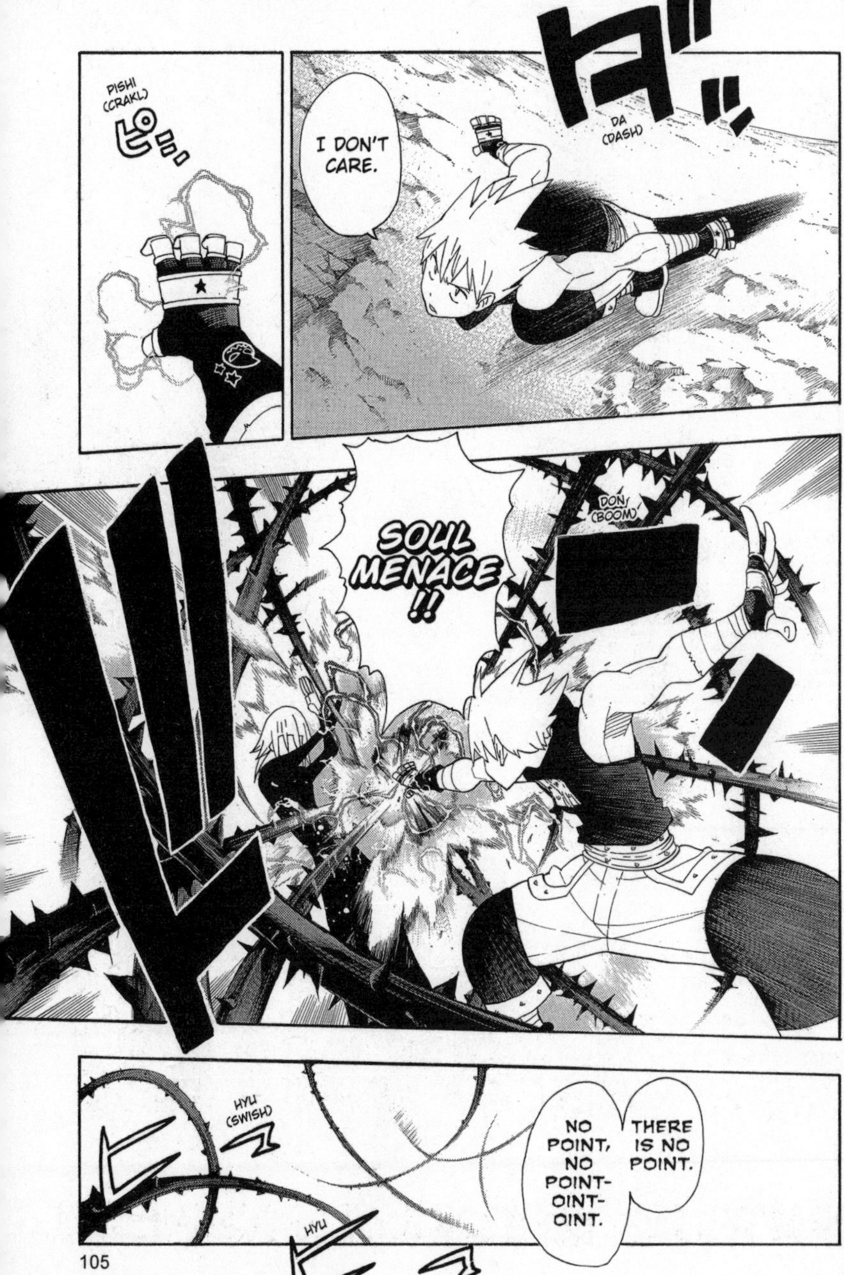
DA (DASH)
I DON'T CARE.
PISHI (CRAKL)
DON (BOOM)
SOUL MENACE!!
THERE IS NO POINT.
NO POINT, NO POINT-OINT-OINT.
HYU (SWISH)
HYU

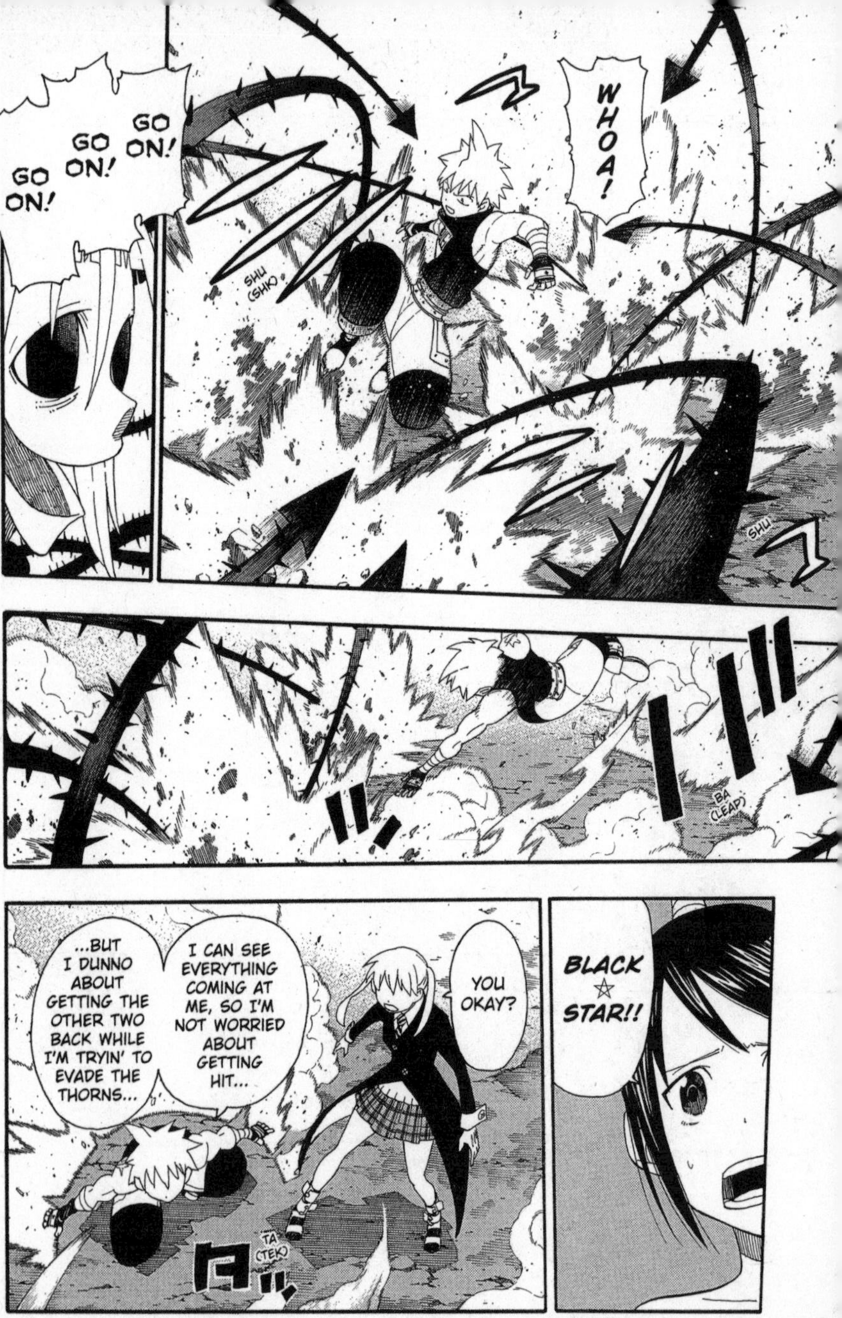
WHOA!
SHU (SHK)
SHU
GO ON!
GO ON!
GO ON!
BA (LEAP)
BLACK☆STAR!!
YOU OKAY?
I CAN SEE EVERYTHING COMING AT ME, SO I'M NOT WORRIED ABOUT GETTING HIT...
...BUT I DUNNO ABOUT GETTING THE OTHER TWO BACK WHILE I'M TRYIN' TO EVADE THE THORNS...
TA (TEK)

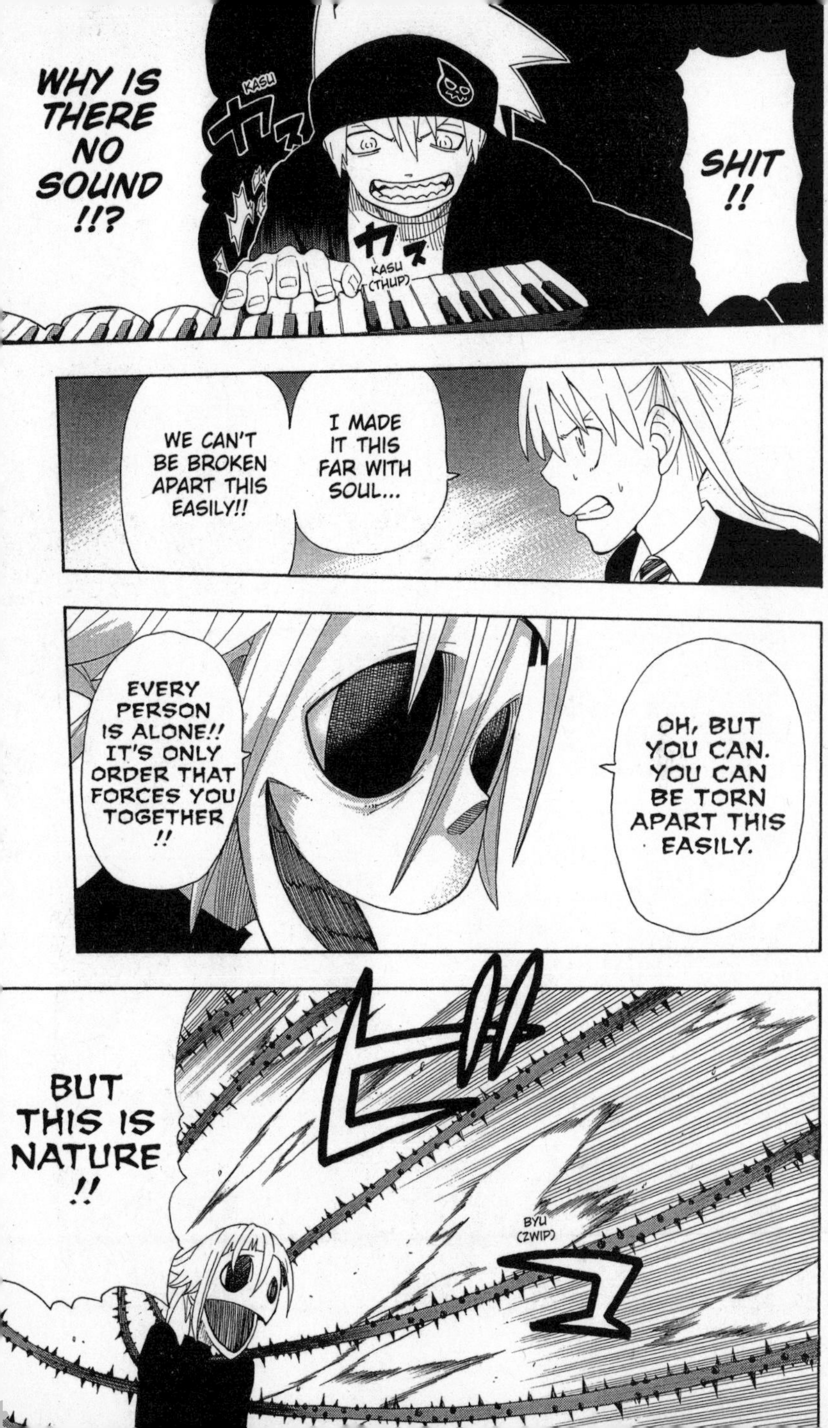
SHIT !!
KASU (THUP)
KASU
WHY IS THERE NO SOUND !!?
I MADE IT THIS FAR WITH SOUL...
WE CAN'T BE BROKEN APART THIS EASILY!!
OH, BUT YOU CAN. YOU CAN BE TORN APART THIS EASILY.
EVERY PERSON IS ALONE!! IT'S ONLY ORDER THAT FORCES YOU TOGETHER !!
BYU (ZWIP)
BUT THIS IS NATURE !!

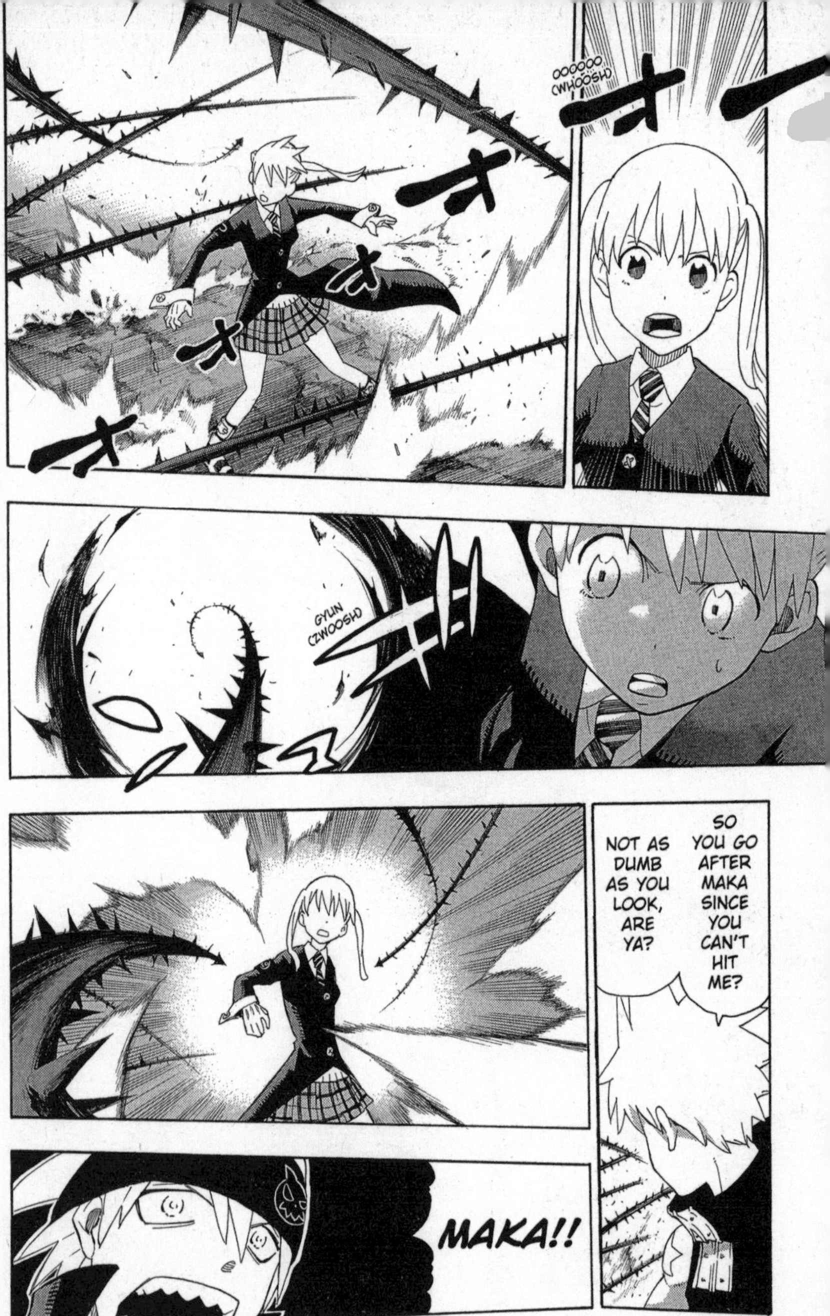
OOOOOO (WHOOSH)
GYUN (ZWOOSH)
SO YOU GO AFTER MAKA SINCE YOU CAN'T HIT ME?
NOT AS DUMB AS YOU LOOK, ARE YA?
MAKA!!

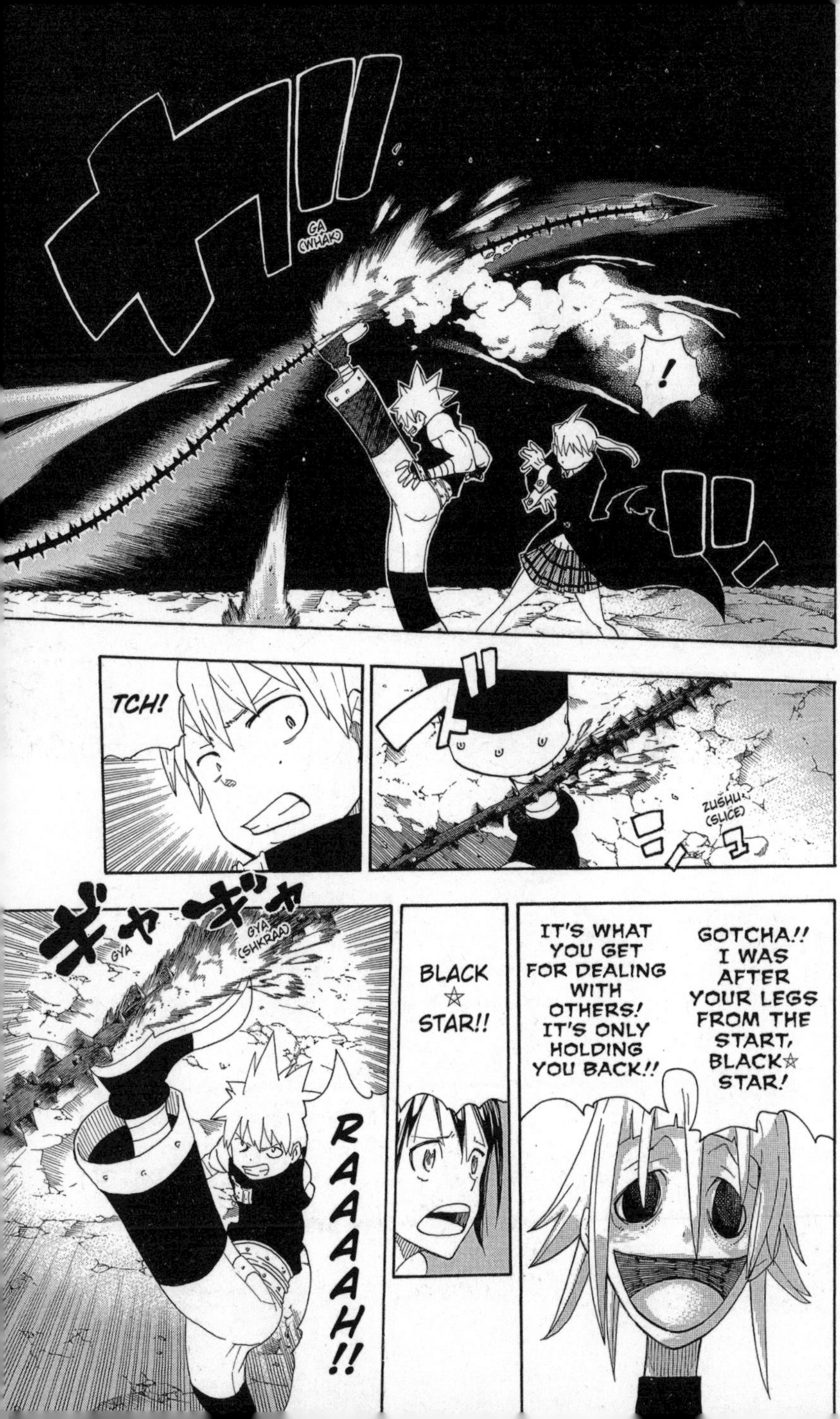
GA (WHAK)
!
ZUSHU (SLICE)
TCH!
GOTCHA!! I WAS AFTER YOUR LEGS FROM THE START, BLACK☆STAR!
IT'S WHAT YOU GET FOR DEALING WITH OTHERS! IT'S ONLY HOLDING YOU BACK!!
BLACK☆STAR!!
GYA GYA (SHKRAA)
RAAAAAH!!

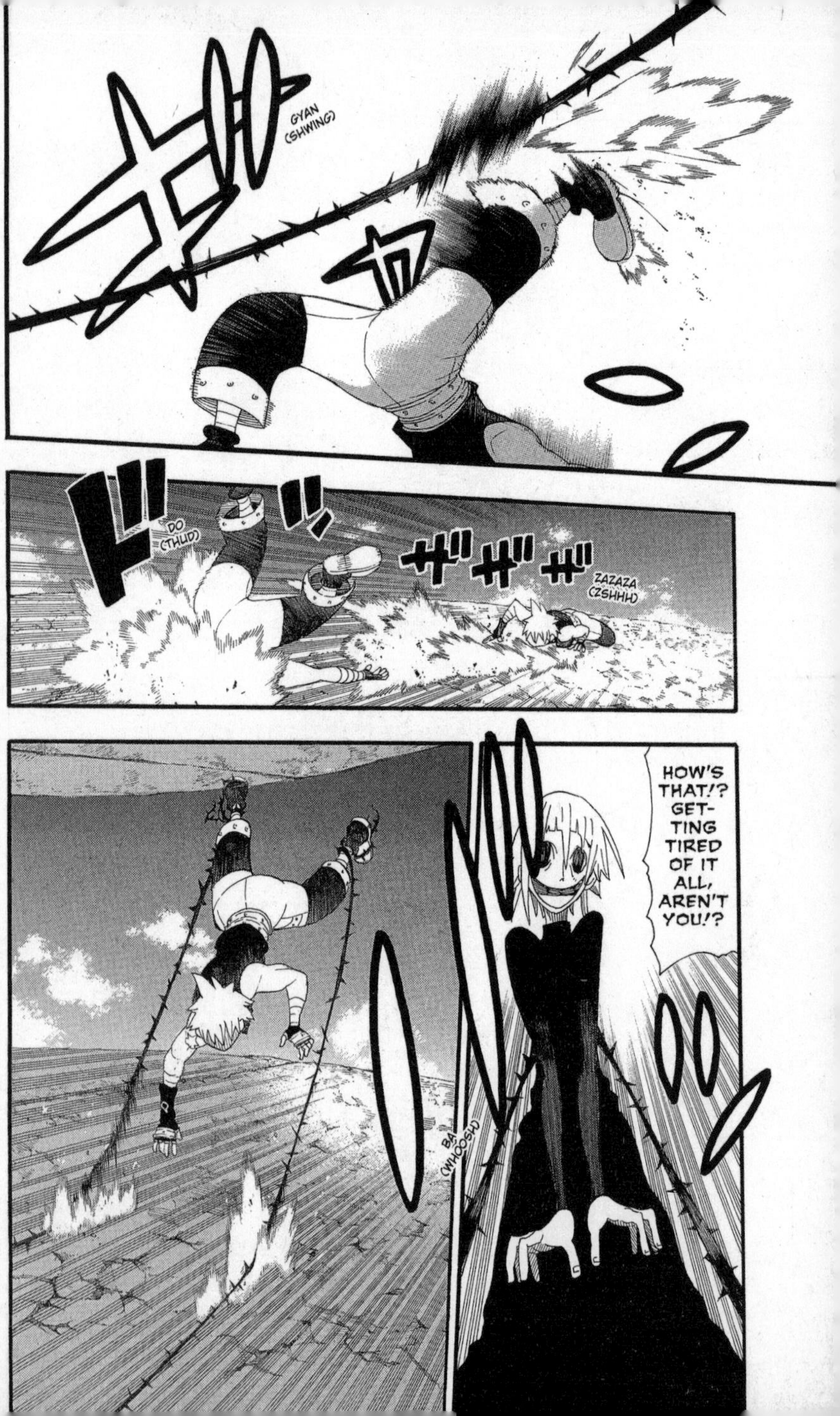
GYAN (SHWING)
DO (THUD)
ZAZAZA (ZSHHH)
HOW'S THAT!? GET-TING TIRED OF IT ALL, AREN'T YOU!?
BA (WHOOSH)

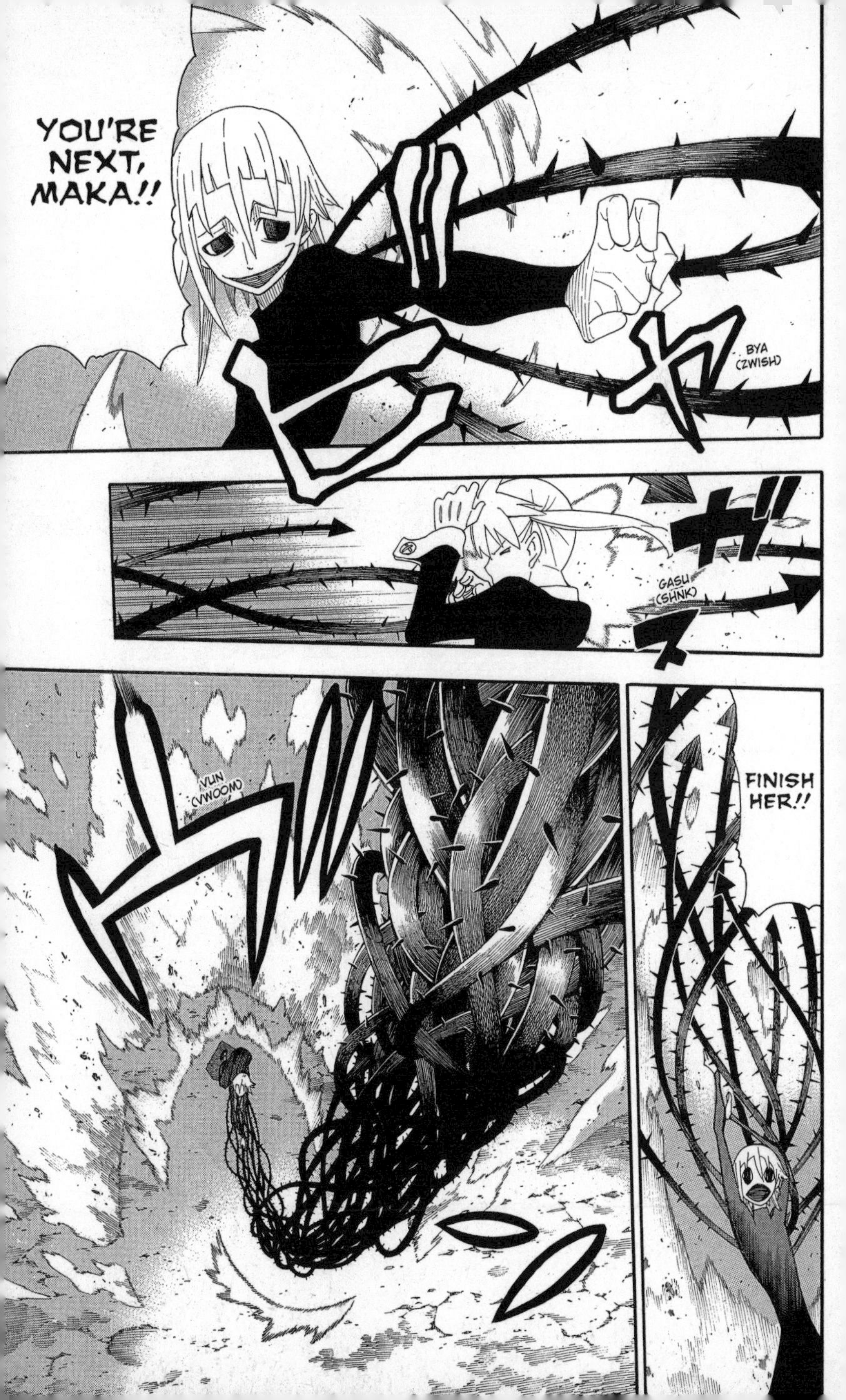
YOU'RE NEXT, MAKA!!
BYA (ZWISH)
GASU (SHNK)
FINISH HER!!
VUN (VWOOM)

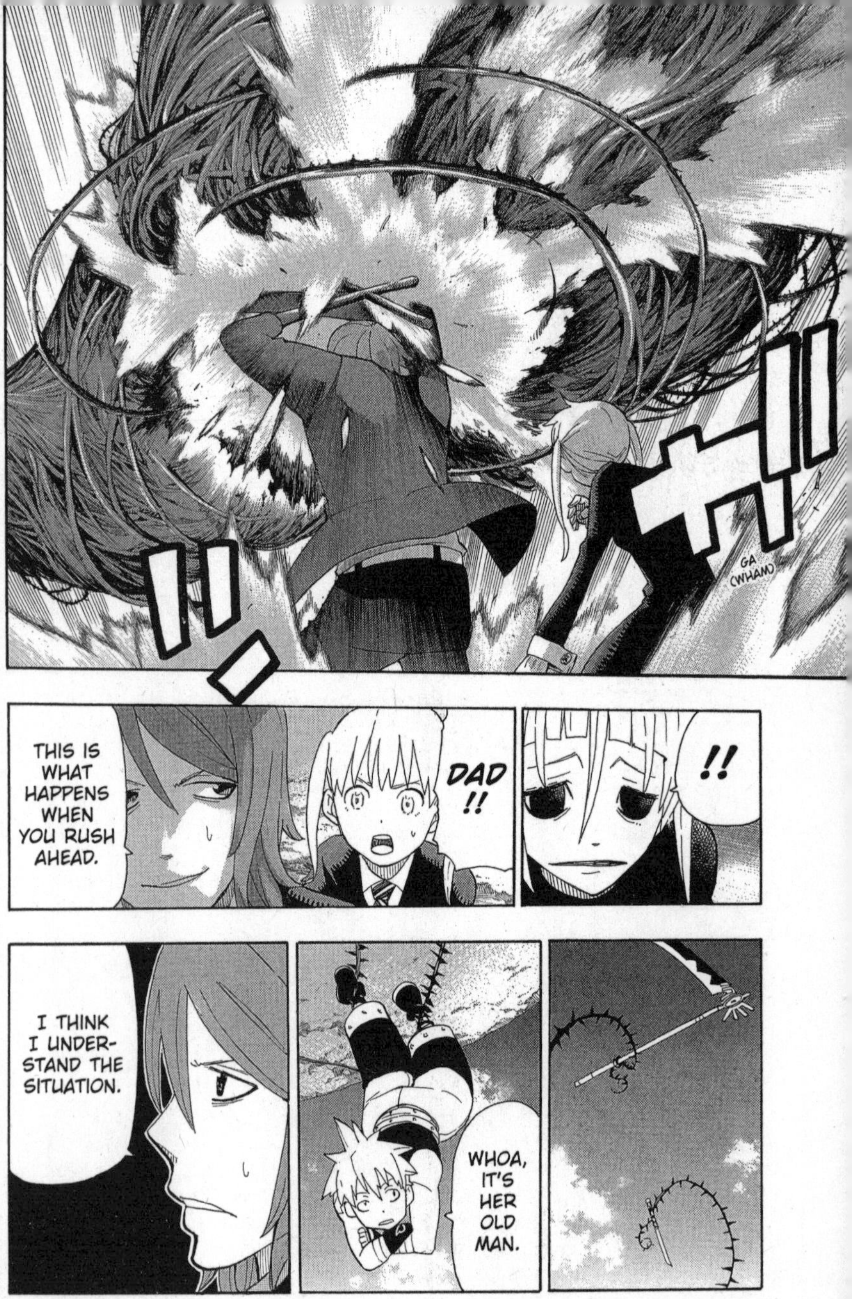
GA (WHAM)
!!
DAD !!
THIS IS WHAT HAPPENS WHEN YOU RUSH AHEAD.
WHOA, IT'S HER OLD MAN.
I THINK I UNDER-STAND THE SITUATION.

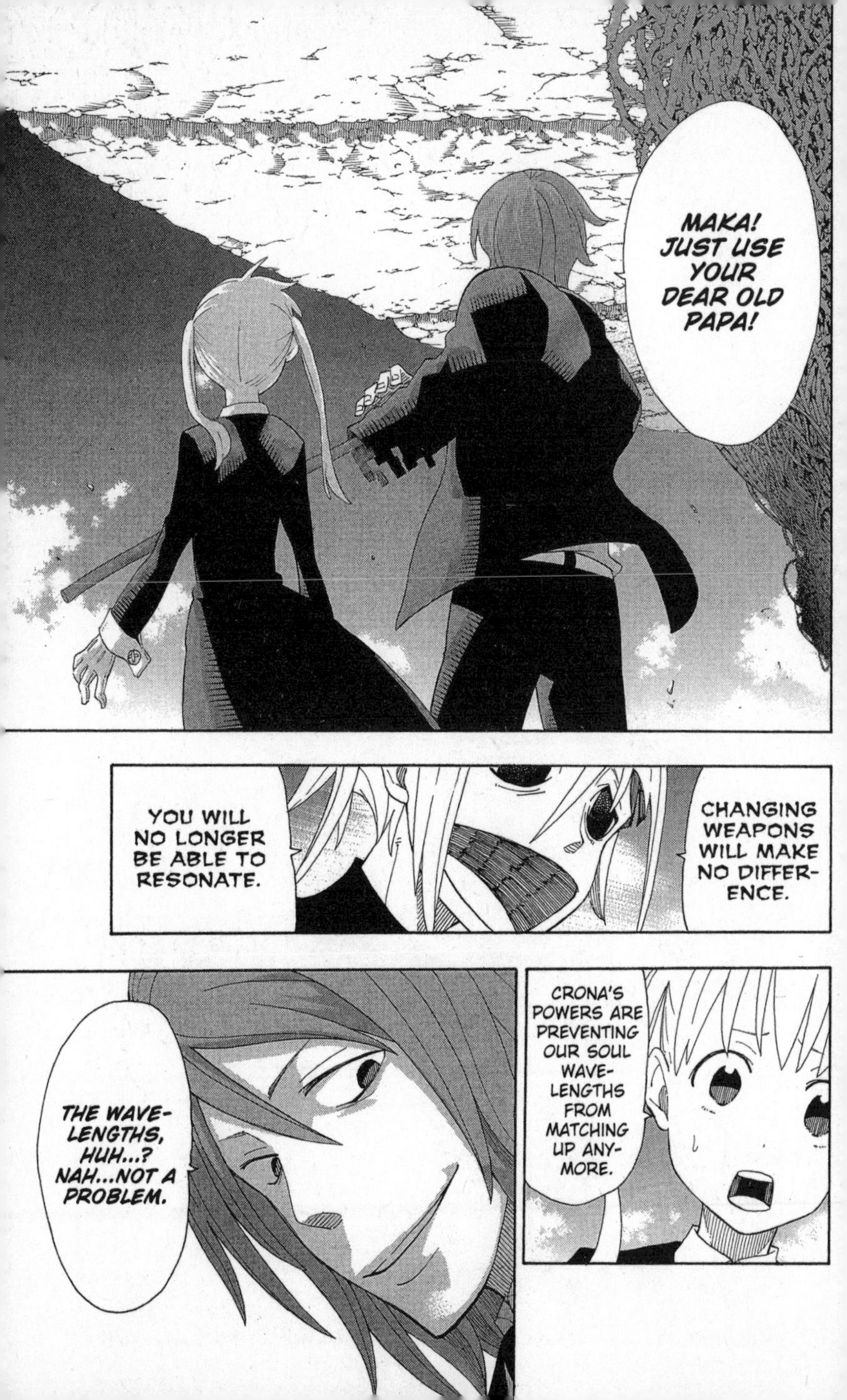
MAKA! JUST USE YOUR DEAR OLD PAPA!
CHANGING WEAPONS WILL MAKE NO DIFFER-ENCE.
YOU WILL NO LONGER BE ABLE TO RESONATE.
CRONA'S POWERS ARE PREVENTING OUR SOUL WAVE-LENGTHS FROM MATCHING UP ANY-MORE.
THE WAVE-LENGTHS, HUH...? NAH...NOT A PROBLEM.

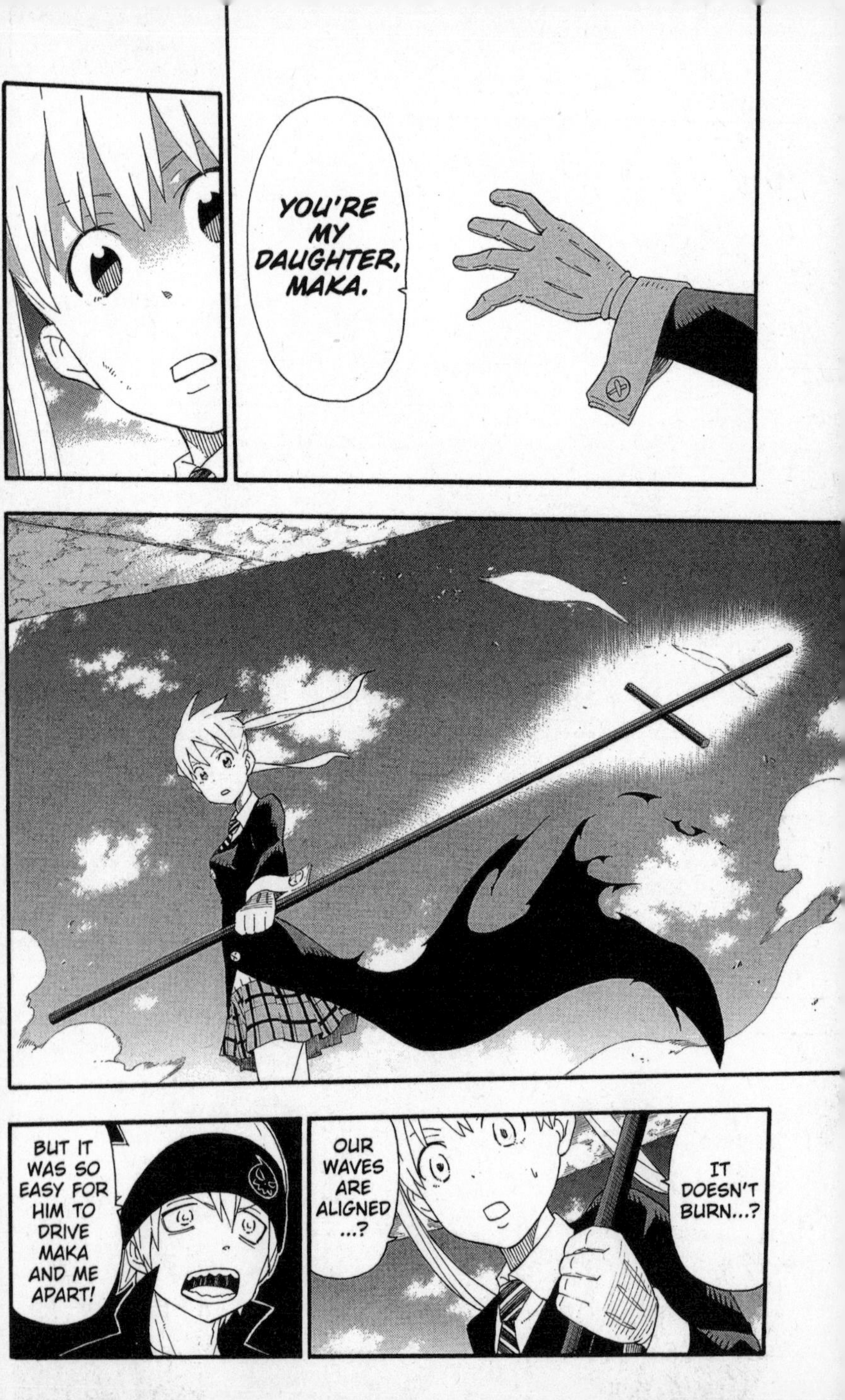
YOU'RE MY DAUGHTER, MAKA.
IT DOESN'T BURN...?
OUR WAVES ARE ALIGNED ...?
BUT IT WAS SO EASY FOR HIM TO DRIVE MAKA AND ME APART!

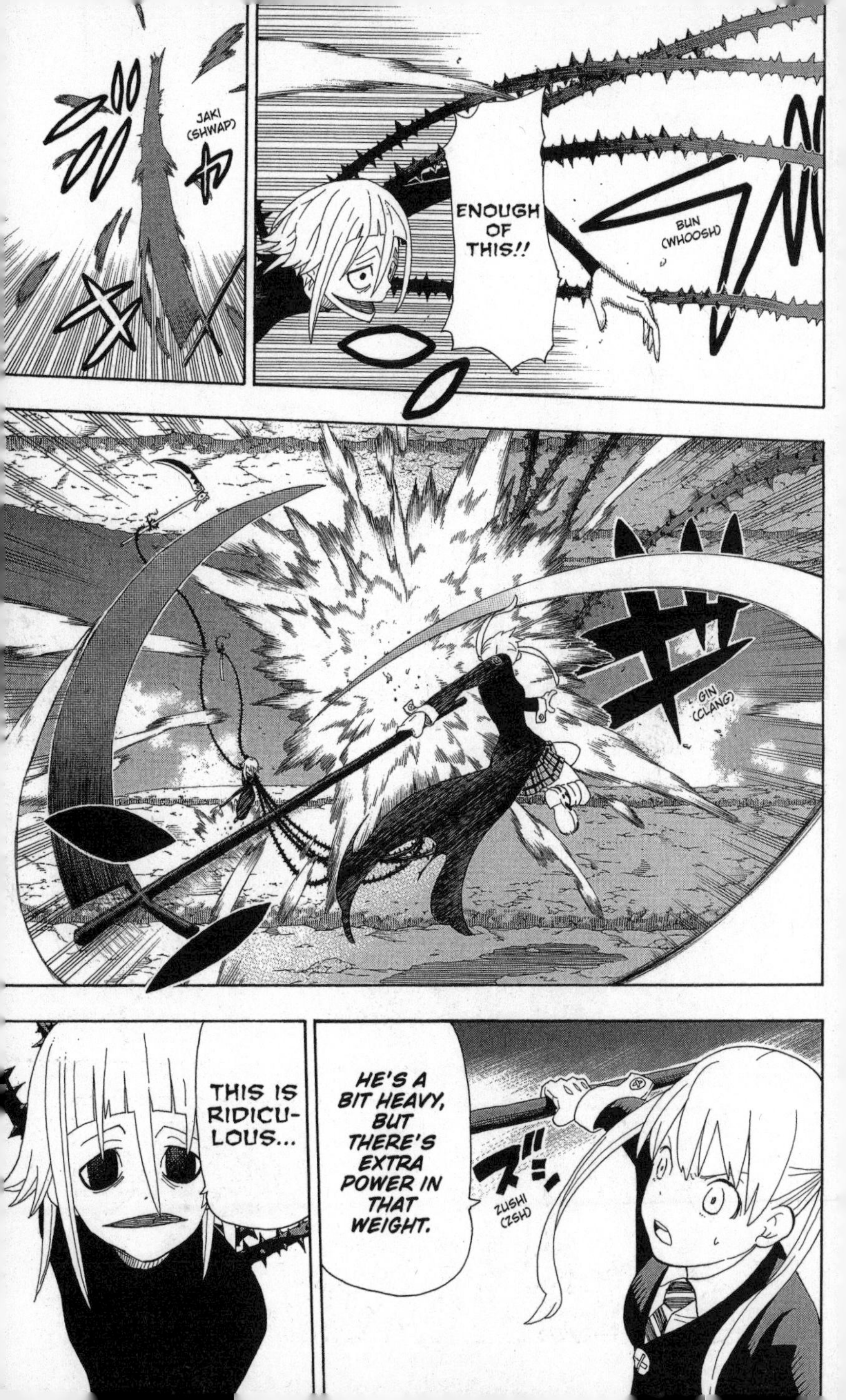
BUN (WHOOSH)
ENOUGH OF THIS!!
JAKI (SHWAP)
GIN (CLANG)
HE'S A BIT HEAVY, BUT THERE'S EXTRA POWER IN THAT WEIGHT.
ZUSHI (ZSH)
THIS IS RIDICULOUS...

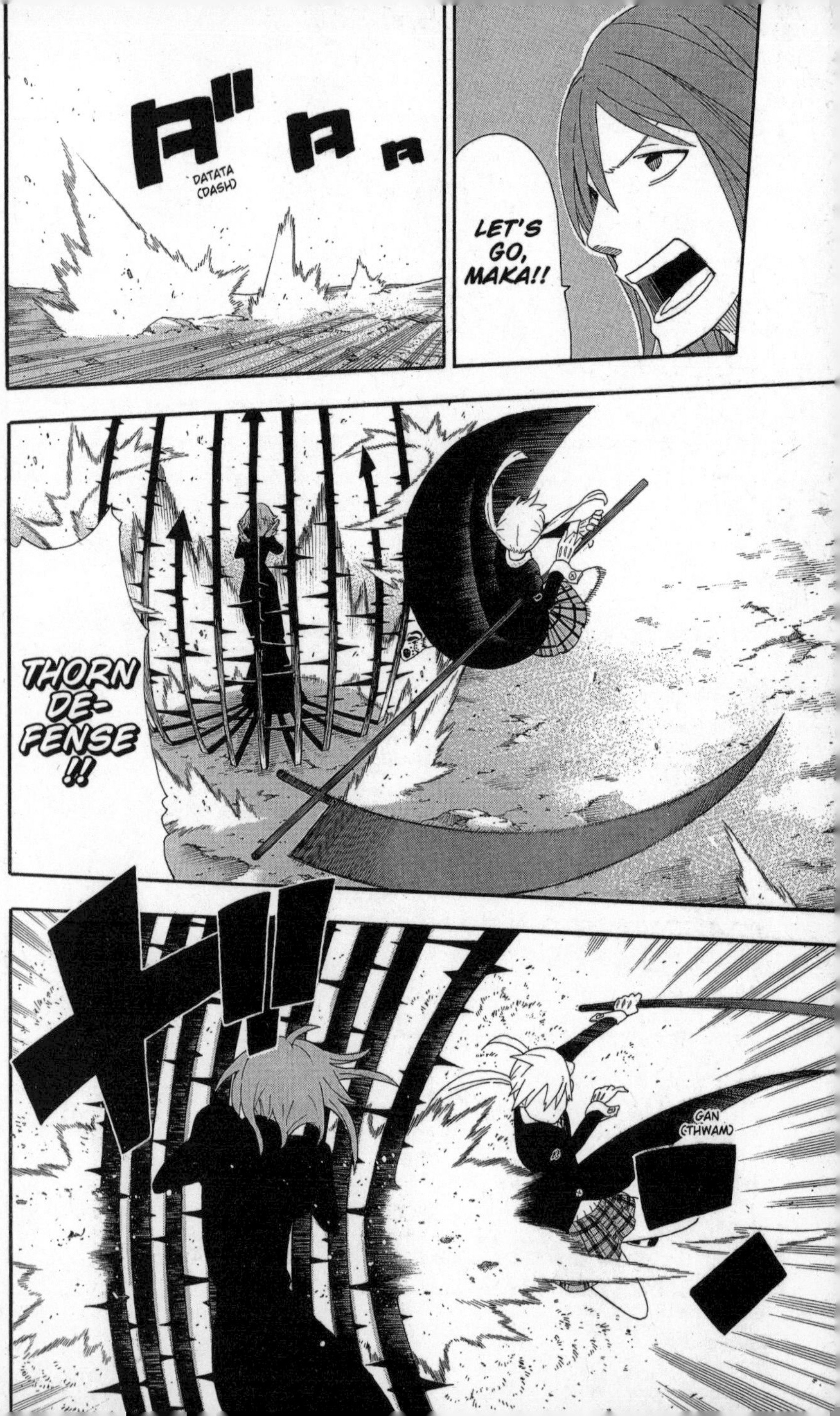
LET'S GO, MAKA!!
DATATA (DASH)
THORN DE-FENSE!!
GAN (THWAM)

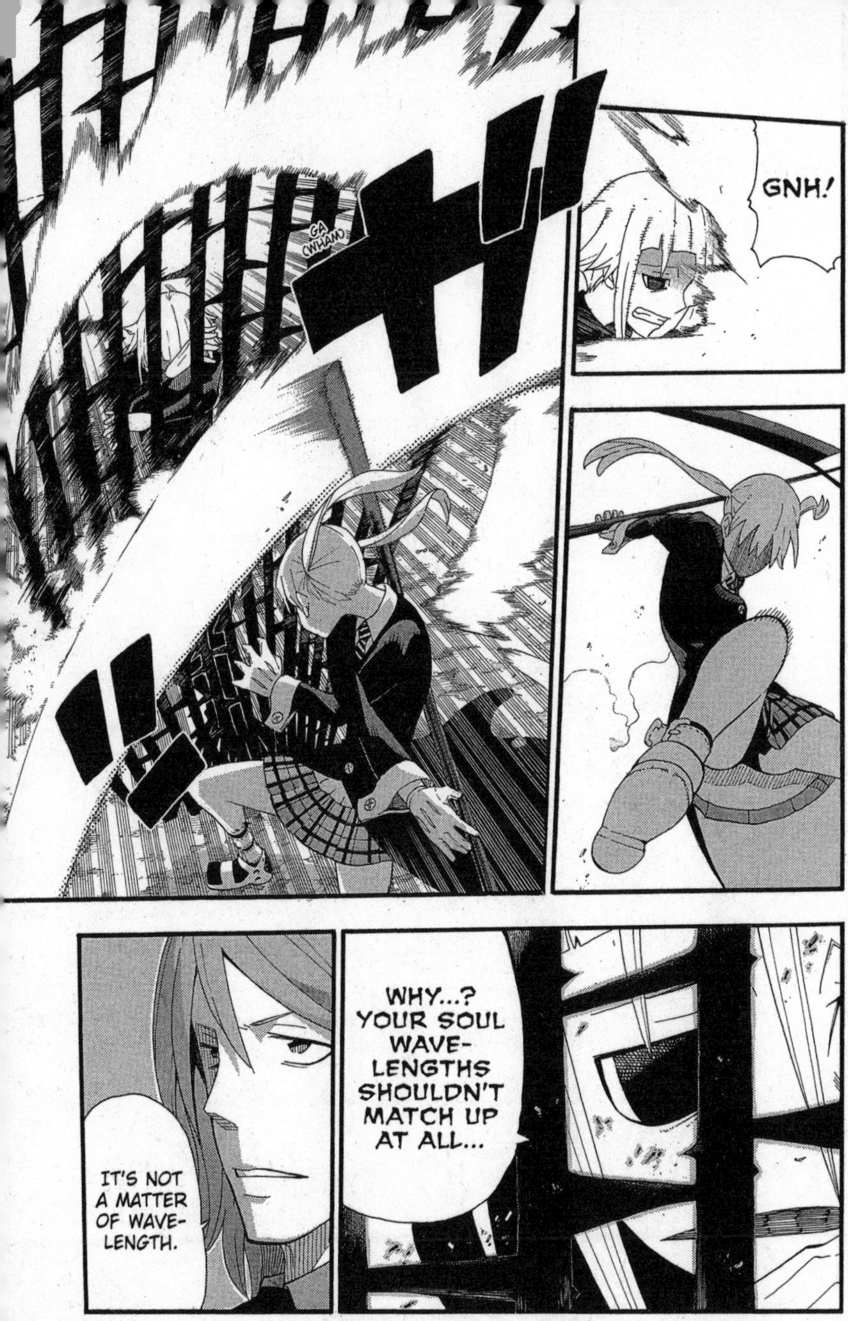
GNH!
GA (WHAM)
WHY...? YOUR SOUL WAVE-LENGTHS SHOULDN'T MATCH UP AT ALL...
IT'S NOT A MATTER OF WAVE-LENGTH.

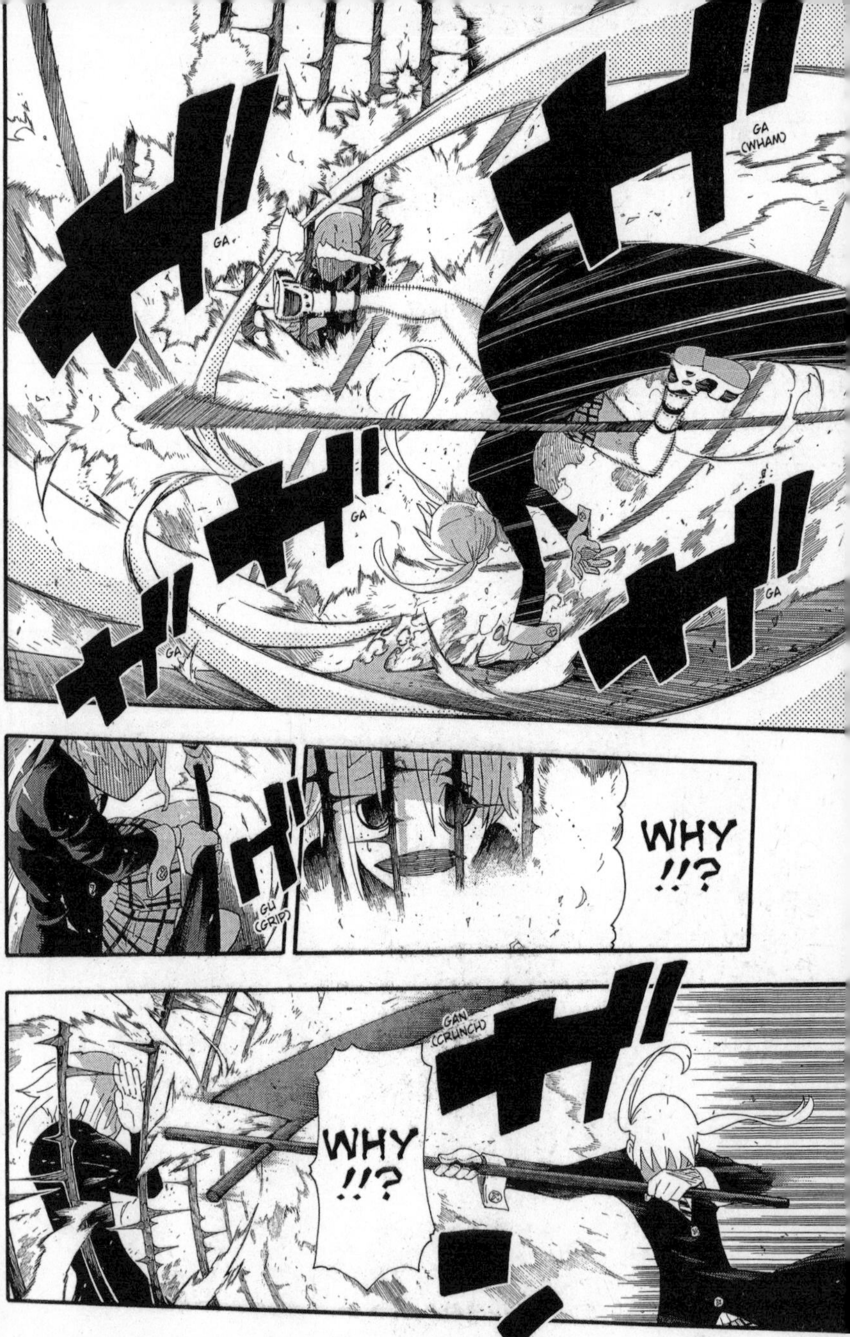
GA (WHAM)
GA
GA
GA
GA
WHY!!?
GU (GRIP)
GAN (CRUNCH)
WHY!!?

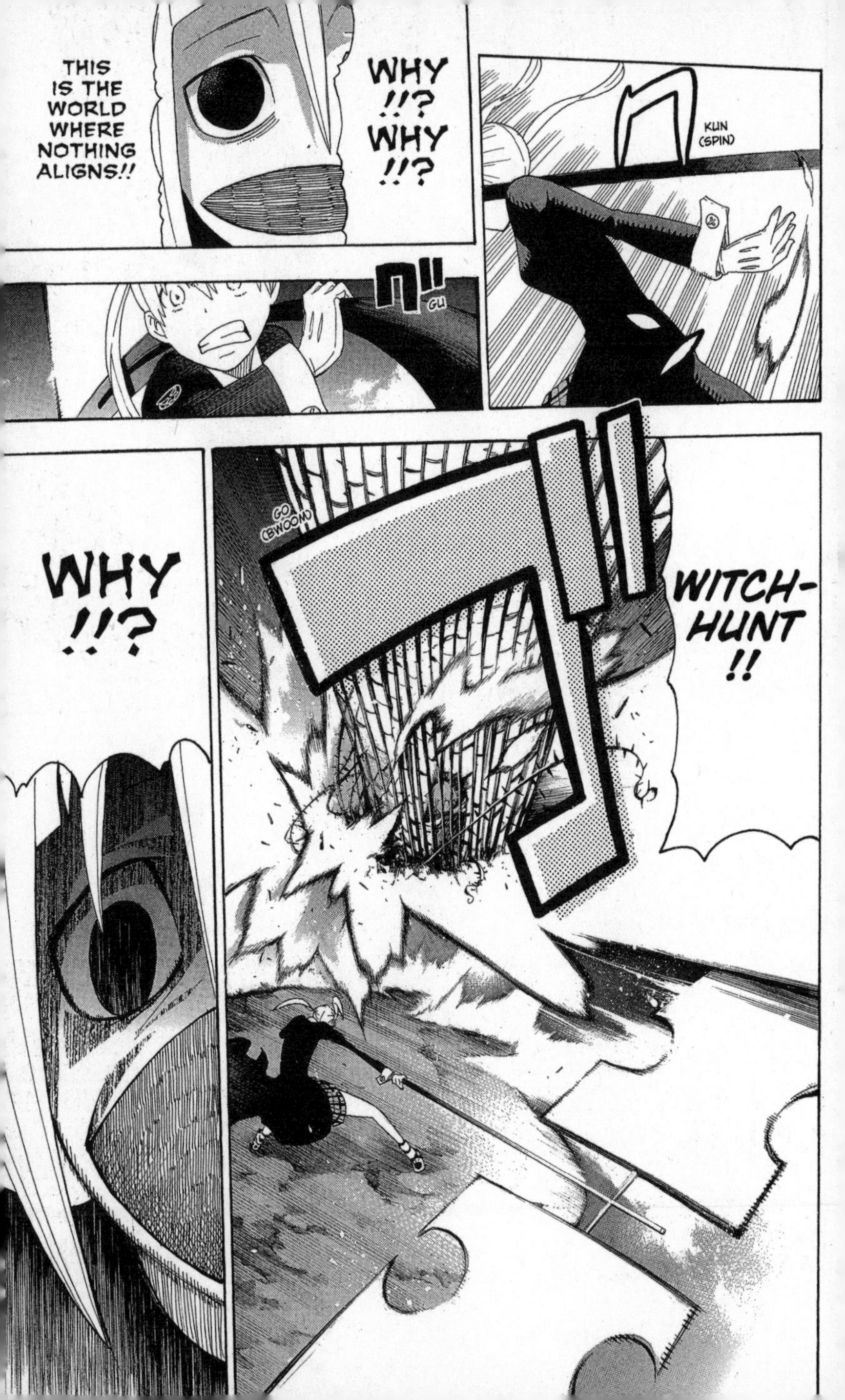
KUN (SPIN)
WHY!!? WHY!!?
THIS IS THE WORLD WHERE NOTHING ALIGNS!!
GU
WITCH-HUNT!!
GO (BWOOM)
WHY!!?

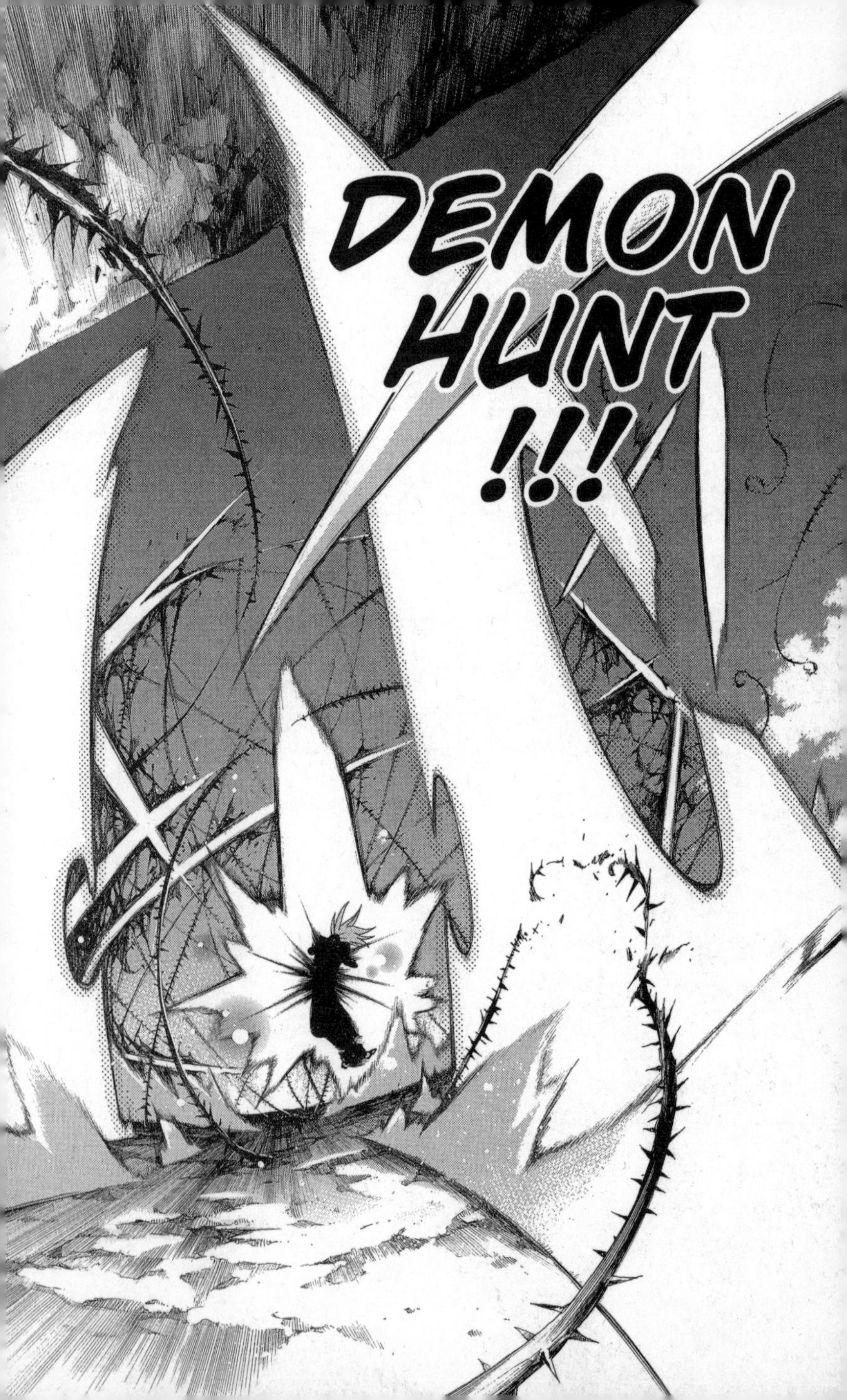
DEMON HUNT !!!

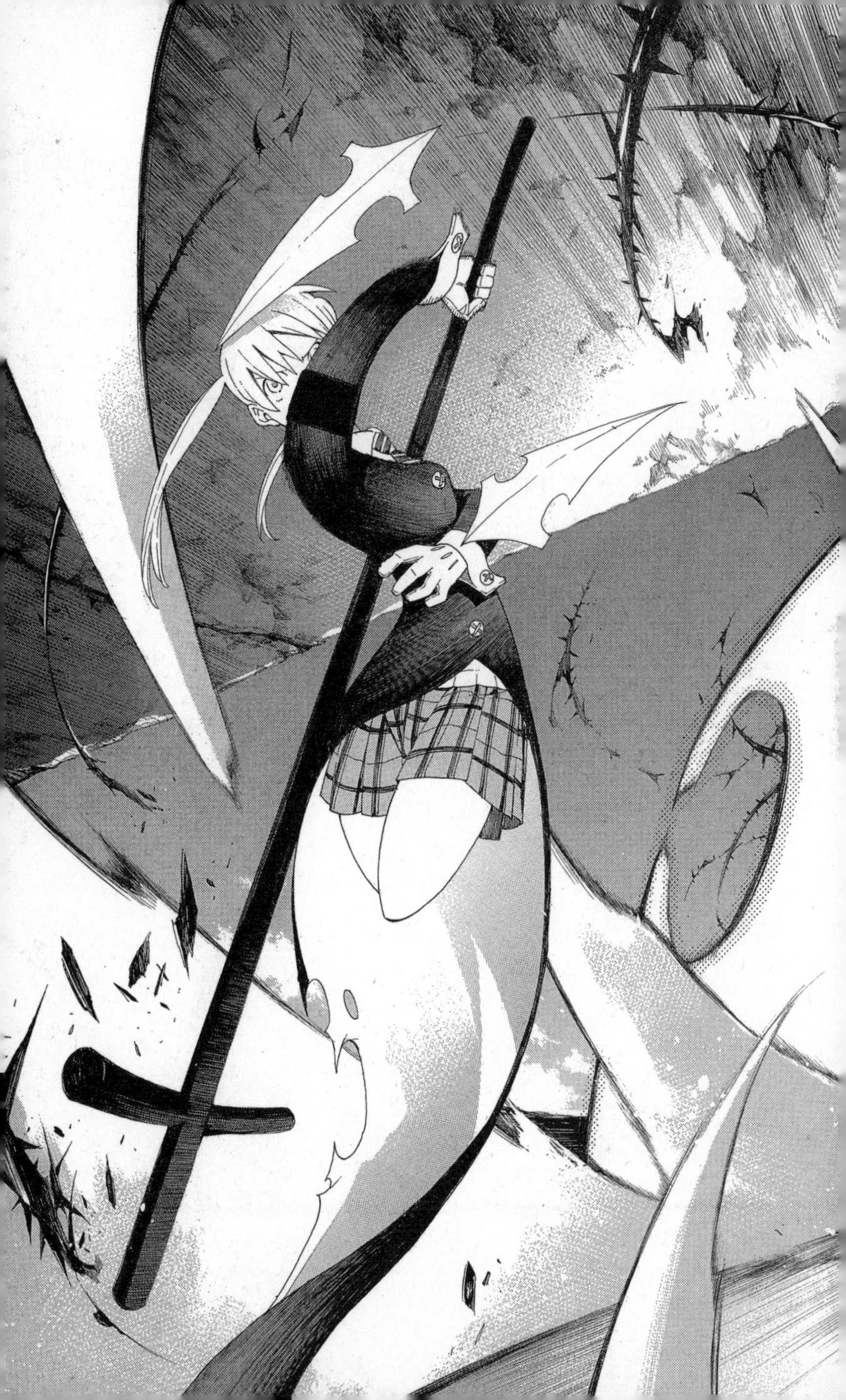

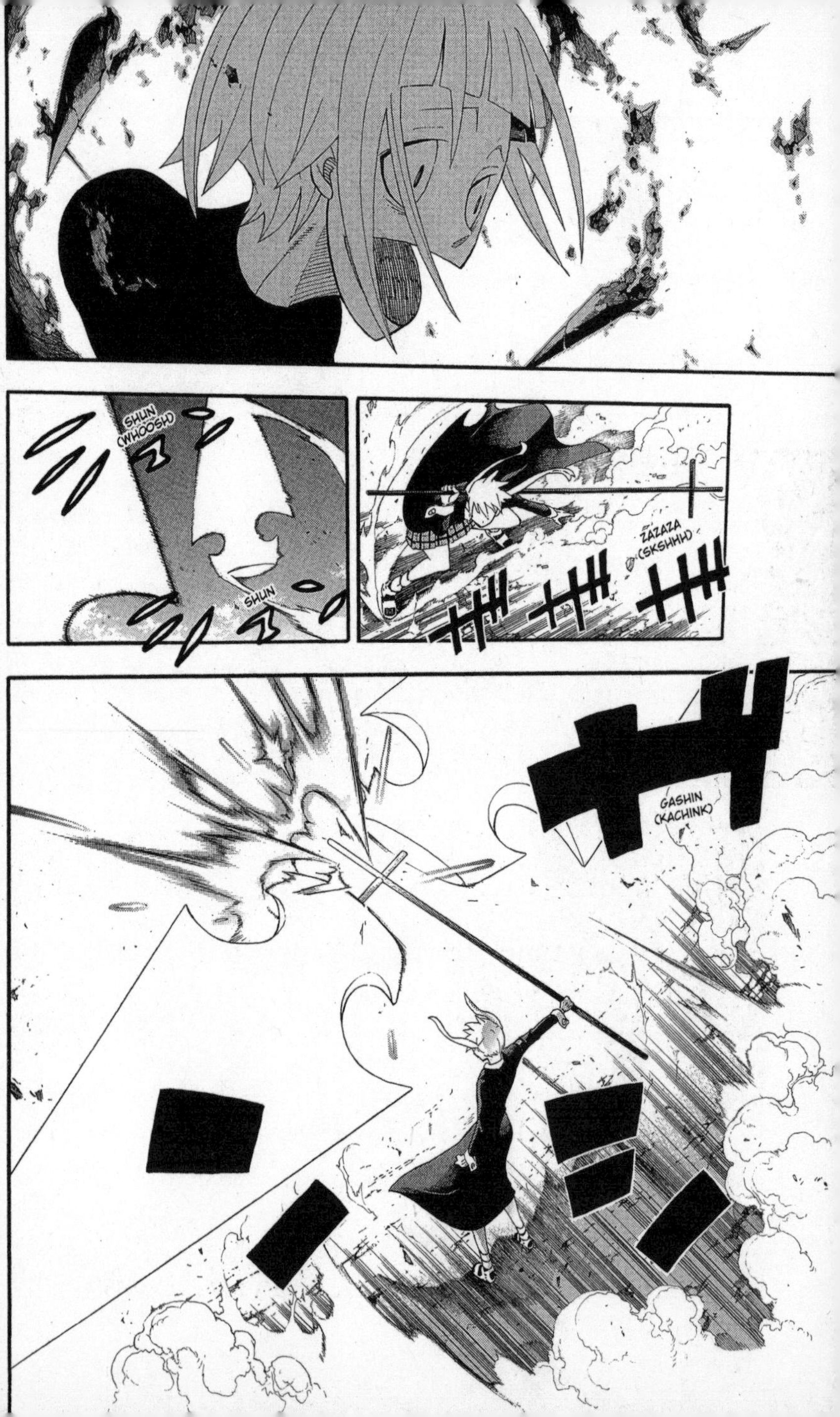
ZAZAZA
(SKSHHH)
SHUN
(WHOOSH)
SHUN
GASHIN
(KACHINK)

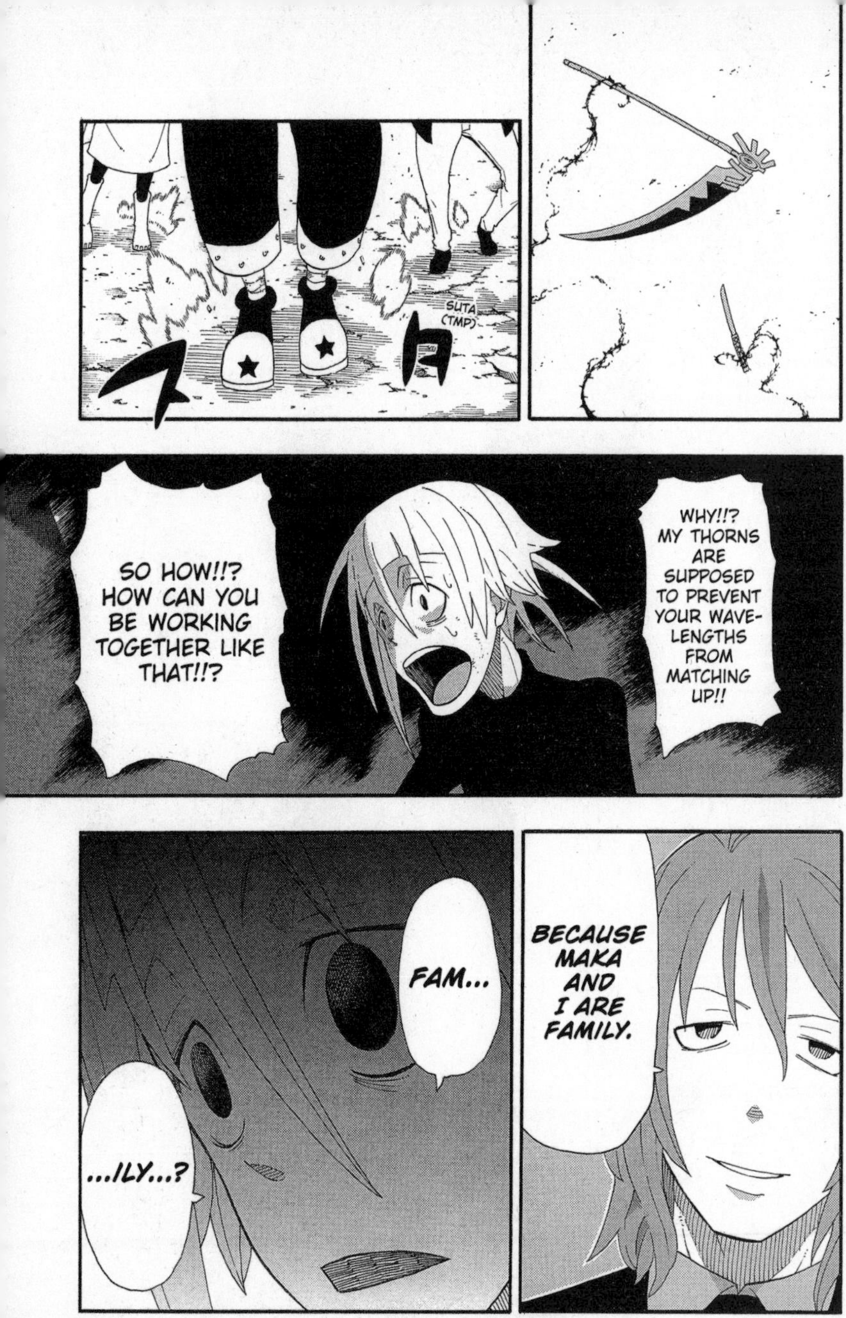
SUTA (TMP)
WHY!!? MY THORNS ARE SUPPOSED TO PREVENT YOUR WAVE-LENGTHS FROM MATCHING UP!!
SO HOW!!? HOW CAN YOU BE WORKING TOGETHER LIKE THAT!!?
BECAUSE MAKA AND I ARE FAMILY.
FAM...
...ILY...?

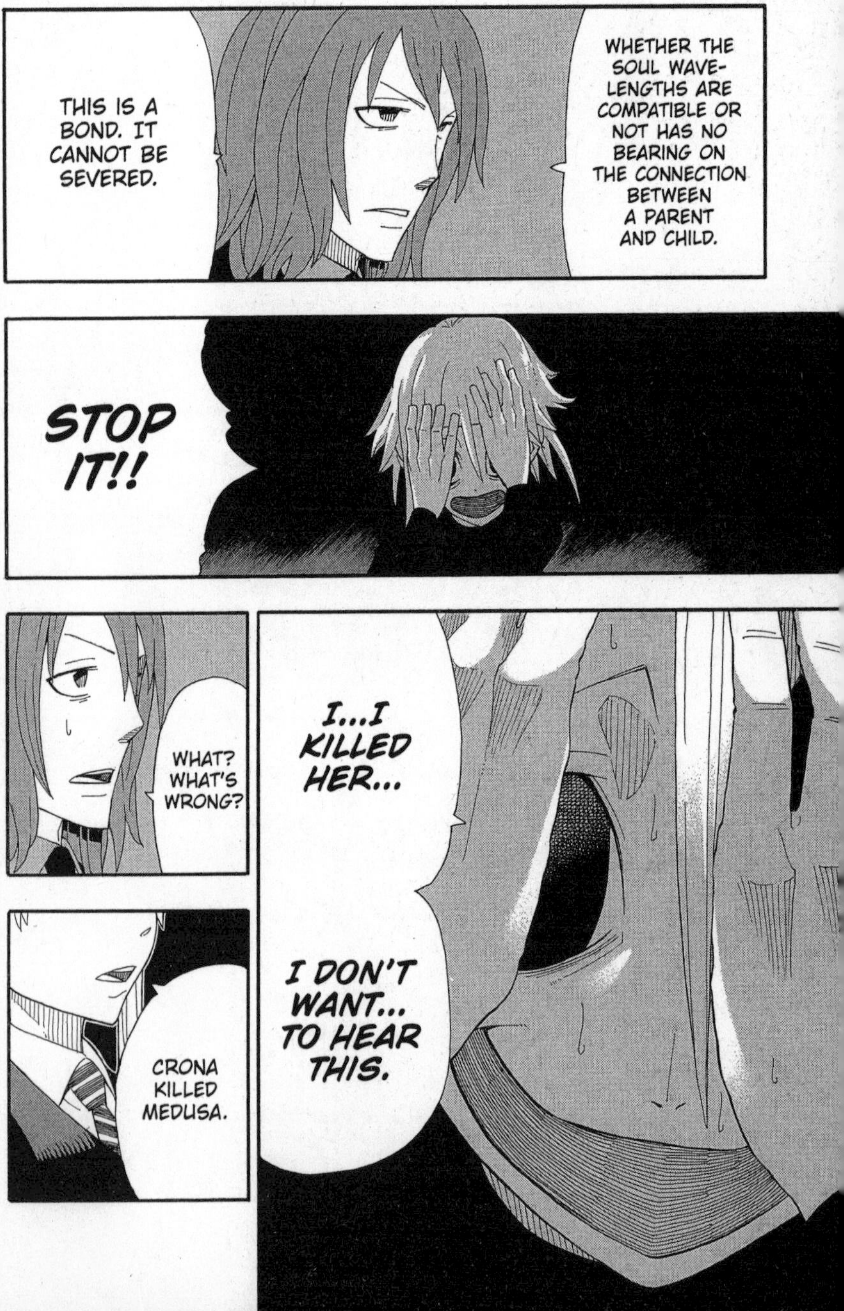
WHETHER THE SOUL WAVE-LENGTHS ARE COMPATIBLE OR NOT HAS NO BEARING ON THE CONNECTION BETWEEN A PARENT AND CHILD.
THIS IS A BOND. IT CANNOT BE SEVERED.
STOP IT!!
I...I KILLED HER...
I DON'T WANT... TO HEAR THIS.
WHAT? WHAT'S WRONG?
CRONA KILLED MEDUSA.

I CUT THAT SOLITARY BOND...THE ONE PERSON I CAN NEVER REPLACE...

SHE WAS MY EVERYTHING... SHE WAS MY ORDER...

HA... HA-HA...

HA...

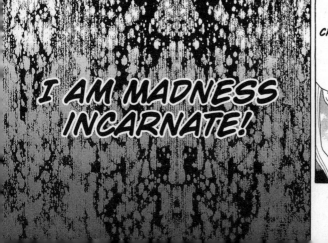

I AM MADNESS INCARNATE!

CRONA ...?

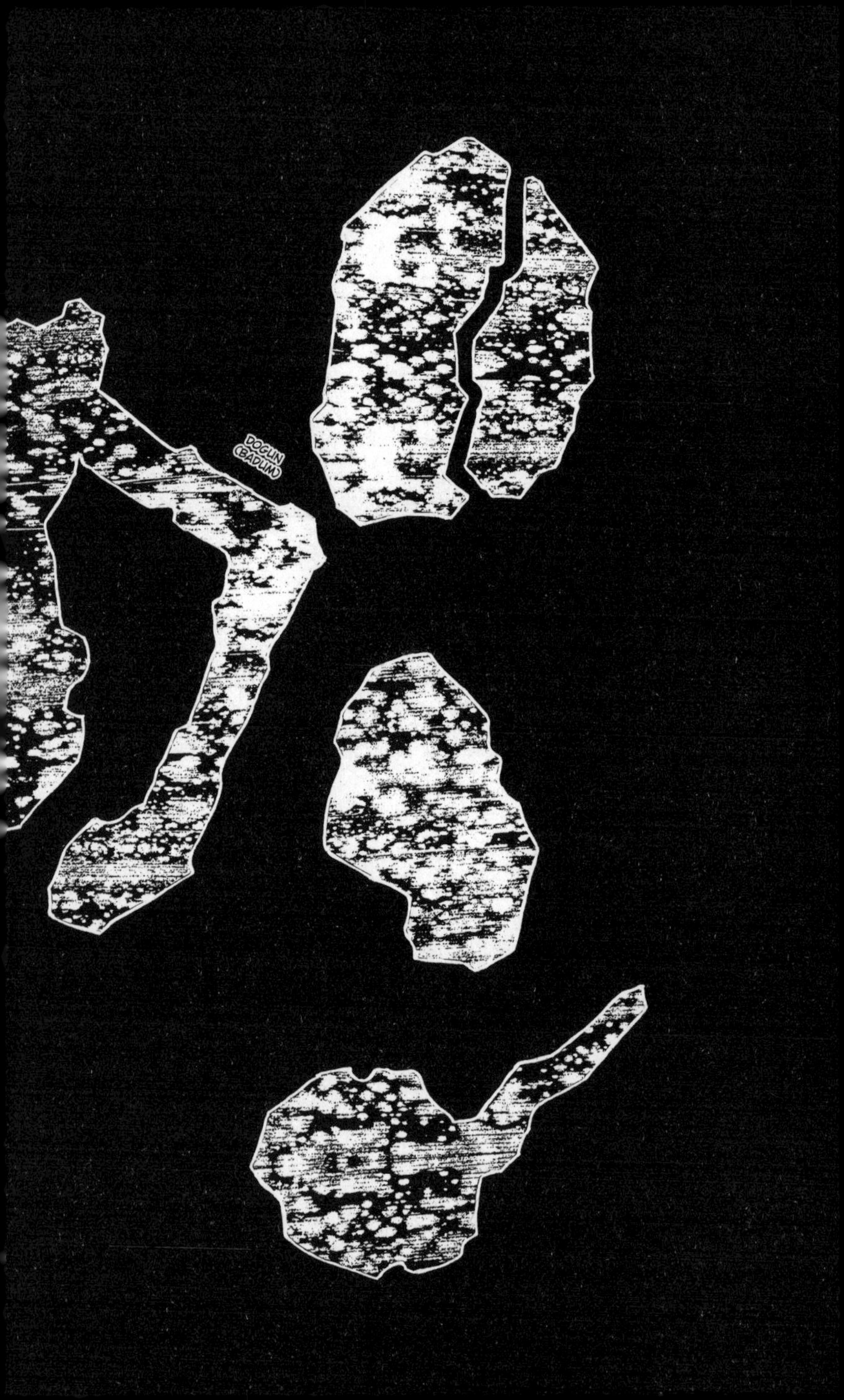
DOGUN
(BADUM)

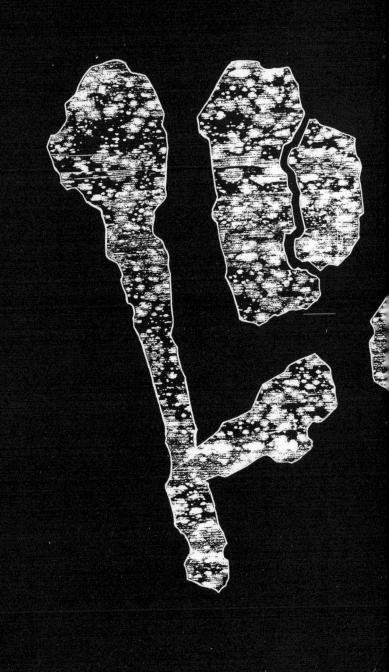

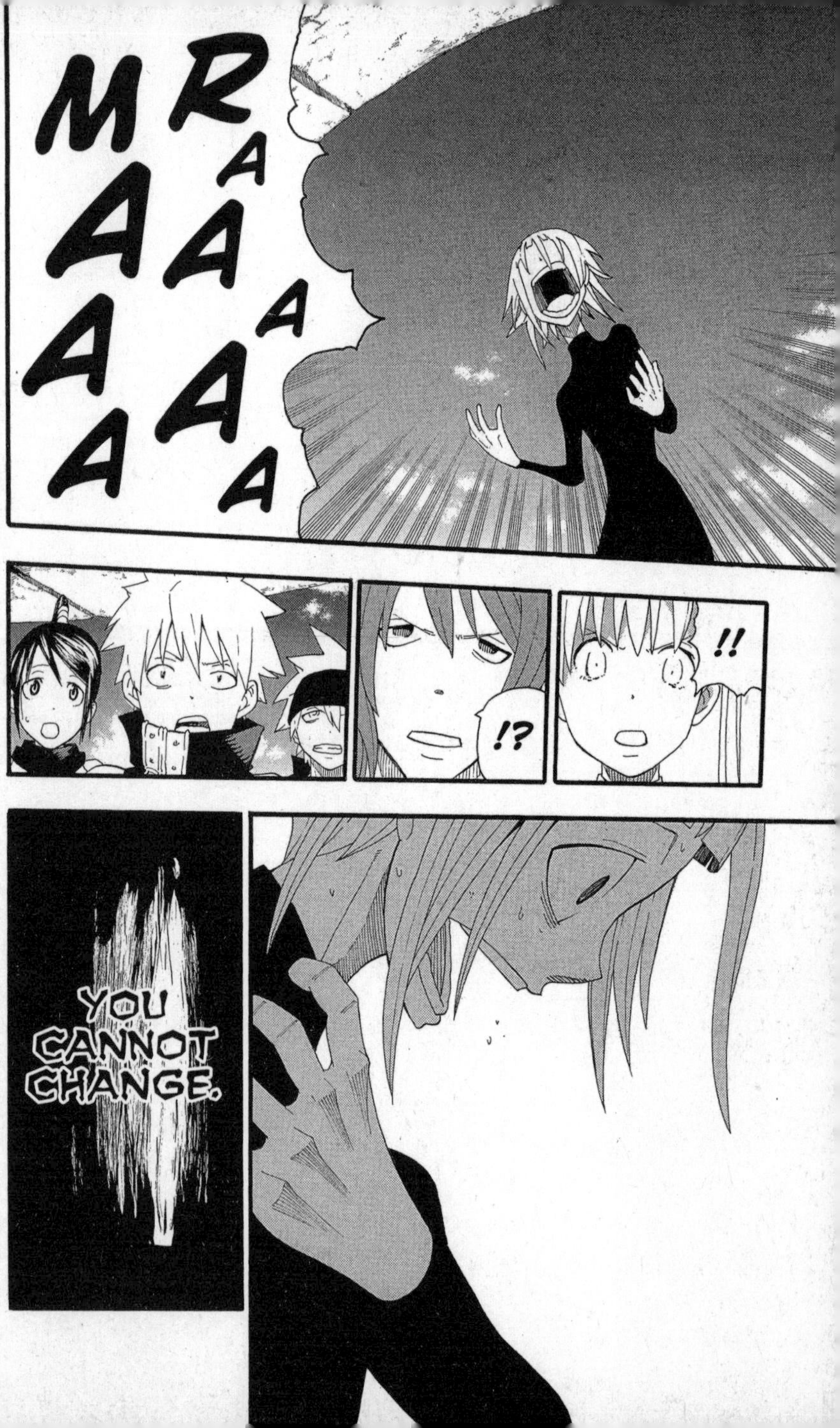
MRAAAAAAAA
!!
!?
YOU CANNOT CHANGE.

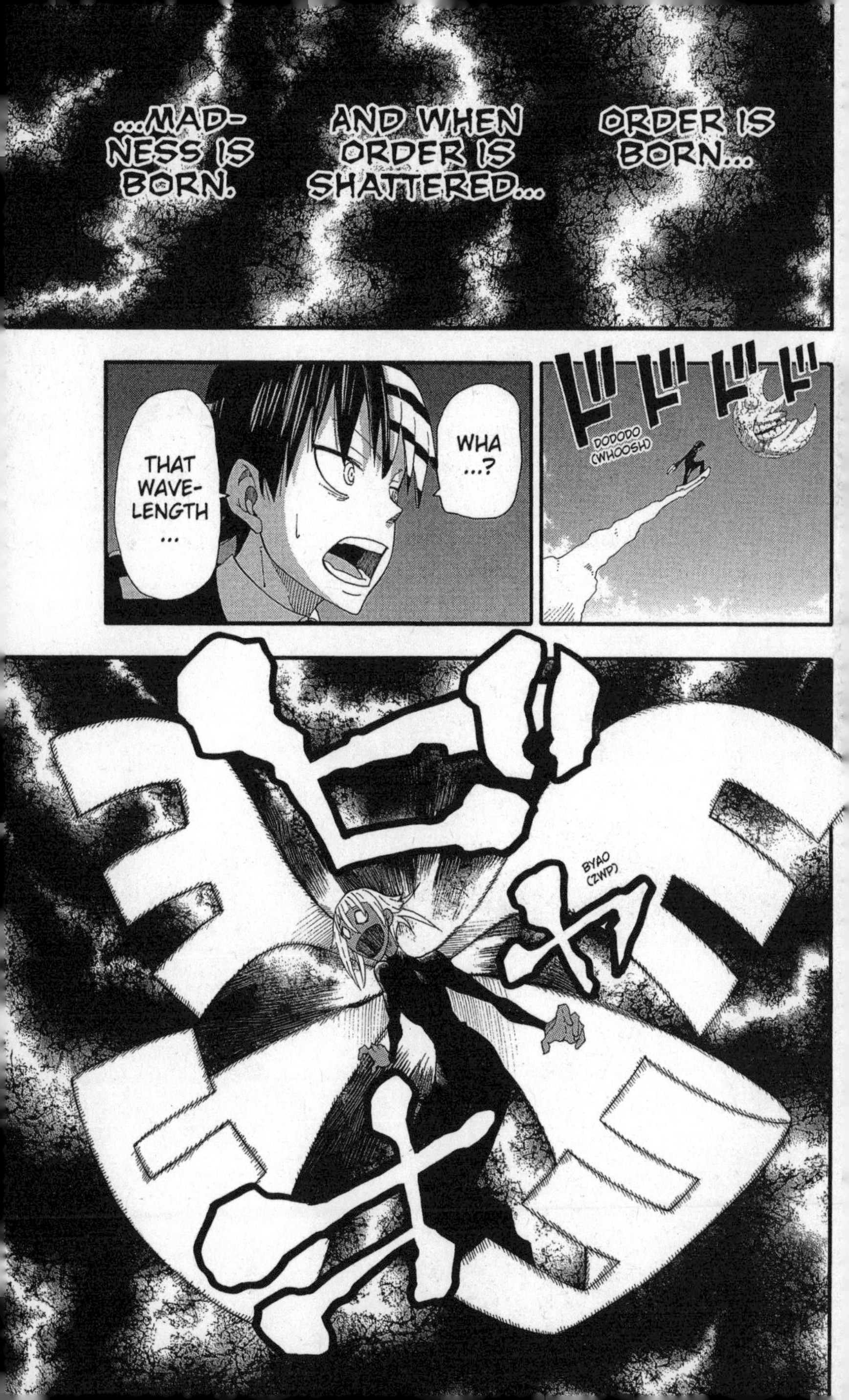
ORDER IS BORN...
AND WHEN ORDER IS SHATTERED...
...MADNESS IS BORN.
ドドドド
DODODO (WHOOSH)
WHA ...?
THAT WAVE-LENGTH ...
BYAO (ZWP)

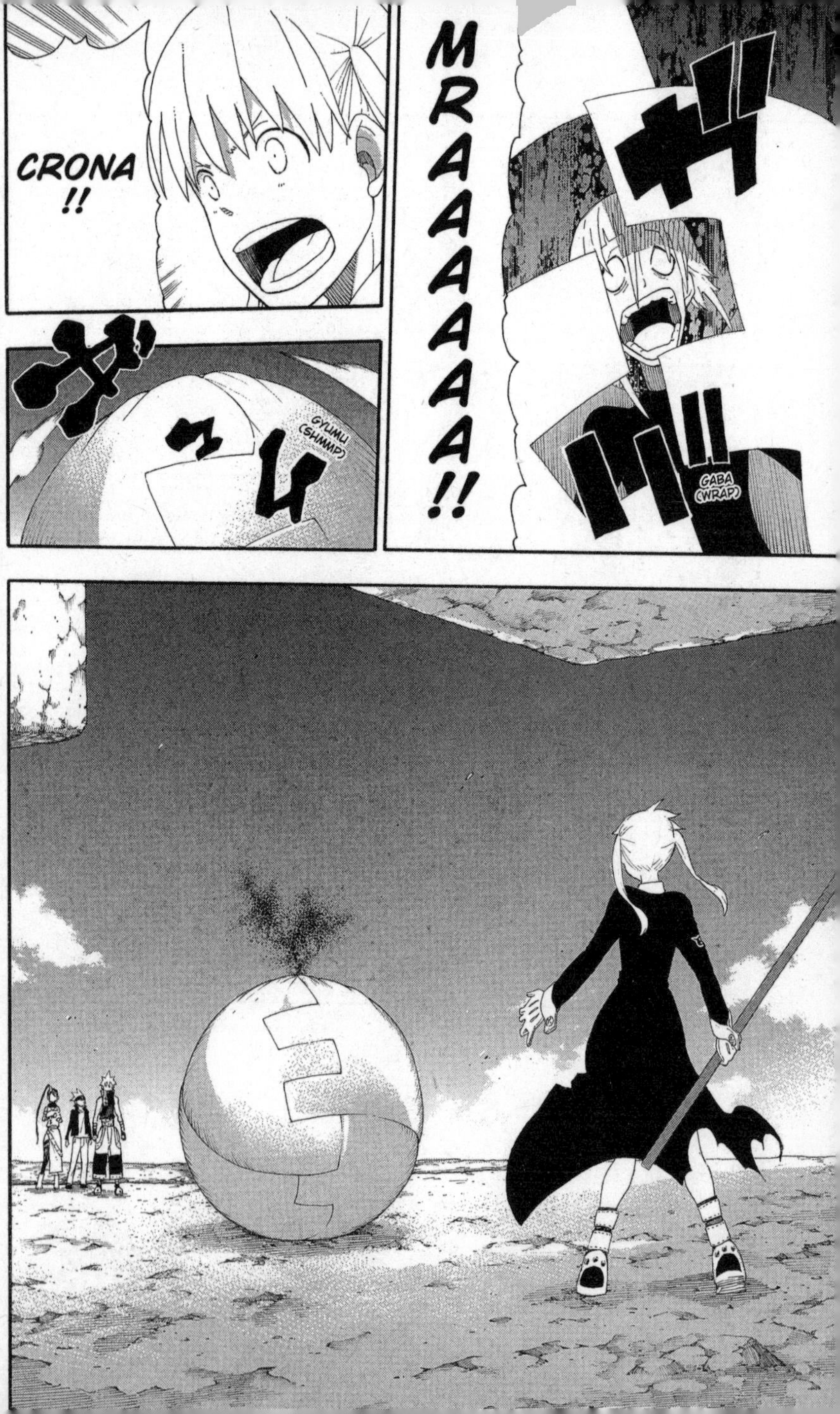

MRAAAAAAAAA!!
GABA (WRAP)
CRONA !!
GYUMU (SHMMP)

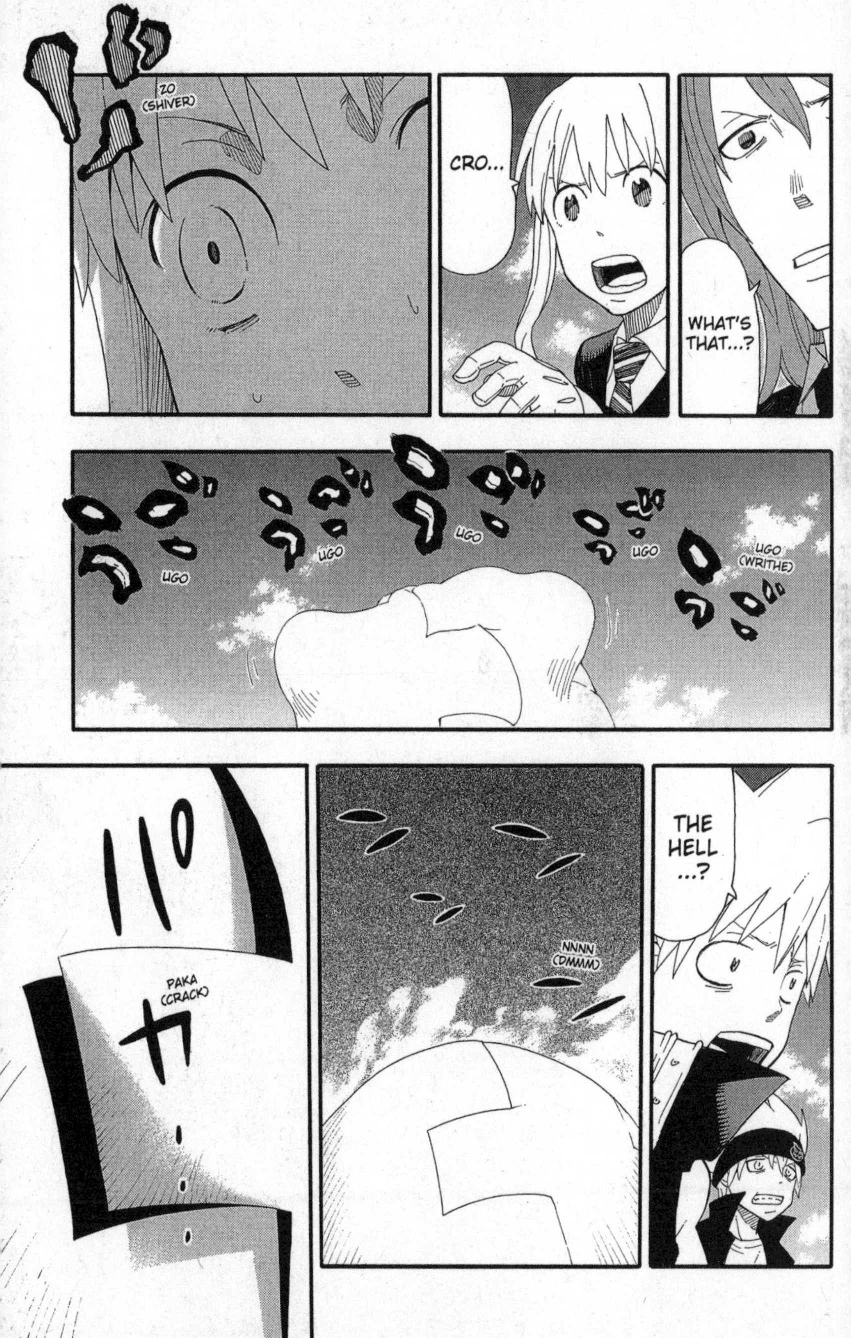
WHAT'S THAT...?
CRO...
ZO (SHIVER)
UGO (WRITHE)
UGO
UGO
UGO
UGO
THE HELL ...?
NNNN (DMMM)
PAKA (CRACK)

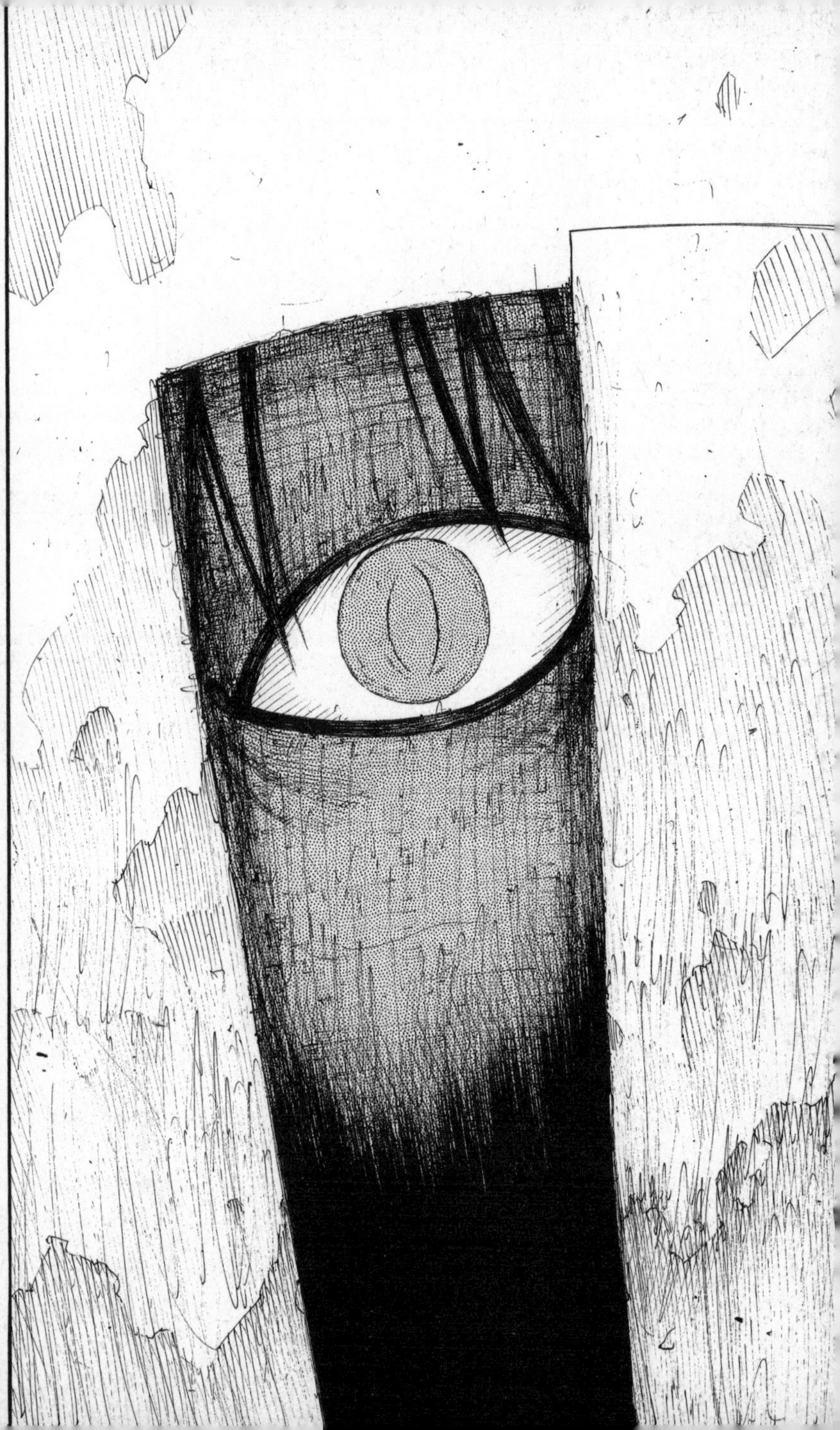

SOUL EATER

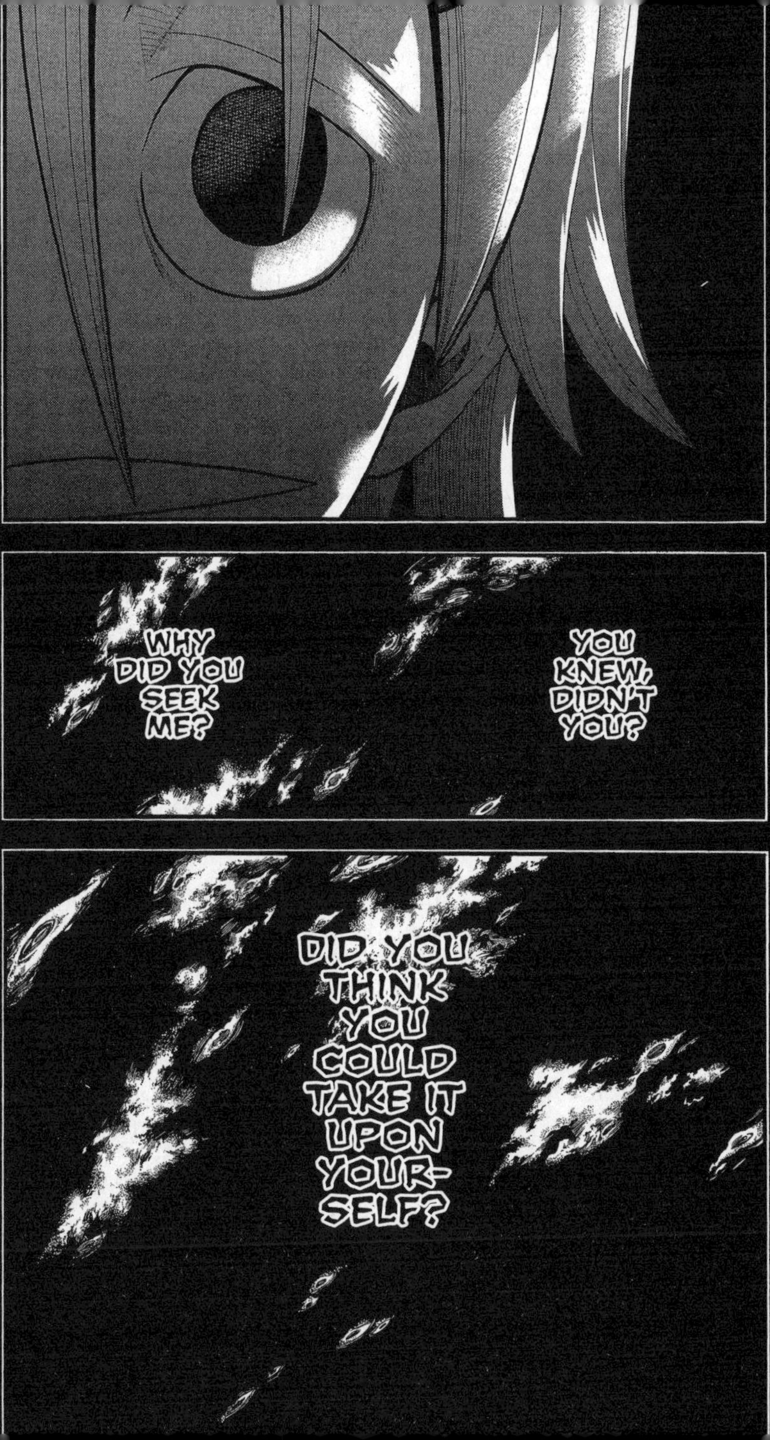
YOU KNEW, DIDN'T YOU?
WHY DID YOU SEEK ME?
DID YOU THINK YOU COULD TAKE IT UPON YOUR-SELF?

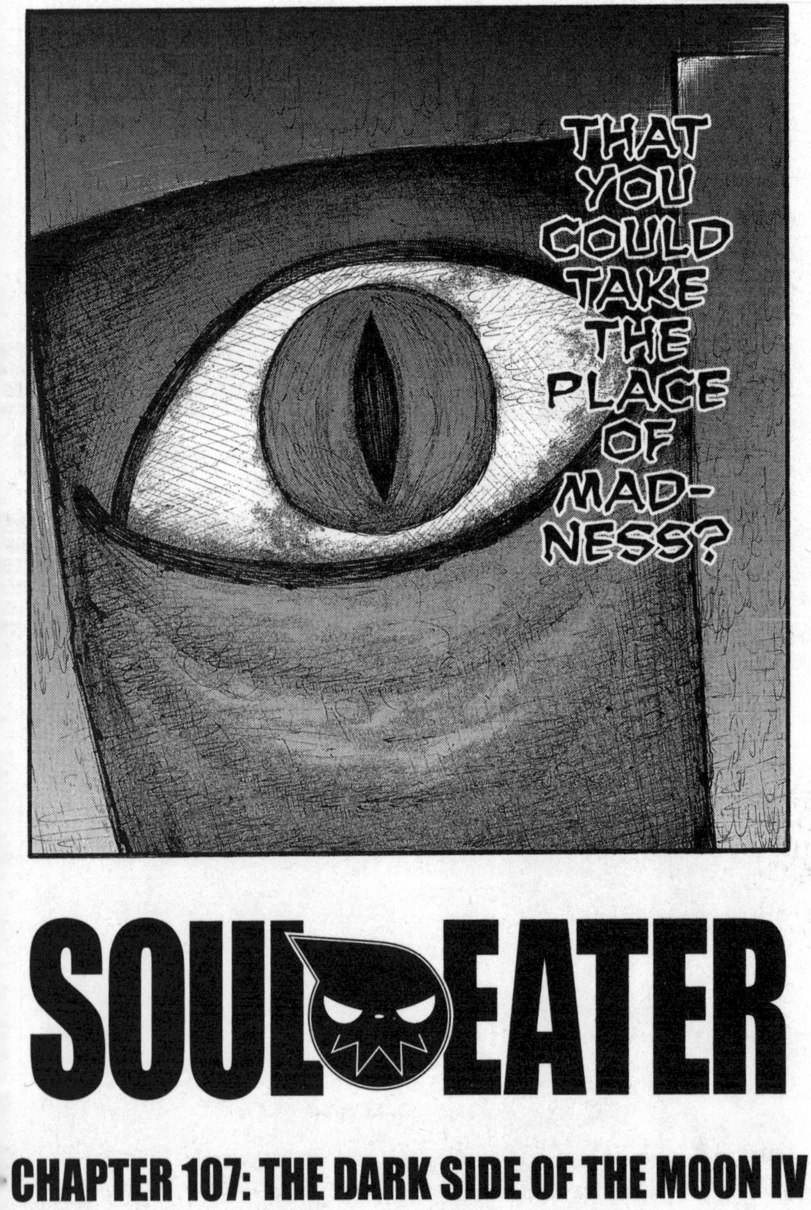
THAT YOU COULD TAKE THE PLACE OF MAD-NESS?

SOUL EATER

CHAPTER 107: THE DARK SIDE OF THE MOON IV

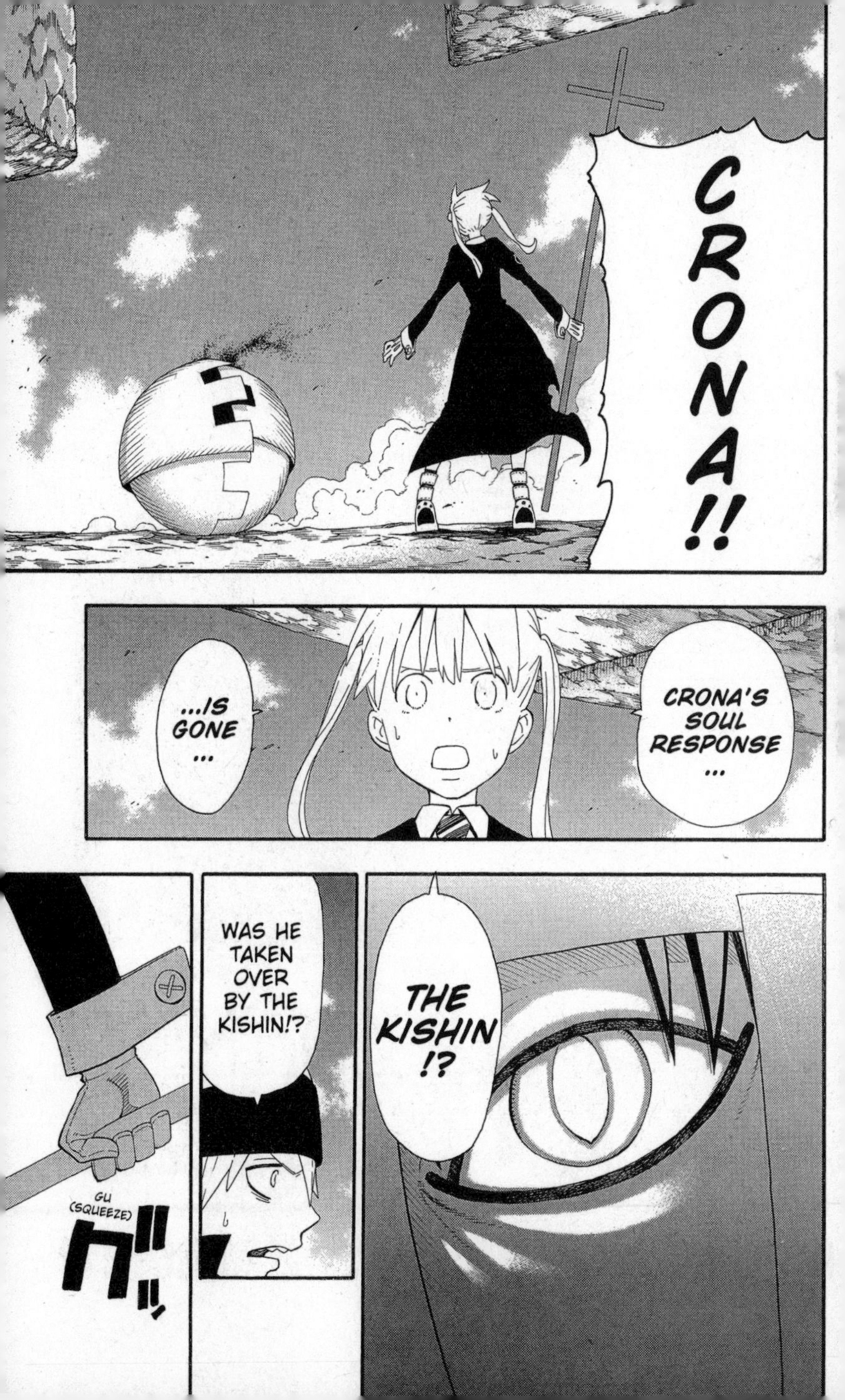
CRONA!!
CRONA'S SOUL RESPONSE ...
...IS GONE ...
THE KISHIN!?
WAS HE TAKEN OVER BY THE KISHIN!?
GU (SQUEEZE)

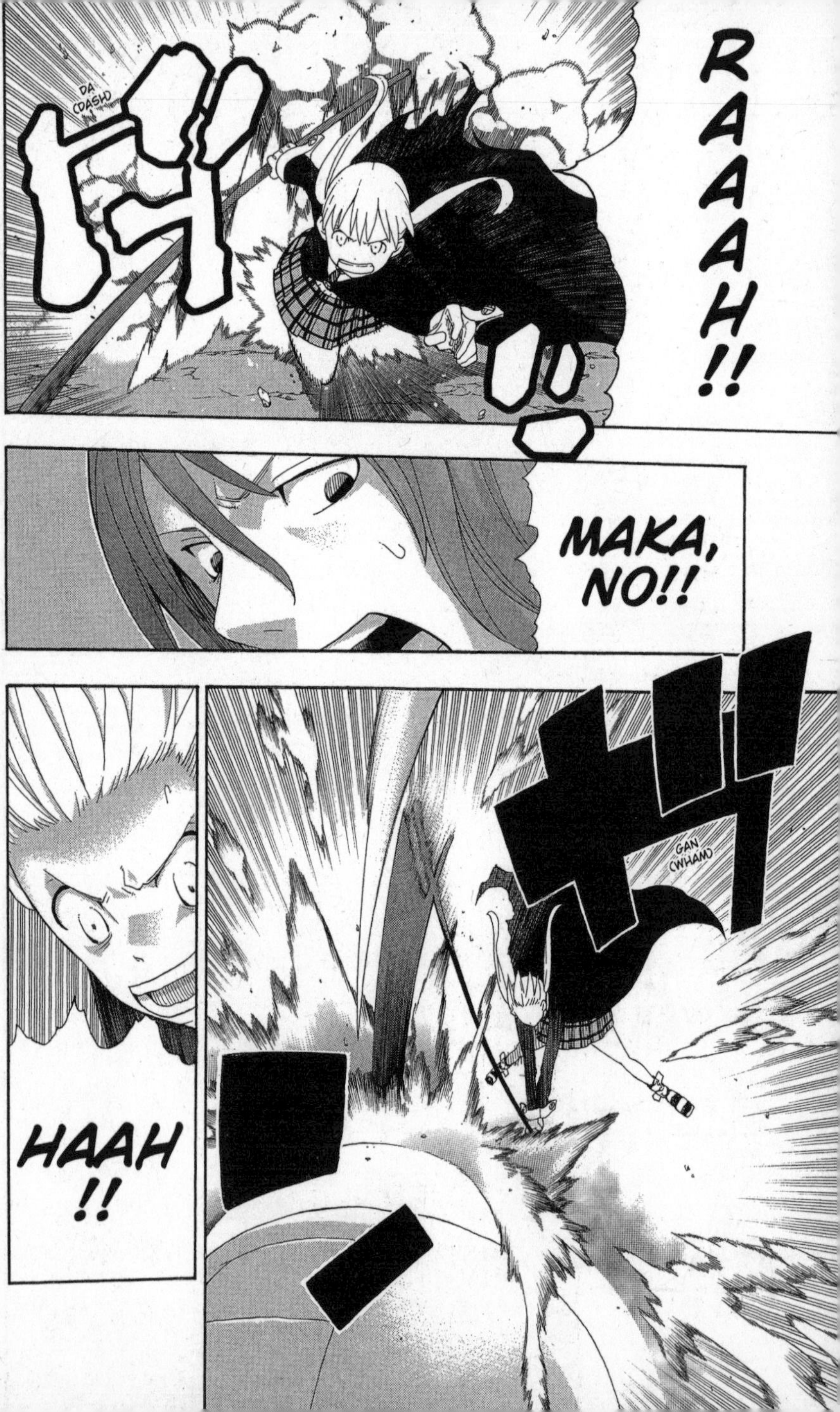
RAAAAH!!
DA (DASH)
MAKA, NO!!
GAN (WHAM)
HAAH!!

BAN
(WHAP)

ZAZA
(SKSH)

WHY
NOT
!!?

IT'S
NO
USE!!

WE
CAN'T
GET
TO
HIM!!

GA
(WHAP)

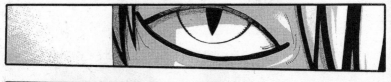

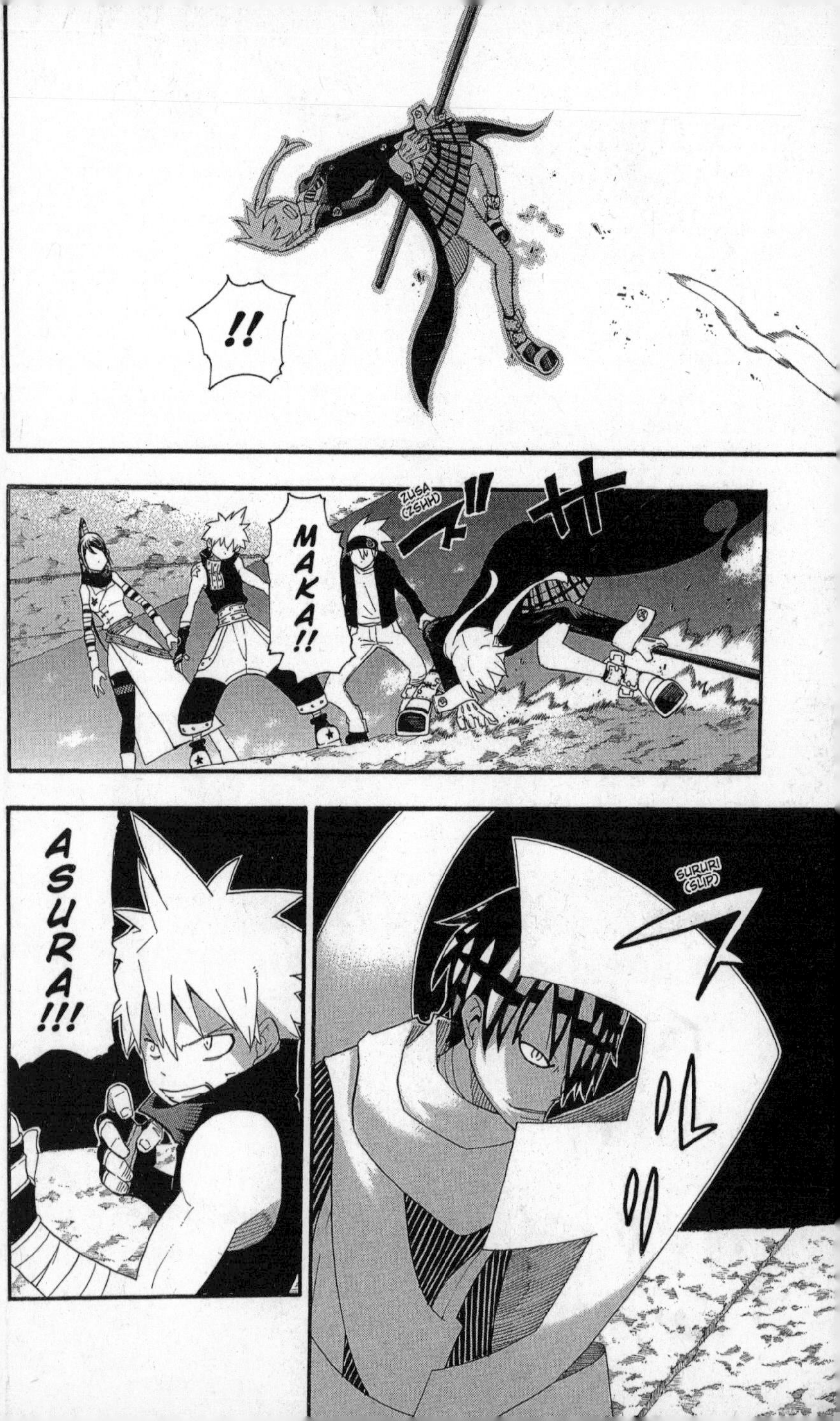
!!
ZUSA (ZSHH)
MAKA!!
SURURI (SLIP)
ASURA!!!

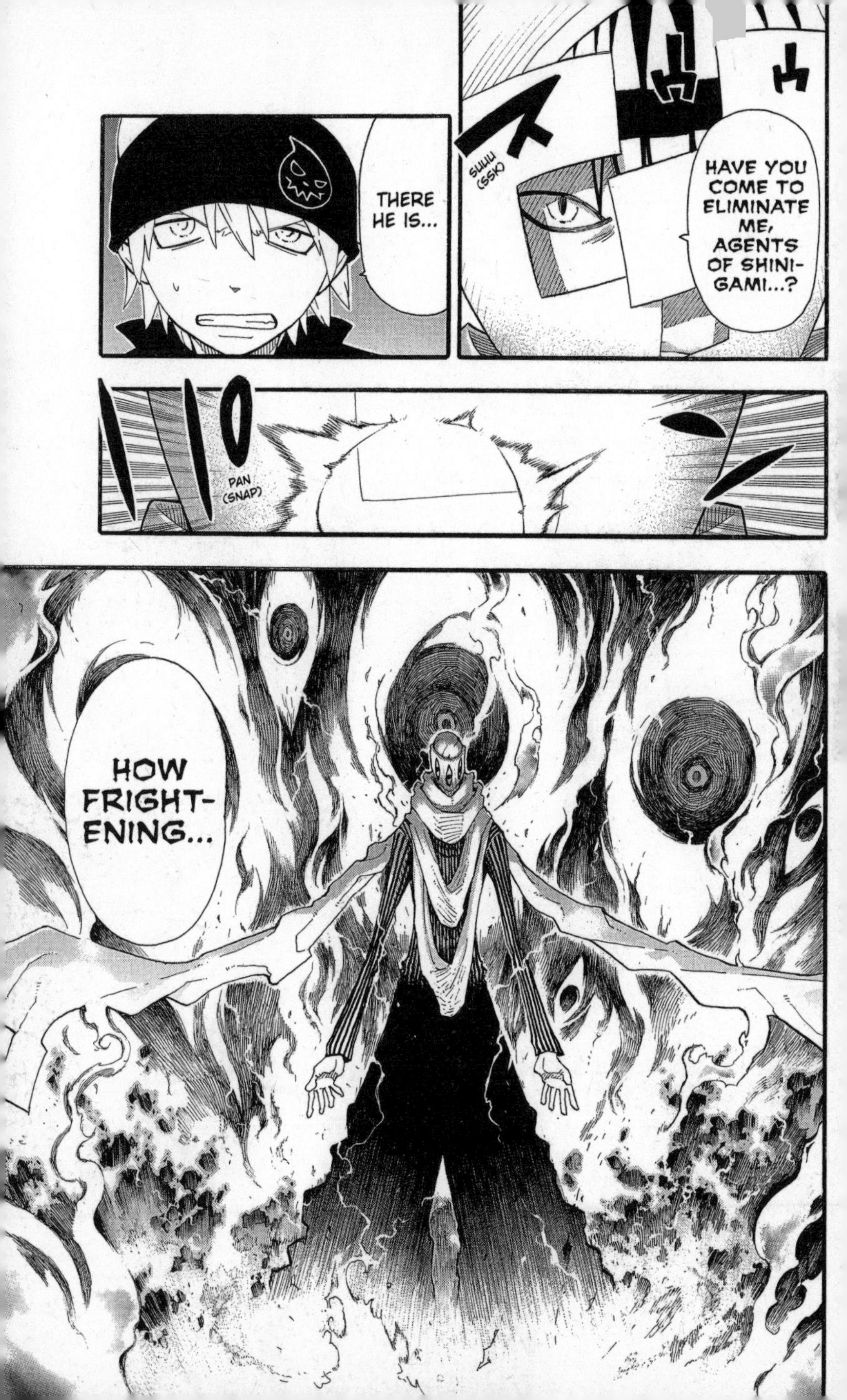
SUUU (SSK)
HAVE YOU COME TO ELIMINATE ME, AGENTS OF SHINI-GAMI...?
THERE HE IS...
PAN (SNAP)
HOW FRIGHT-ENING...

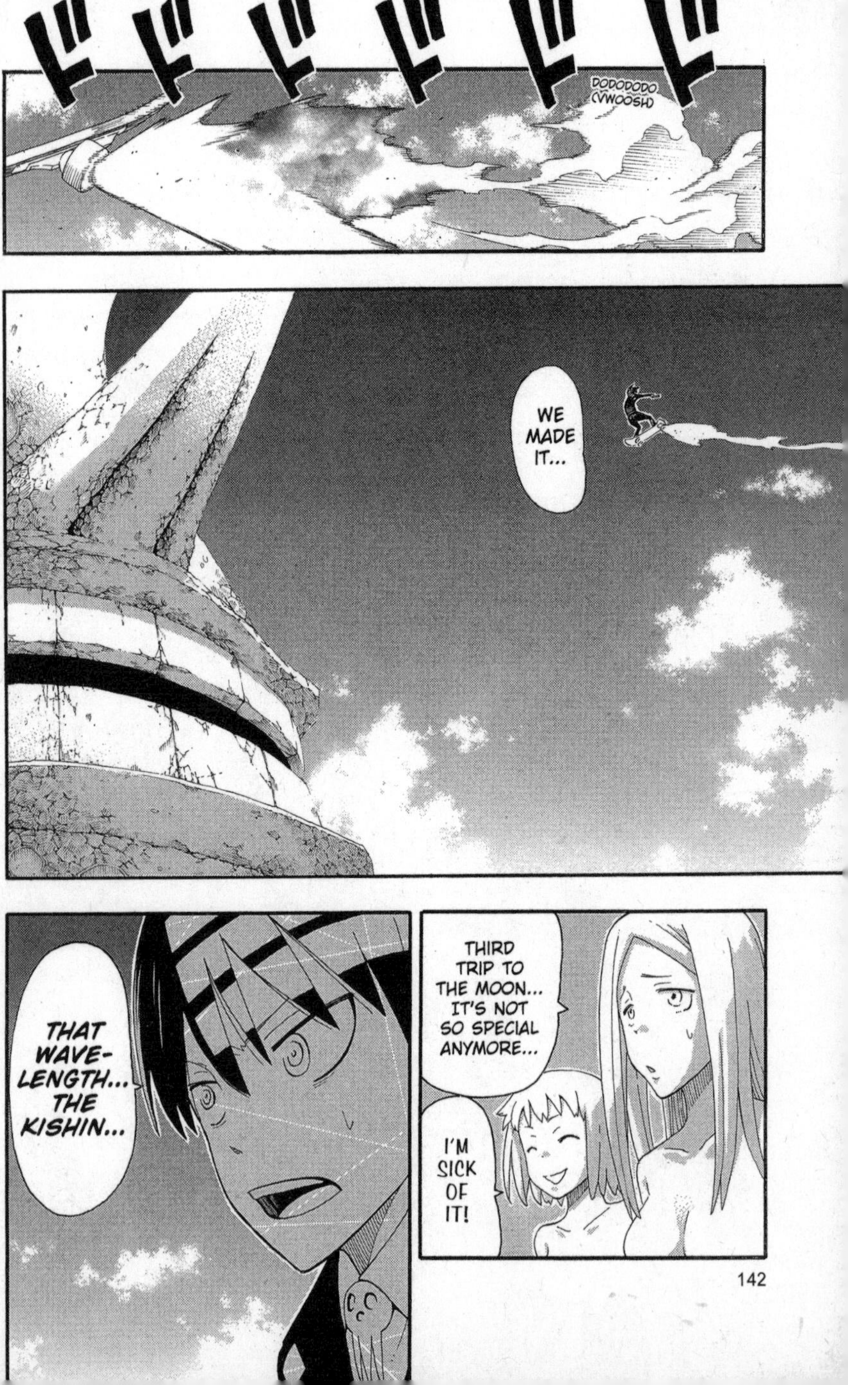
ドドドドドド
DODODODO (VWOOSH)
WE MADE IT...
THIRD TRIP TO THE MOON... IT'S NOT SO SPECIAL ANYMORE...
I'M SICK OF IT!
THAT WAVE-LENGTH... THE KISHIN...

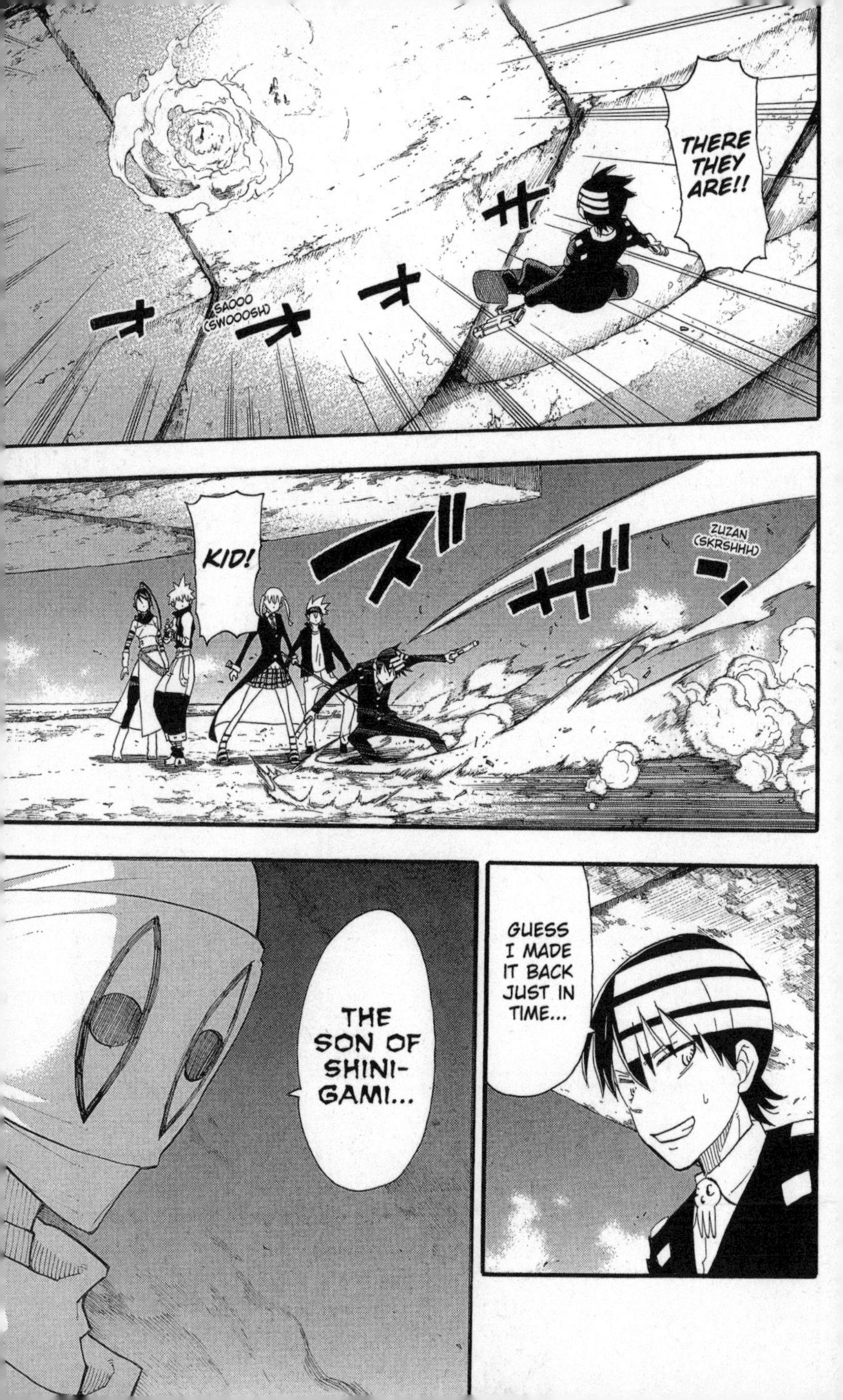
THERE THEY ARE!!
SAOOO (SWOOOSH)
KID!
ZUZAN (SKRSHHH)
GUESS I MADE IT BACK JUST IN TIME...
THE SON OF SHINI-GAMI...

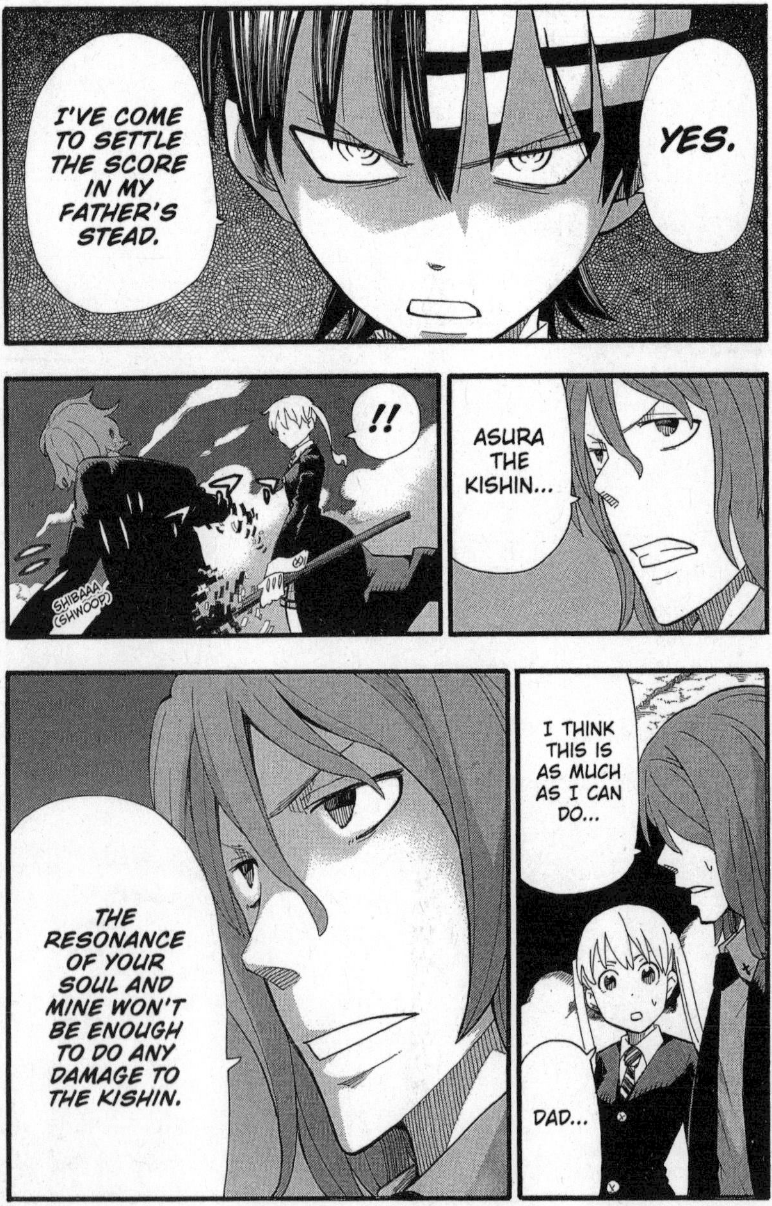
YES.
I'VE COME TO SETTLE THE SCORE IN MY FATHER'S STEAD.
ASURA THE KISHIN...
!!
SHIBAAA (SHWOOP)
I THINK THIS IS AS MUCH AS I CAN DO...
DAD...
THE RESONANCE OF YOUR SOUL AND MINE WON'T BE ENOUGH TO DO ANY DAMAGE TO THE KISHIN.

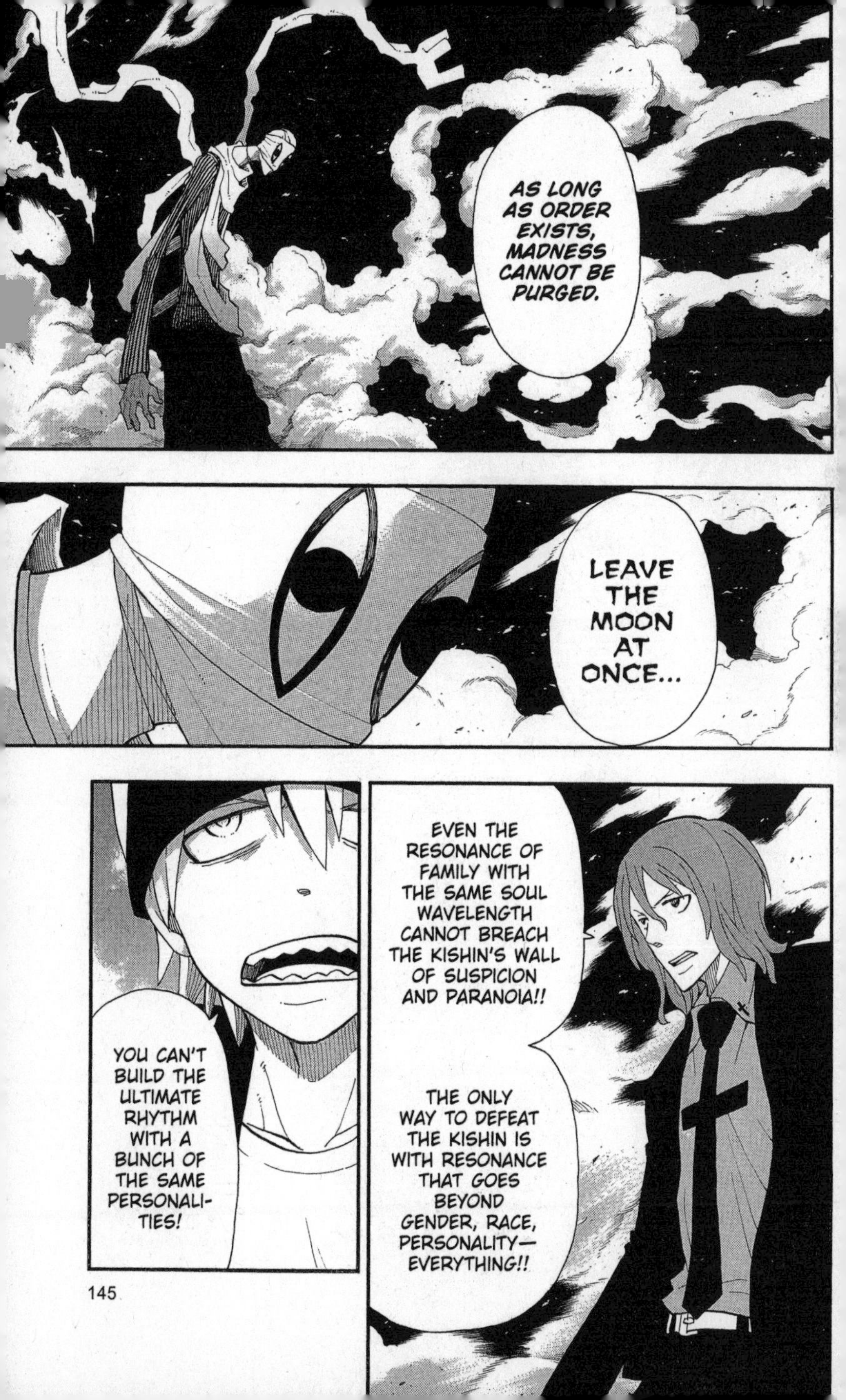
AS LONG AS ORDER EXISTS, MADNESS CANNOT BE PURGED.
LEAVE THE MOON AT ONCE...
EVEN THE RESONANCE OF FAMILY WITH THE SAME SOUL WAVELENGTH CANNOT BREACH THE KISHIN'S WALL OF SUSPICION AND PARANOIA!!
THE ONLY WAY TO DEFEAT THE KISHIN IS WITH RESONANCE THAT GOES BEYOND GENDER, RACE, PERSONALITY—EVERYTHING!!
YOU CAN'T BUILD THE ULTIMATE RHYTHM WITH A BUNCH OF THE SAME PERSONALI-TIES!

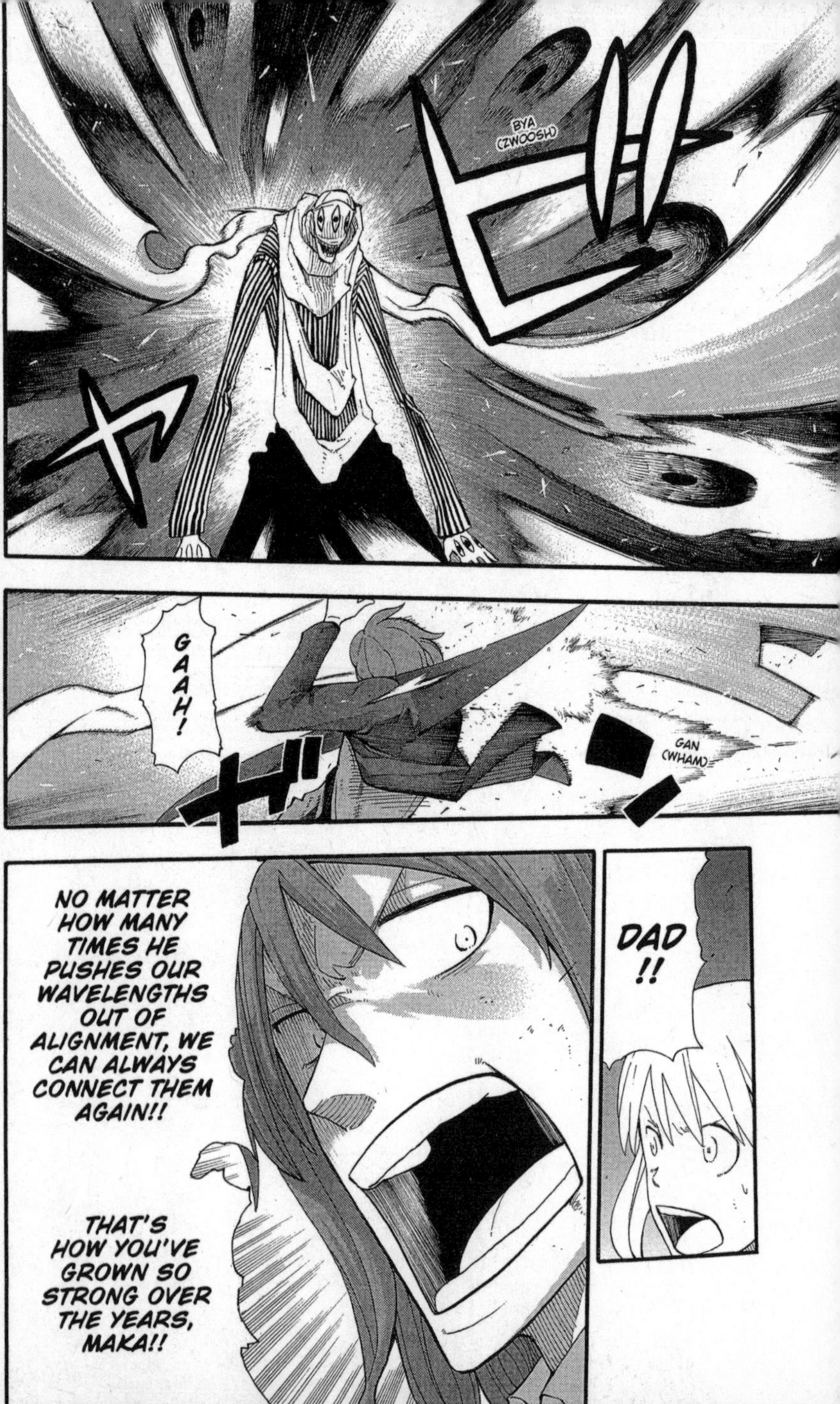
BYA (ZWOOSH)
GAN (WHAM)
GAAH!
DAD!!
NO MATTER HOW MANY TIMES HE PUSHES OUR WAVELENGTHS OUT OF ALIGNMENT, WE CAN ALWAYS CONNECT THEM AGAIN!!
THAT'S HOW YOU'VE GROWN SO STRONG OVER THE YEARS, MAKA!!

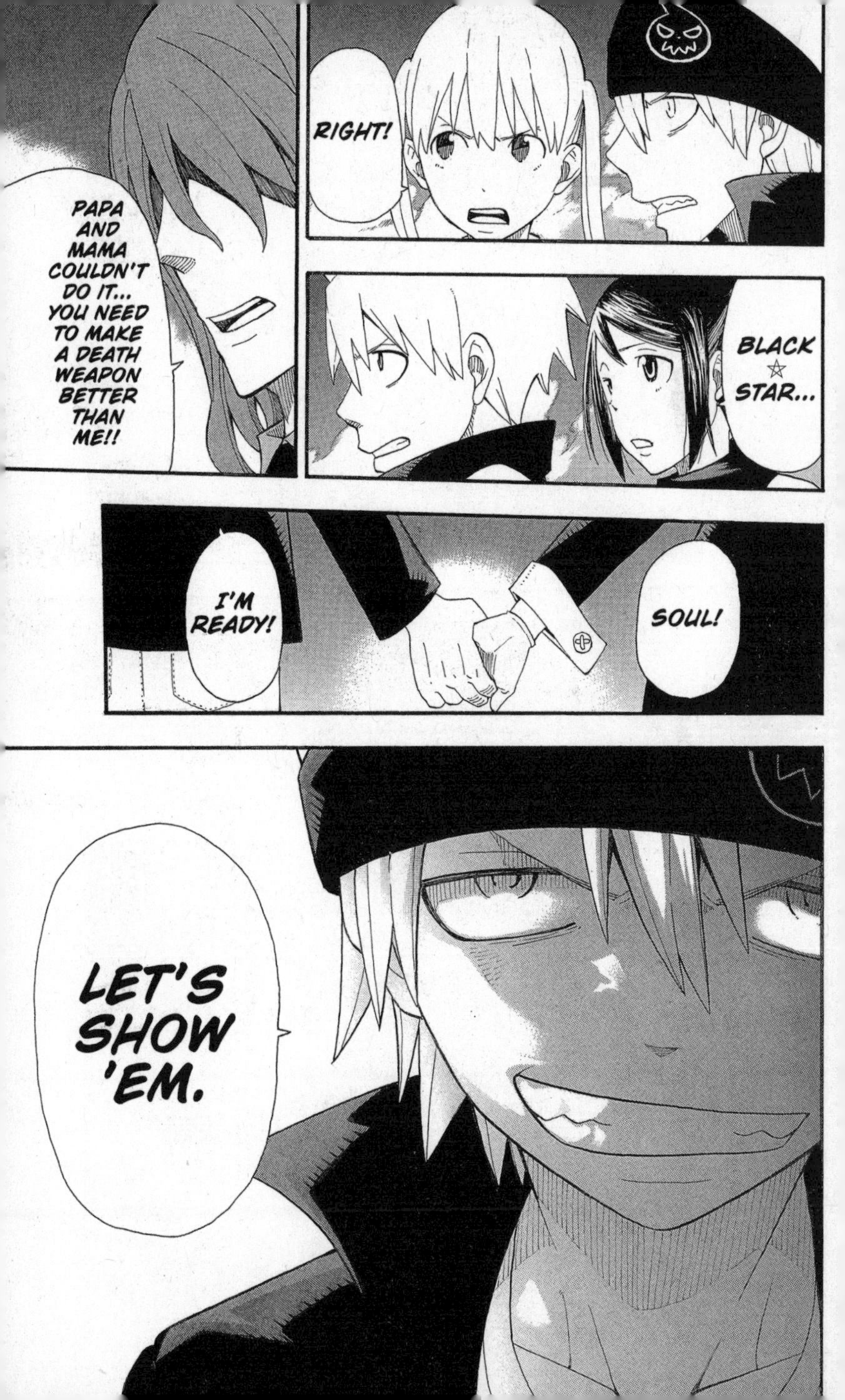
RIGHT!
BLACK ☆ STAR...
PAPA AND MAMA COULDN'T DO IT... YOU NEED TO MAKE A DEATH WEAPON BETTER THAN ME!!
SOUL!
I'M READY!
LET'S SHOW 'EM.

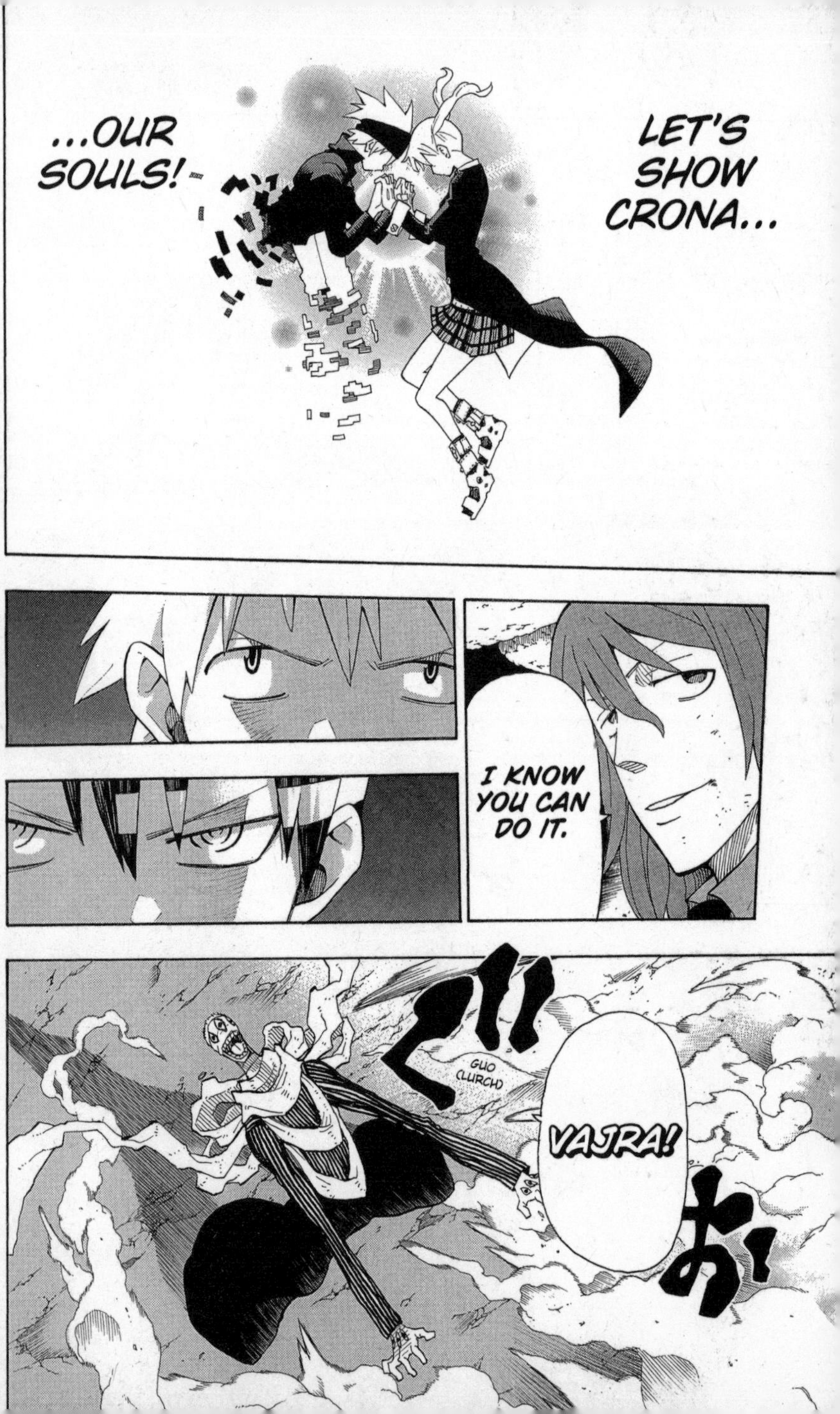
LET'S SHOW CRONA...
...OUR SOULS!
I KNOW YOU CAN DO IT.
VAJRA!
GUO (LURCH)

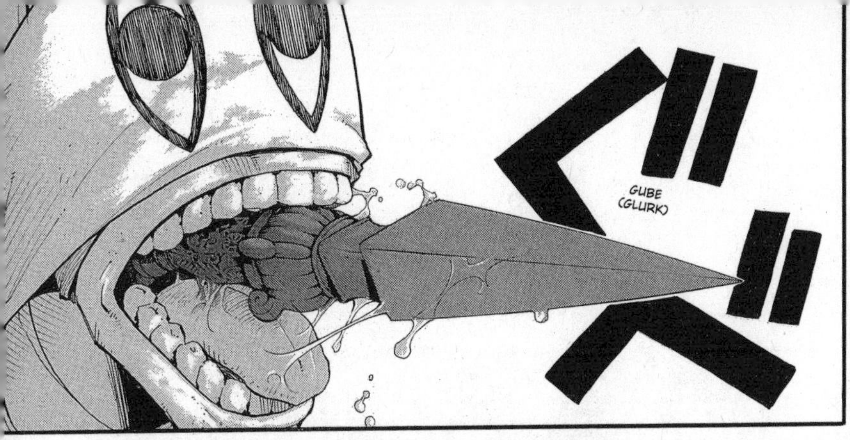
GUBE
(GLURK)
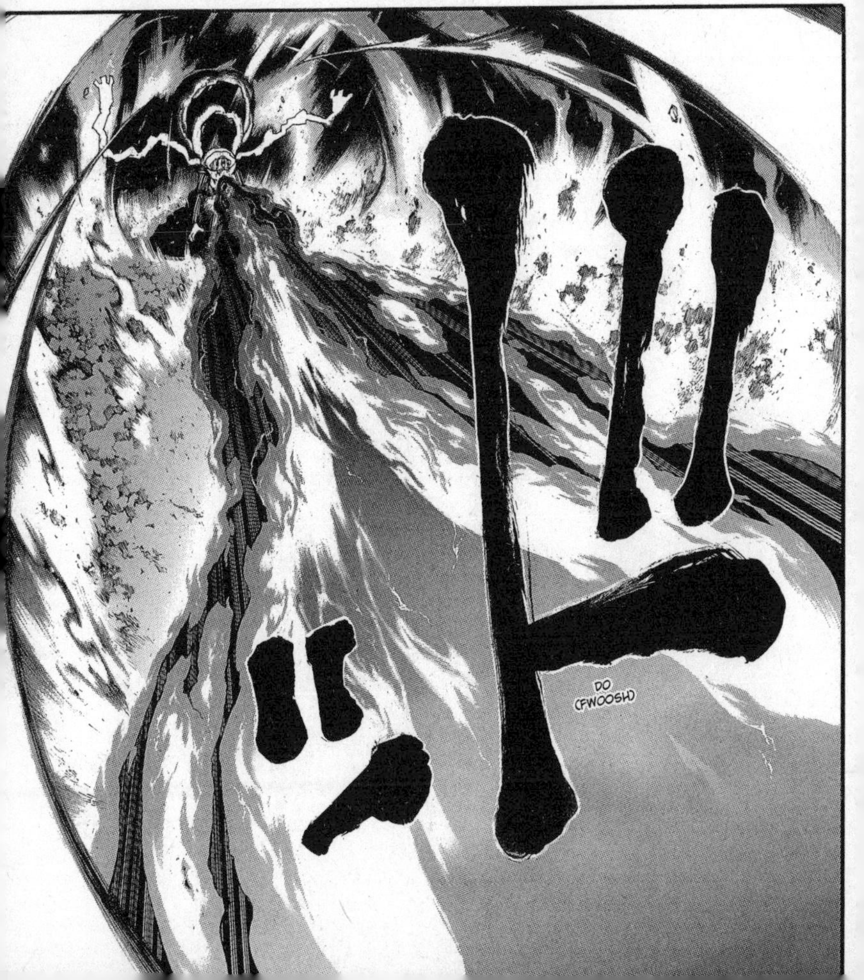
DO
(FWOOSH)

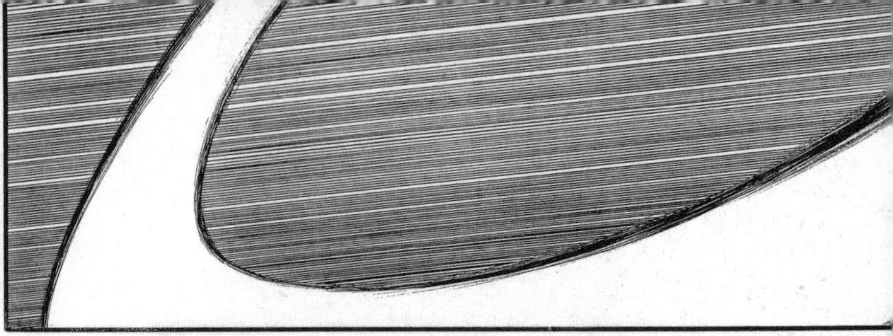

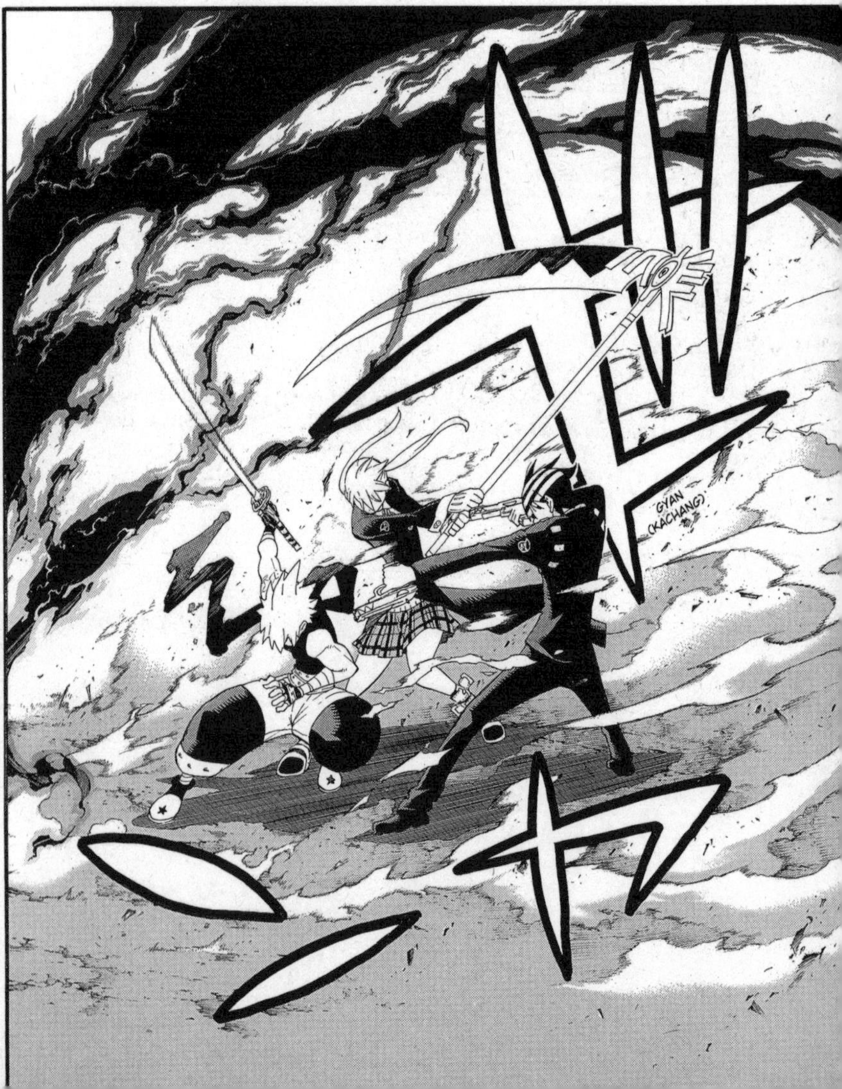
GYAN
(KACHANG)

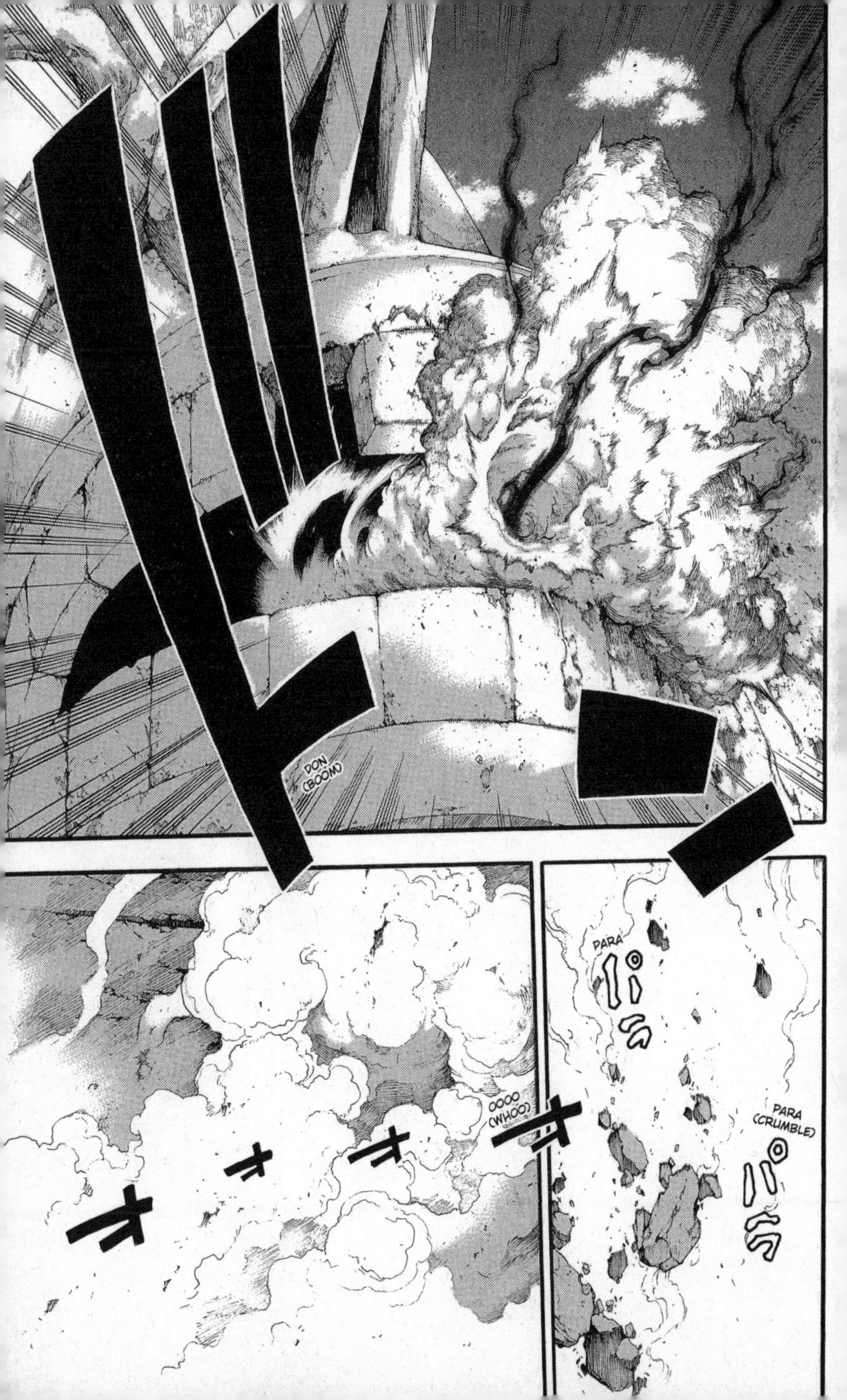
DON (BOOM)
PARA
PARA (CRUMBLE)
OOOO (WHOO)

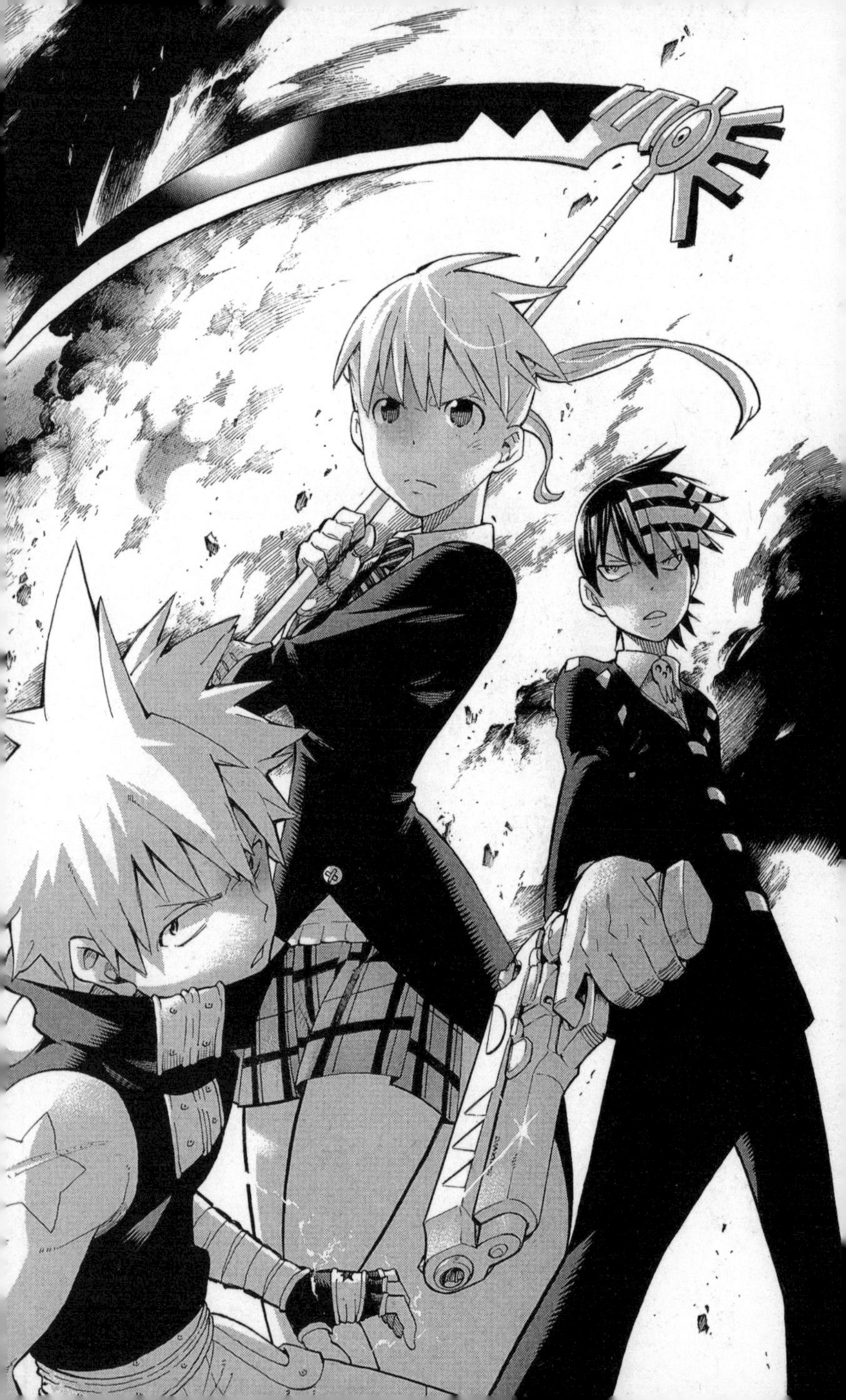

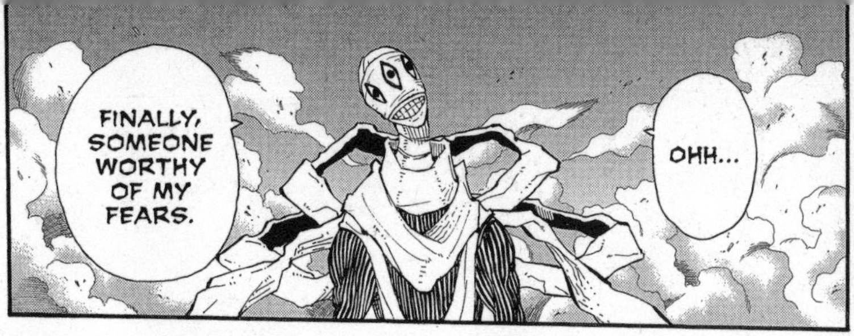
OHH...
FINALLY, SOMEONE WORTHY OF MY FEARS.

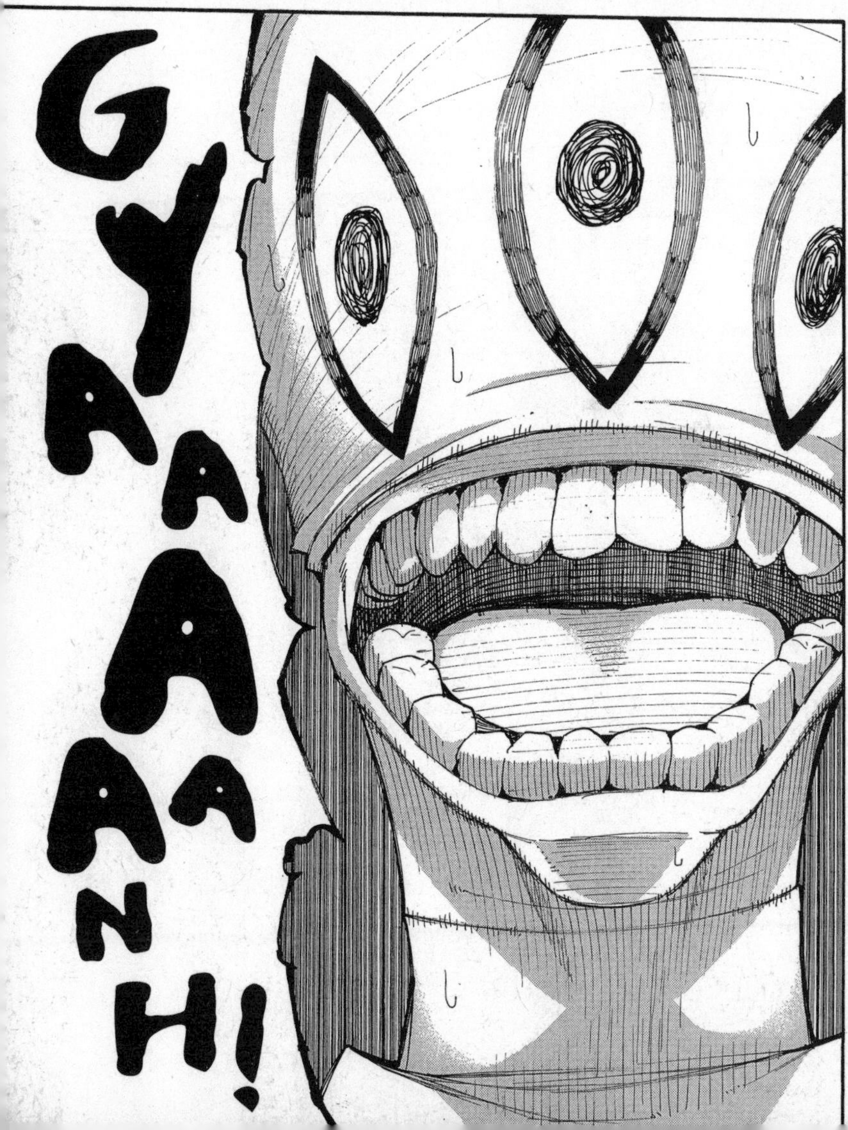
GYAAAAANH!

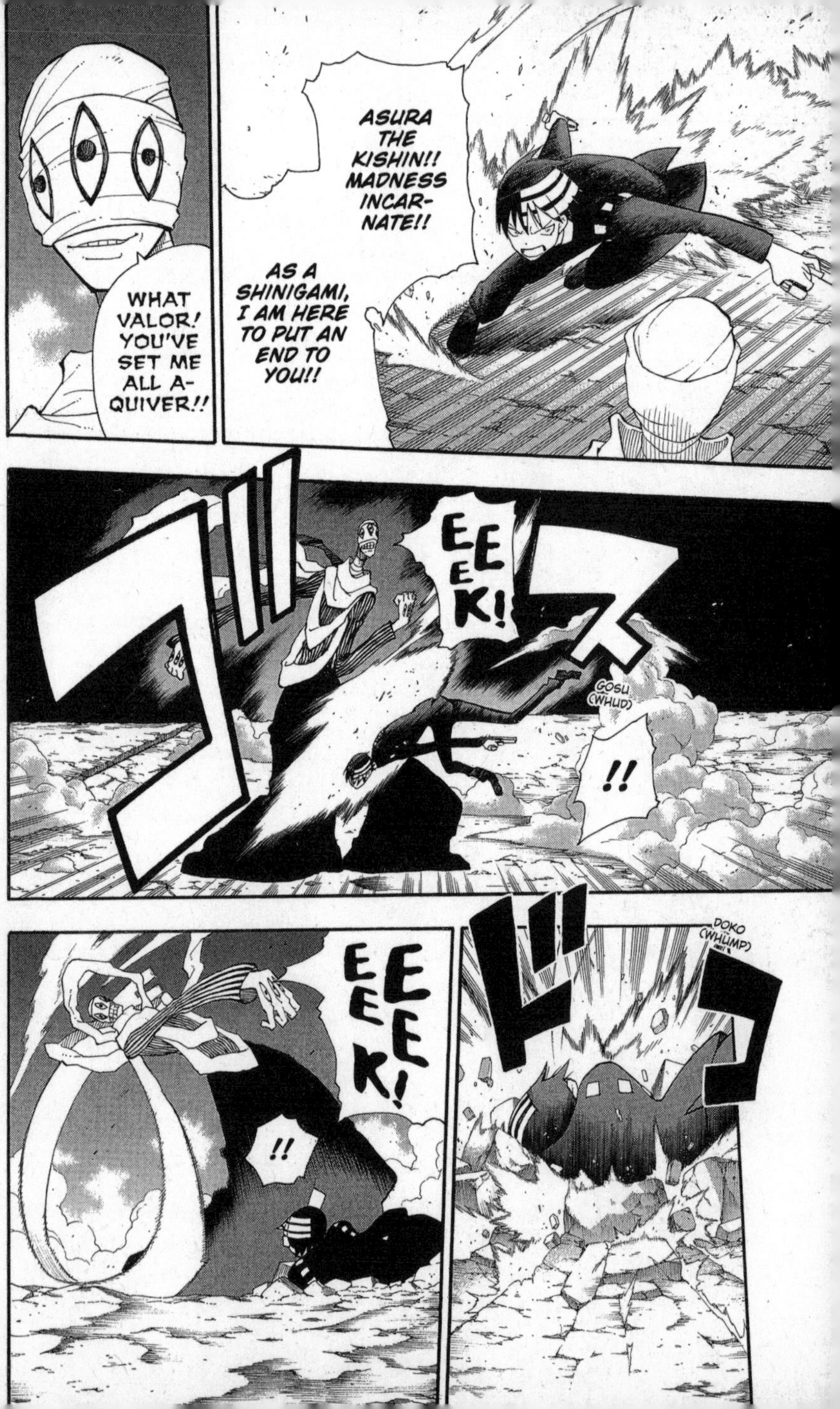
ASURA THE KISHIN!! MADNESS INCARNATE!!
AS A SHINIGAMI, I AM HERE TO PUT AN END TO YOU!!
WHAT VALOR! YOU'VE SET ME ALL A-QUIVER!!
EEEK!
GOSU (WHUD)
!!
DOKO (WHUMP)
EEEEK!
!!

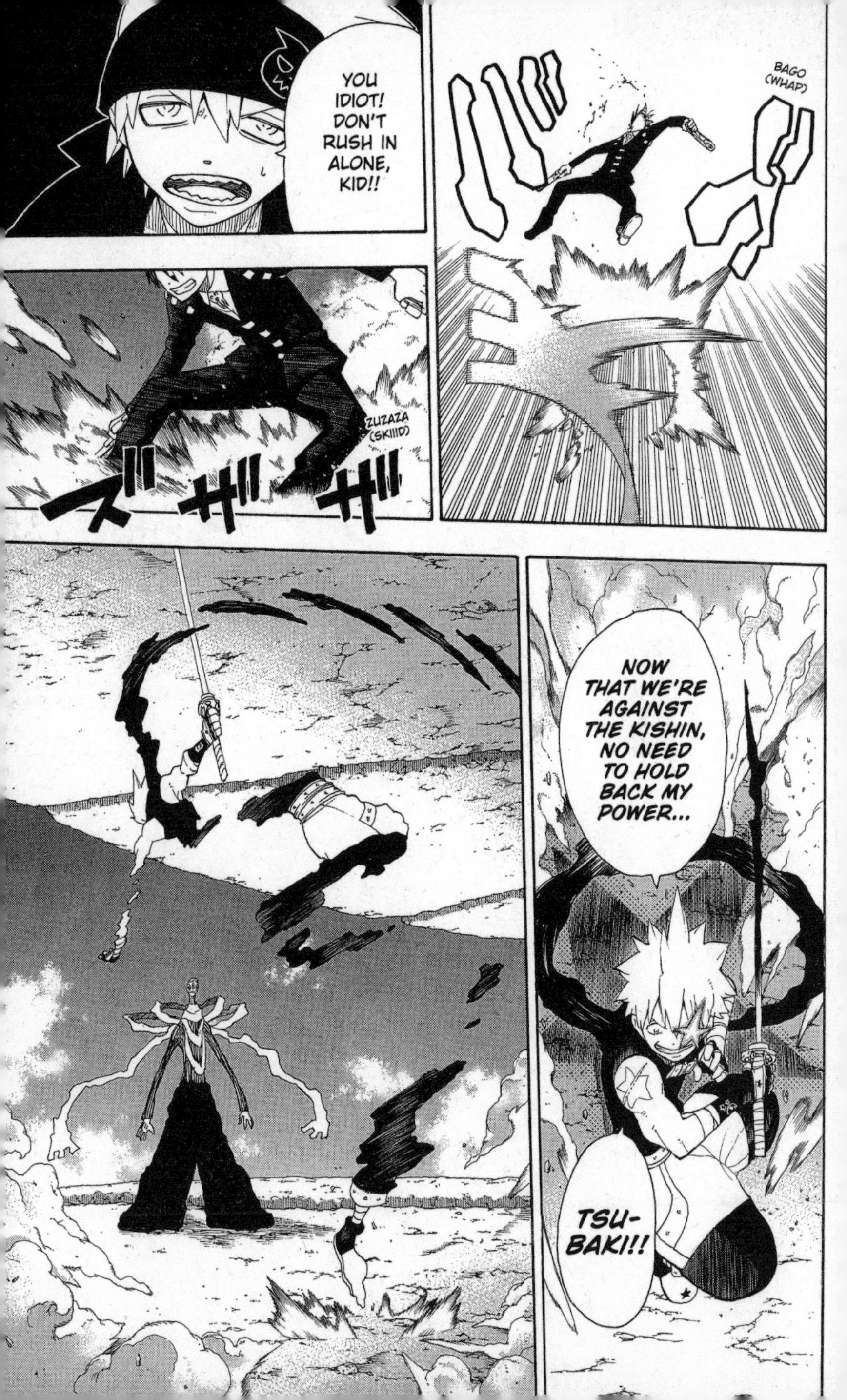
BAGO (WHAP)
YOU IDIOT! DON'T RUSH IN ALONE, KID!!
ZUZAZA (SKIIID)
NOW THAT WE'RE AGAINST THE KISHIN, NO NEED TO HOLD BACK MY POWER...
TSU-BAKI!!

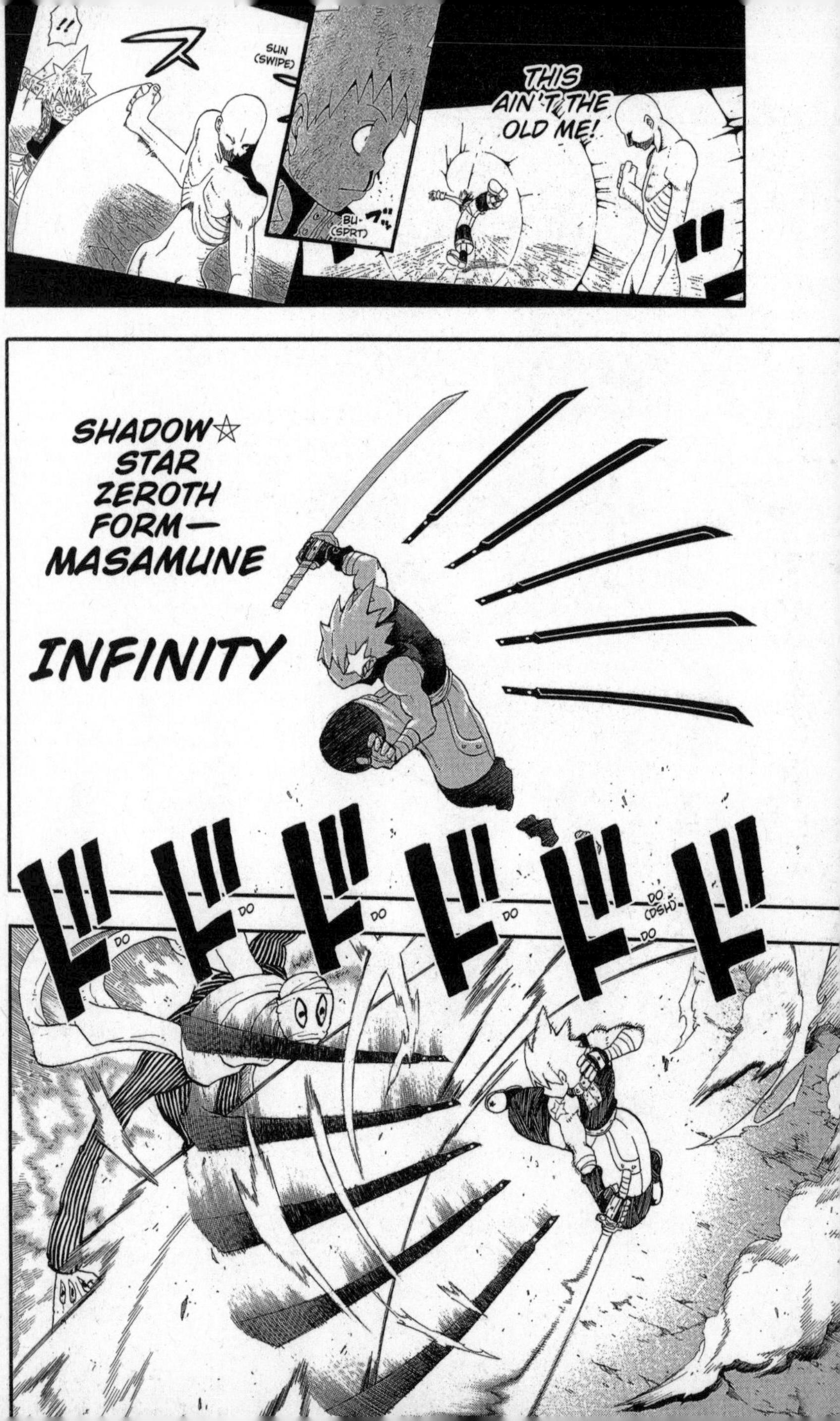
THIS AIN'T THE OLD ME!
BU (SPRT)
!!
SUN (SWIPE)
SHADOW☆STAR ZEROTH FORM— MASAMUNE
INFINITY
DO (DSH)
DO
DO
DO
DO
DO

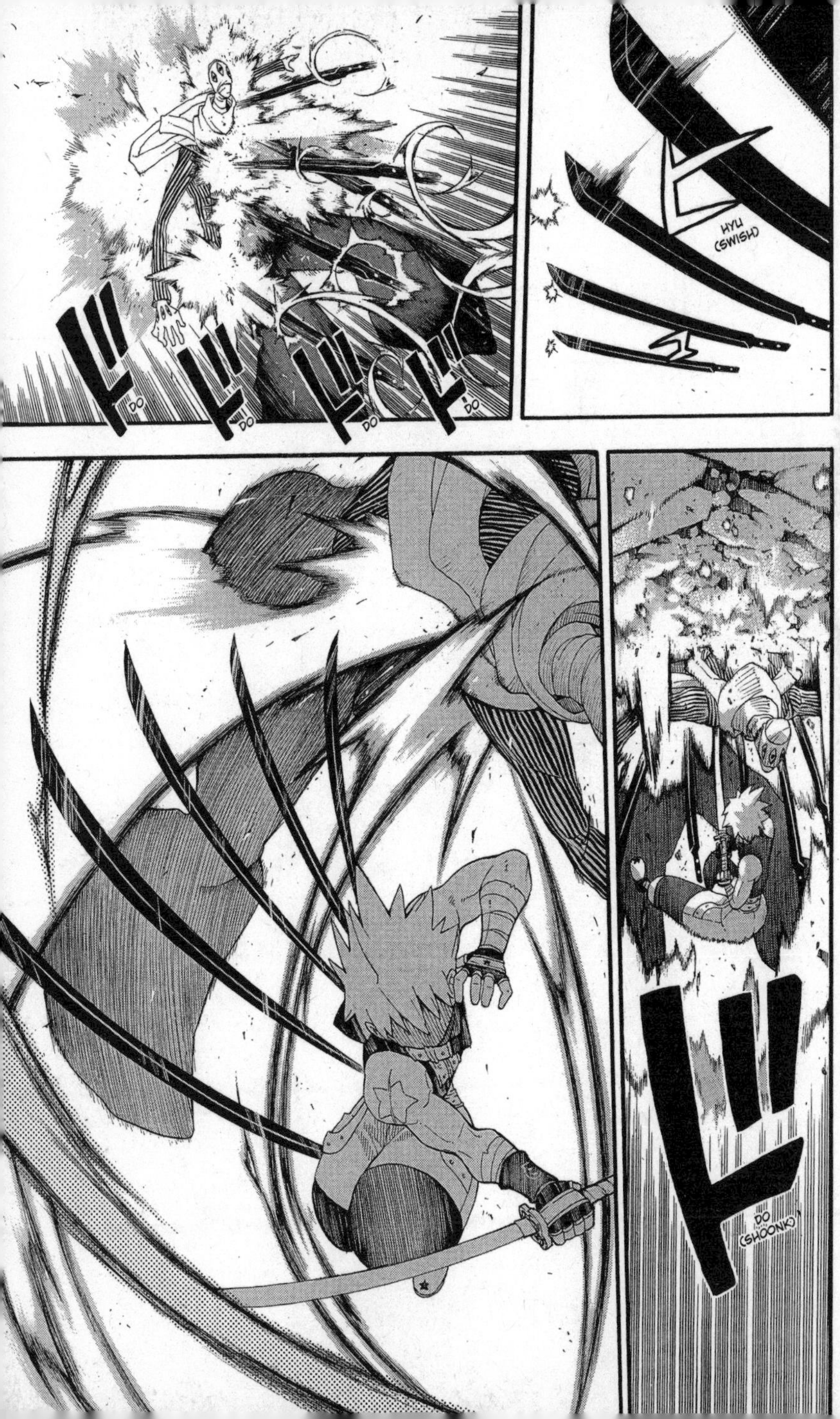
HYU (SWISH)
DO
DO
DO
DO
DO (SHOONK)

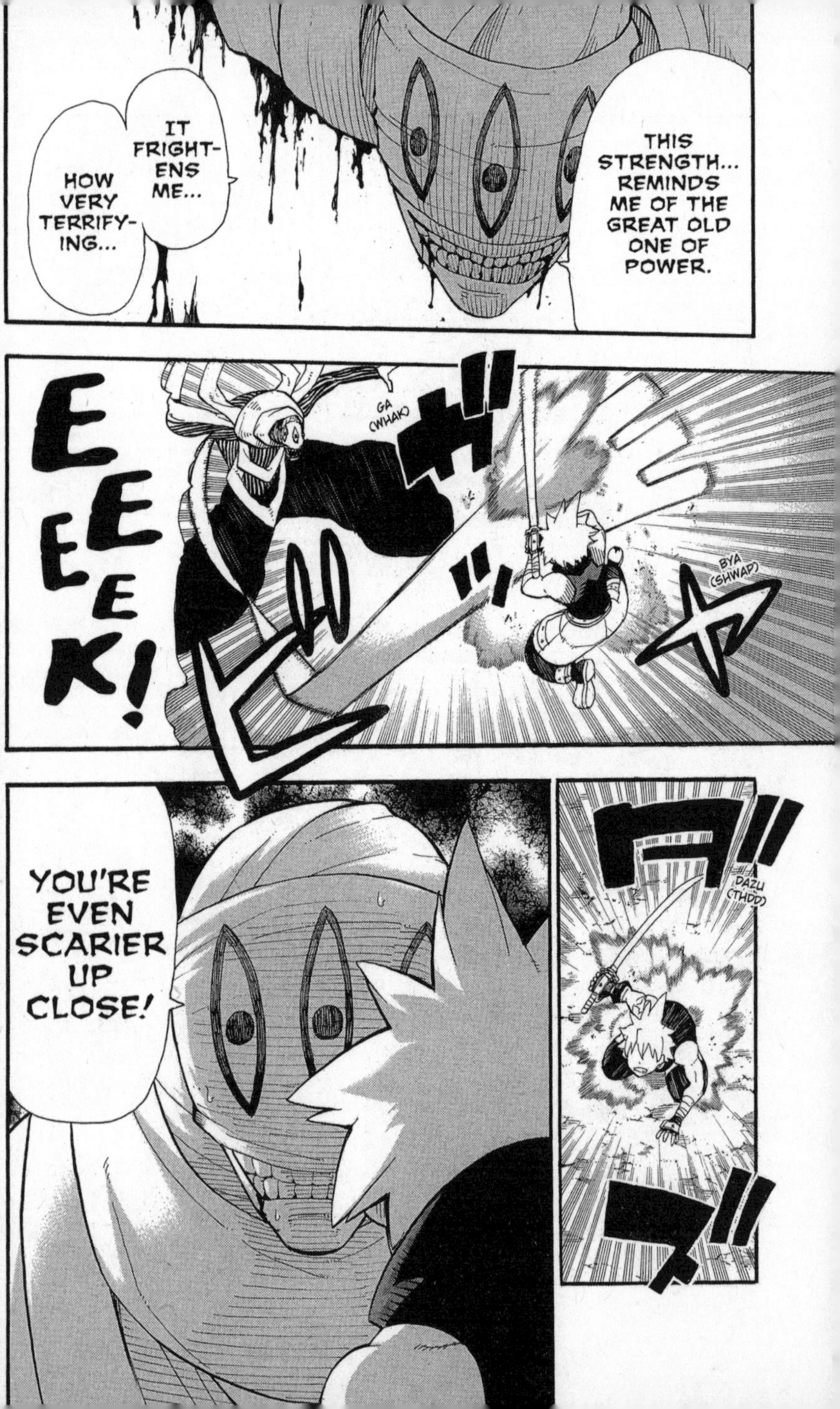
THIS STRENGTH... REMINDS ME OF THE GREAT OLD ONE OF POWER.
IT FRIGHT-ENS ME...
HOW VERY TERRIFY-ING...
BYA (SHWAP)
GA (WHAK)
EEEEK!
DAZU (THDD)
YOU'RE EVEN SCARIER UP CLOSE!

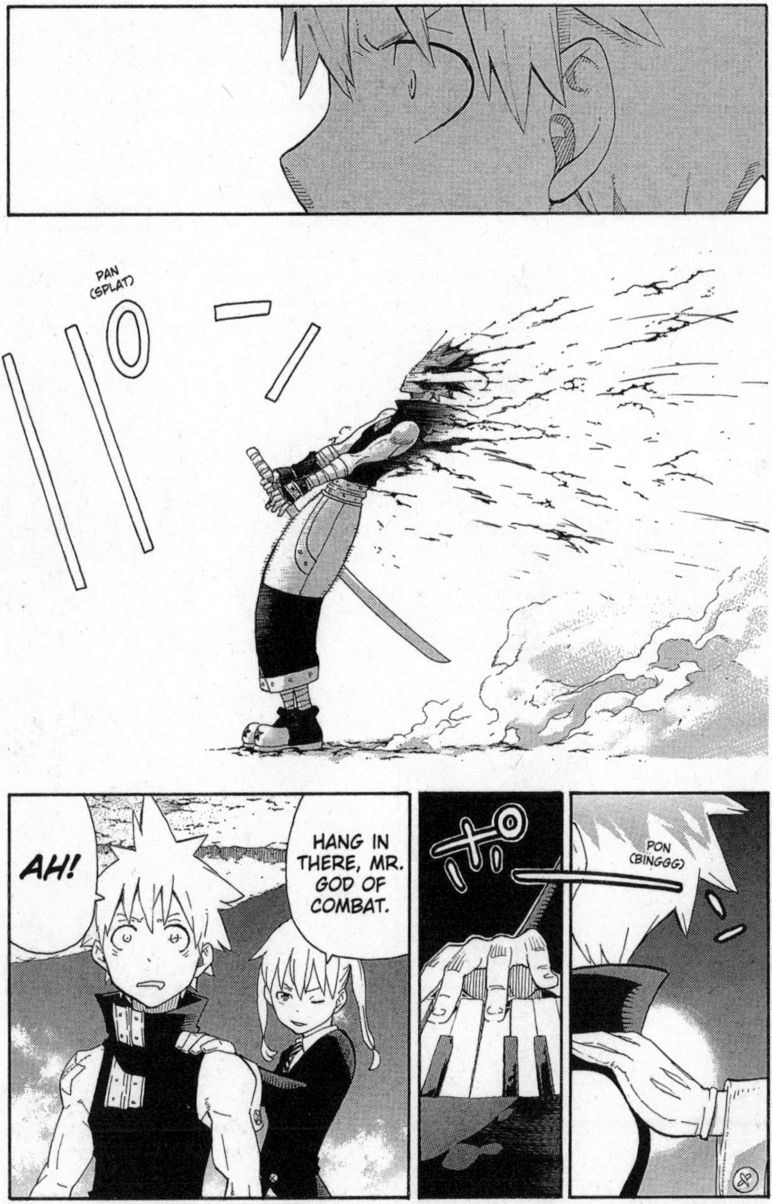
PAN
(SPLAT)
PON
(BINGGG)
HANG IN THERE, MR. GOD OF COMBAT.
AH!

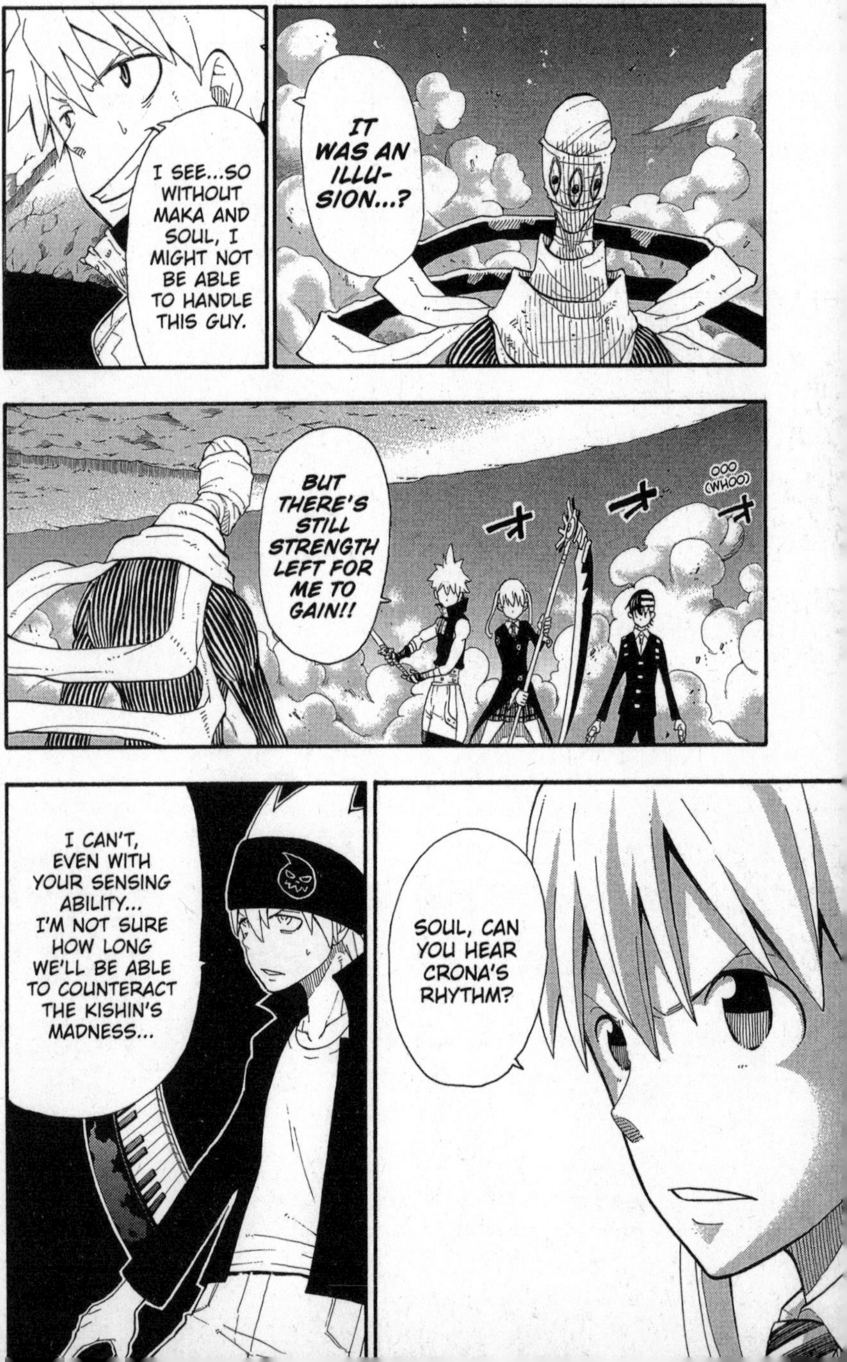
IT WAS AN ILLUSION...?
I SEE...SO WITHOUT MAKA AND SOUL, I MIGHT NOT BE ABLE TO HANDLE THIS GUY.
OOO (WHOO)
BUT THERE'S STILL STRENGTH LEFT FOR ME TO GAIN!!
SOUL, CAN YOU HEAR CRONA'S RHYTHM?
I CAN'T, EVEN WITH YOUR SENSING ABILITY... I'M NOT SURE HOW LONG WE'LL BE ABLE TO COUNTERACT THE KISHIN'S MADNESS...

YOU CAN'T DROWN OUT MADNESS WITH THAT TINY KEY-BOARD...

HE'S GOT BLACK BLOOD, YOU'VE GOT BLACK BLOOD.

I'VE GOT A BIG ONE JUST IN HERE, ALL TUNED UP AND READY TO BLAST.

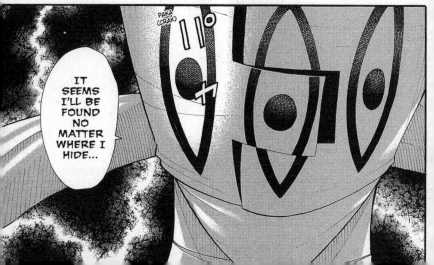

PAKA CCRAKO

IT SEEMS I'LL BE FOUND NO MATTER WHERE I HIDE...

SO I WILL USE THIS MADNESS TO ERASE EVERY-THING.

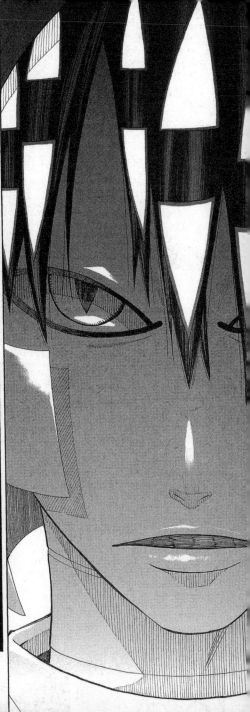

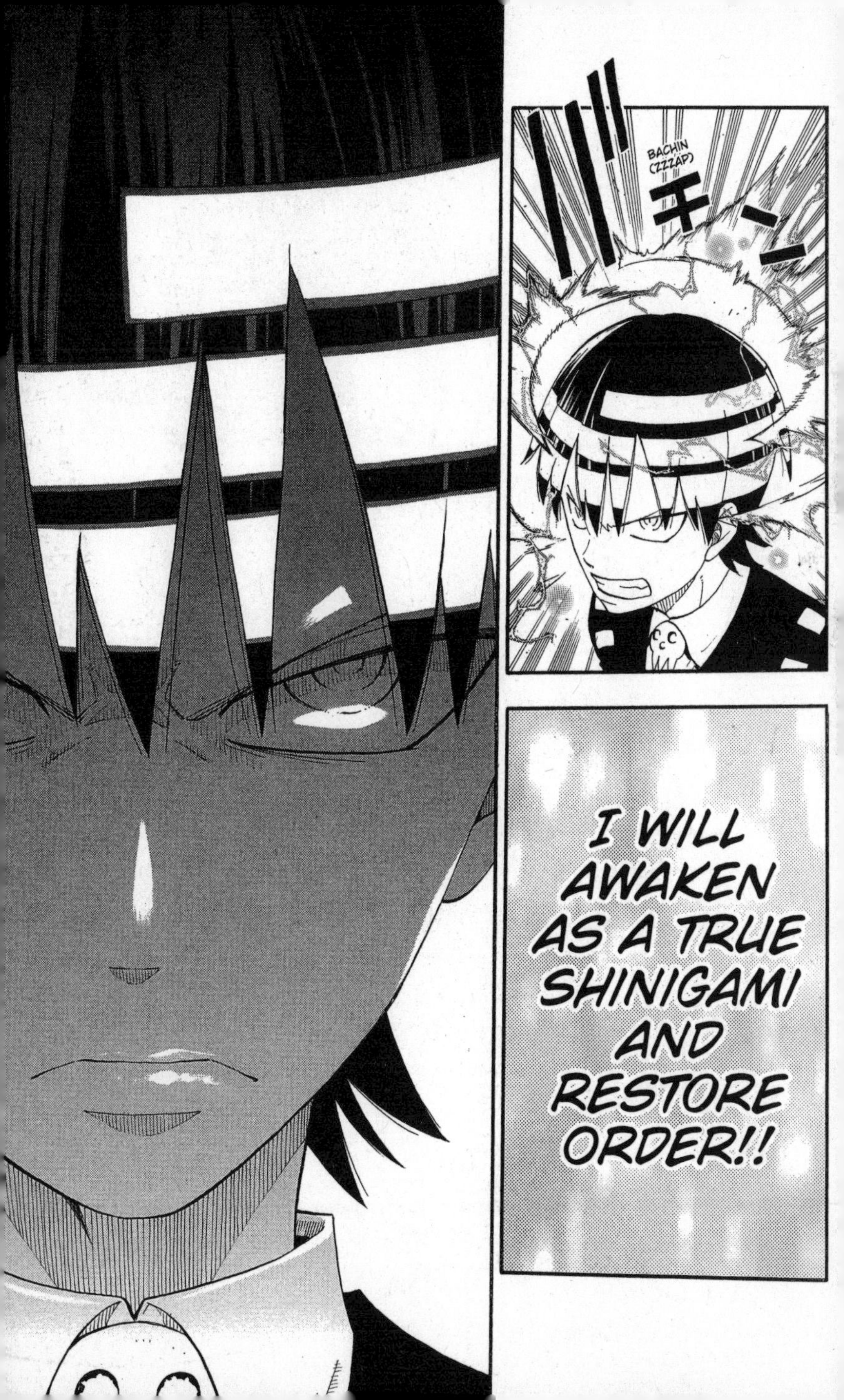
BACHIN
(ZZZAP)
I WILL AWAKEN AS A TRUE SHINIGAMI AND RESTORE ORDER!!

PAKI
(CRAK)

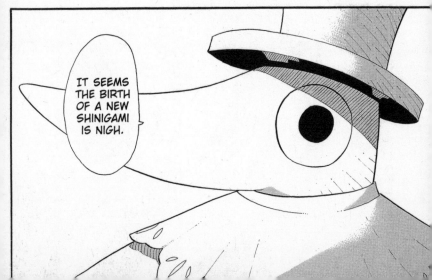

IT SEEMS THE BIRTH OF A NEW SHINIGAMI IS NIGH.

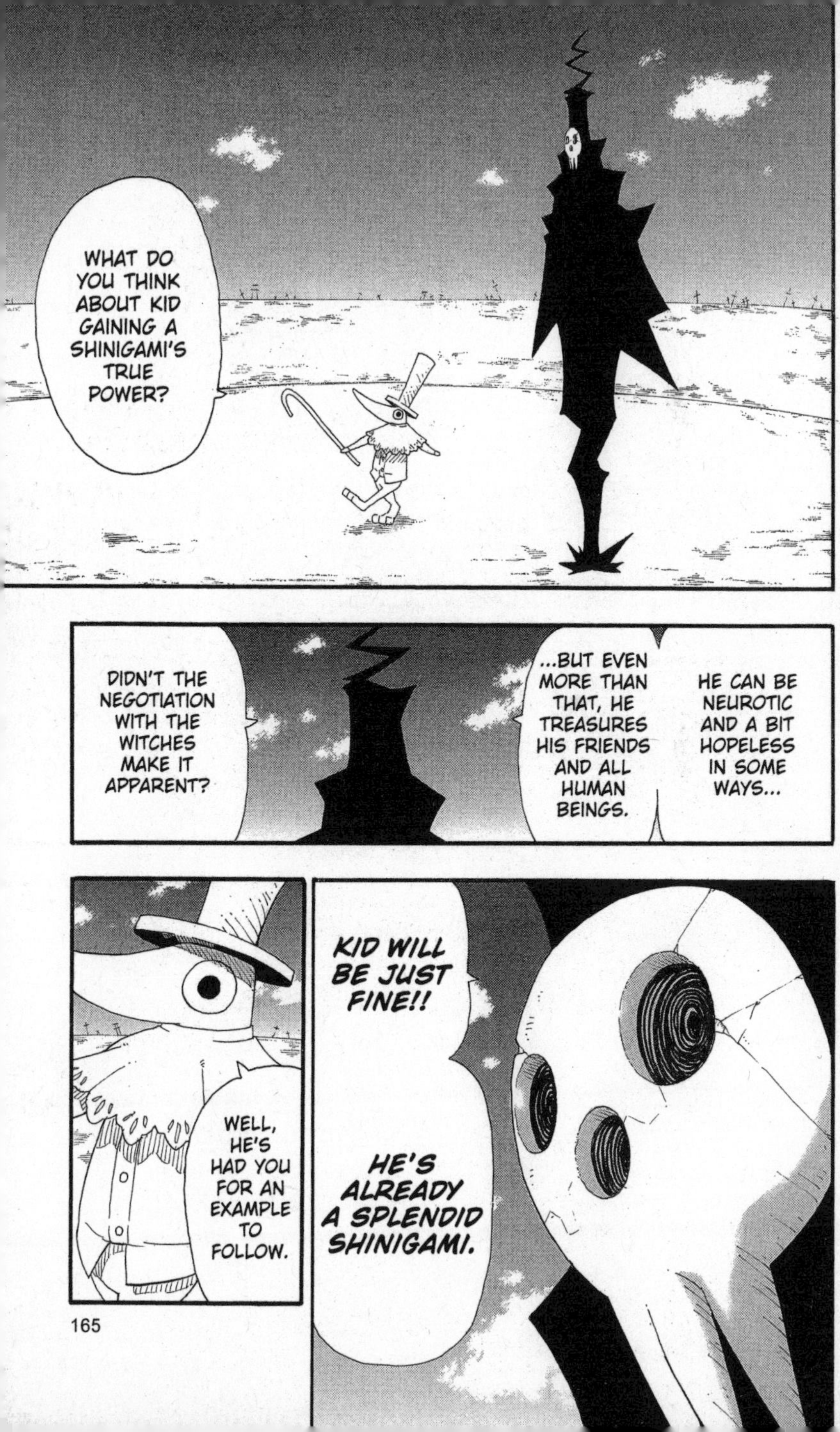
WHAT DO YOU THINK ABOUT KID GAINING A SHINIGAMI'S TRUE POWER?
HE CAN BE NEUROTIC AND A BIT HOPELESS IN SOME WAYS...
...BUT EVEN MORE THAN THAT, HE TREASURES HIS FRIENDS AND ALL HUMAN BEINGS.
DIDN'T THE NEGOTIATION WITH THE WITCHES MAKE IT APPARENT?
KID WILL BE JUST FINE!!
HE'S ALREADY A SPLENDID SHINIGAMI.
WELL, HE'S HAD YOU FOR AN EXAMPLE TO FOLLOW.

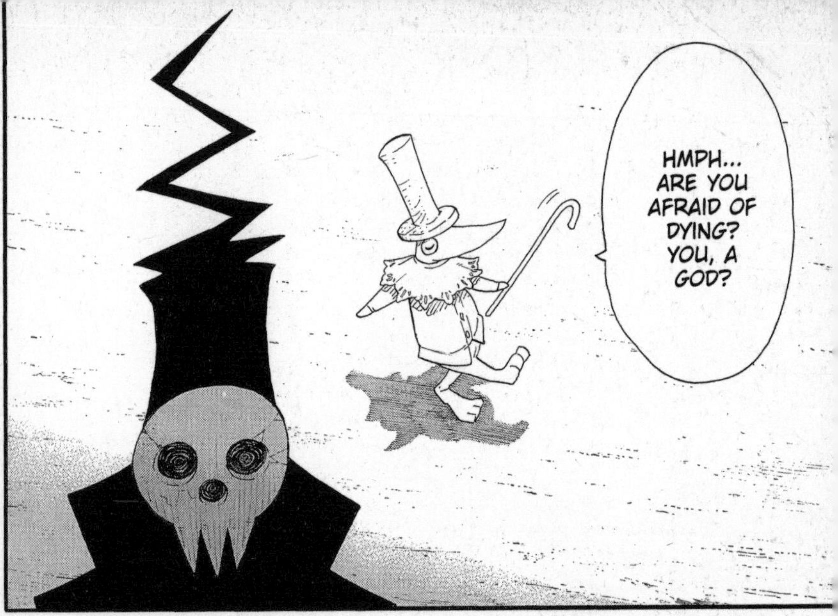
HMPH... ARE YOU AFRAID OF DYING? YOU, A GOD?

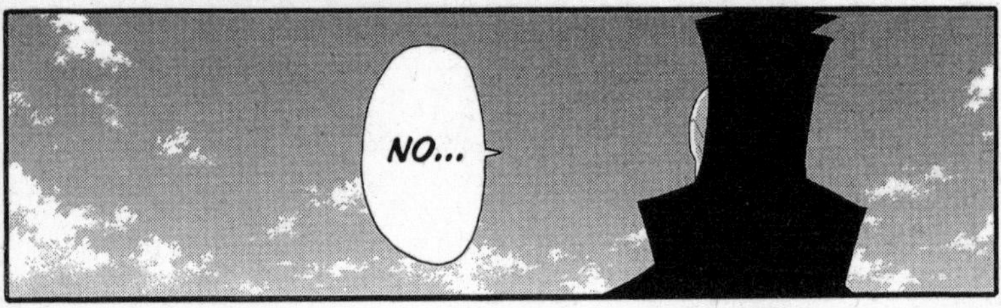
NO...

I'VE ALREADY GIVEN AWAY MY FEAR ALONG WITH EVERYTHING ELSE...

SOUL EATER 24 END

Translation Notes

Common Honorifics

no honorific: Indicates familiarity or closeness; if used without permission or reason, addressing someone in this manner would constitute an insult.

-san: The Japanese equivalent of Mr./Mrs./Miss. If a situation calls for politeness, this is the fail-safe honorific.

-sama: Conveys great respect; may also indicate that the social status of the speaker is lower than that of the addressee.

-dono: Like -sama, using -dono is an indication of respect for the addressee.

-kun: Used most often when referring to boys, this indicates affection or familiarity. Occasionally used by older men among their peers, but it may also be used by anyone referring to a person of lower standing.

-chan: An affectionate honorific indicating familiarity used mostly in reference to girls; also used in reference to cute persons or animals of either gender.

-senpai: A suffix used to address upperclassmen or more experienced coworkers.

-sensei: A respectful term for teachers, artists, or high-level professionals.

Page 92
While in the Western world a **baby tooth** that falls out is traditionally placed under a child's pillow to be retrieved by the tooth fairy, Japan has its own customs. If the tooth is from the bottom jaw, it is thrown onto the roof, and if it's from the top jaw, it's tossed into the crawlspace beneath the house (usually underneath the wooden porch facing the backyard). They are thrown in the opposite direction to inspire the next tooth to grow into its proper place, downward or upward.

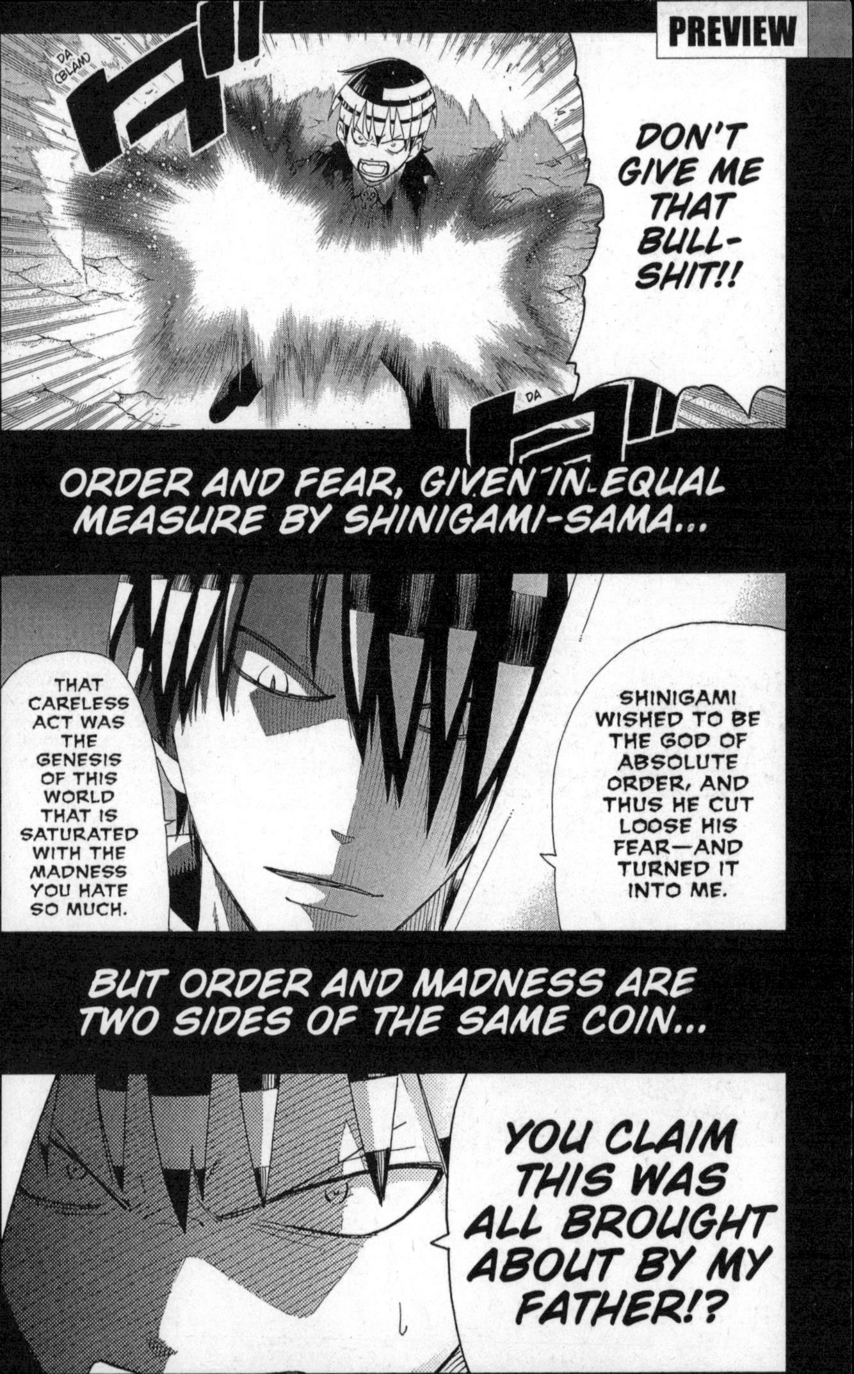
DA (BLAM)
DON'T GIVE ME THAT BULL-SHIT!!
DA
ORDER AND FEAR, GIVEN IN EQUAL MEASURE BY SHINIGAMI-SAMA...
SHINIGAMI WISHED TO BE THE GOD OF ABSOLUTE ORDER, AND THUS HE CUT LOOSE HIS FEAR—AND TURNED IT INTO ME.
THAT CARELESS ACT WAS THE GENESIS OF THIS WORLD THAT IS SATURATED WITH THE MADNESS YOU HATE SO MUCH.
BUT ORDER AND MADNESS ARE TWO SIDES OF THE SAME COIN...
YOU CLAIM THIS WAS ALL BROUGHT ABOUT BY MY FATHER!?

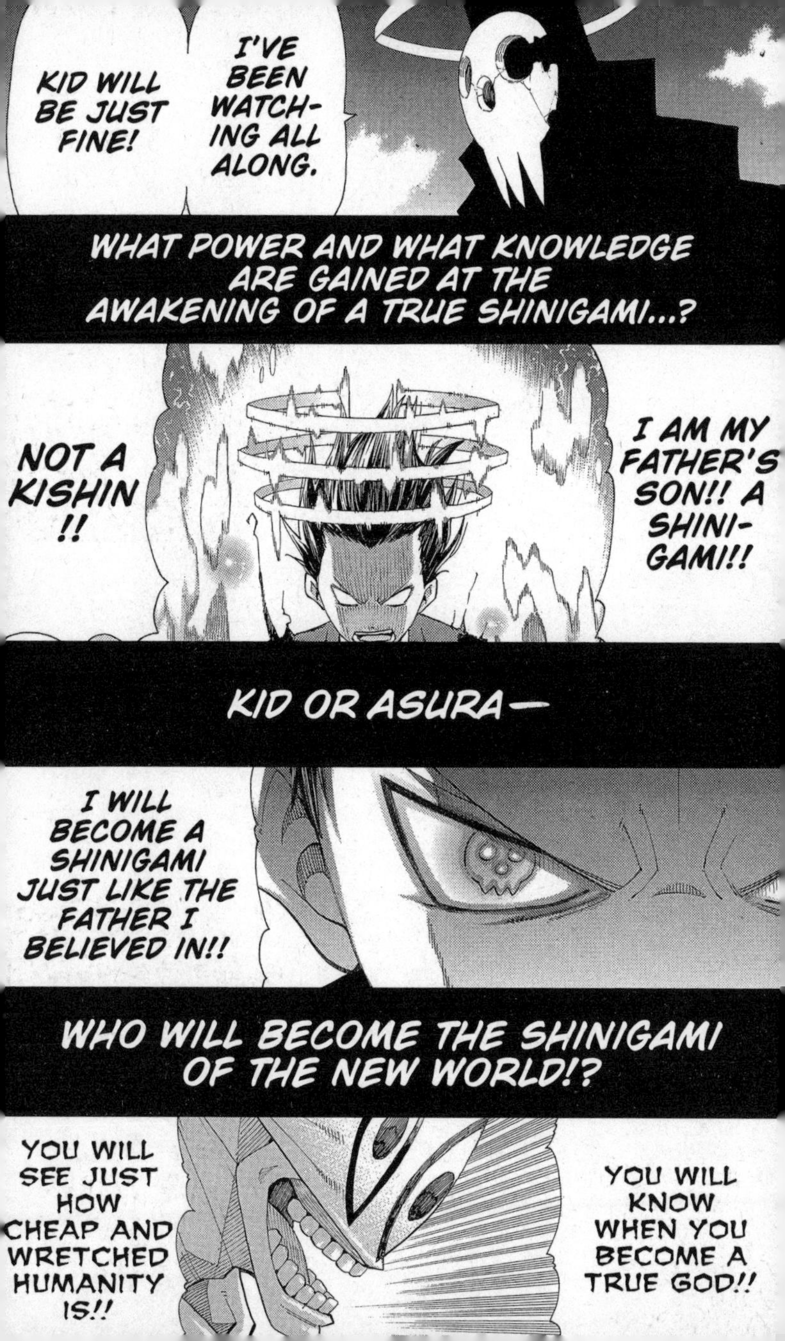
I'VE BEEN WATCHING ALL ALONG.
KID WILL BE JUST FINE!
WHAT POWER AND WHAT KNOWLEDGE ARE GAINED AT THE AWAKENING OF A TRUE SHINIGAMI...?
I AM MY FATHER'S SON!! A SHINIGAMI!!
NOT A KISHIN!!
KID OR ASURA—
I WILL BECOME A SHINIGAMI JUST LIKE THE FATHER I BELIEVED IN!!
WHO WILL BECOME THE SHINIGAMI OF THE NEW WORLD!?
YOU WILL KNOW WHEN YOU BECOME A TRUE GOD!!
YOU WILL SEE JUST HOW CHEAP AND WRETCHED HUMANITY IS!!

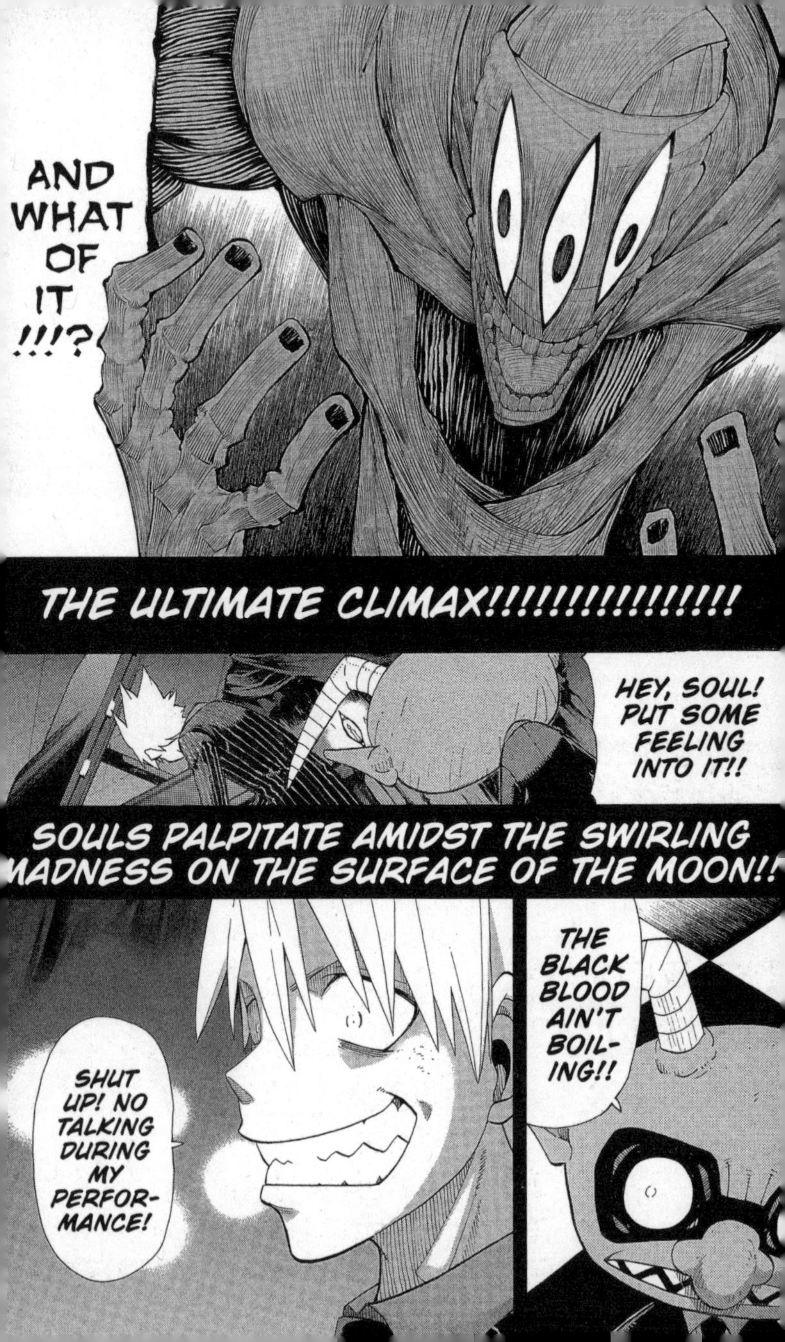
AND WHAT OF IT!!!?
THE ULTIMATE CLIMAX!!!!!!!!!!!!!!!!
HEY, SOUL! PUT SOME FEELING INTO IT!!
SOULS PALPITATE AMIDST THE SWIRLING MADNESS ON THE SURFACE OF THE MOON!!
THE BLACK BLOOD AIN'T BOIL-ING!!
SHUT UP! NO TALKING DURING MY PERFOR-MANCE!

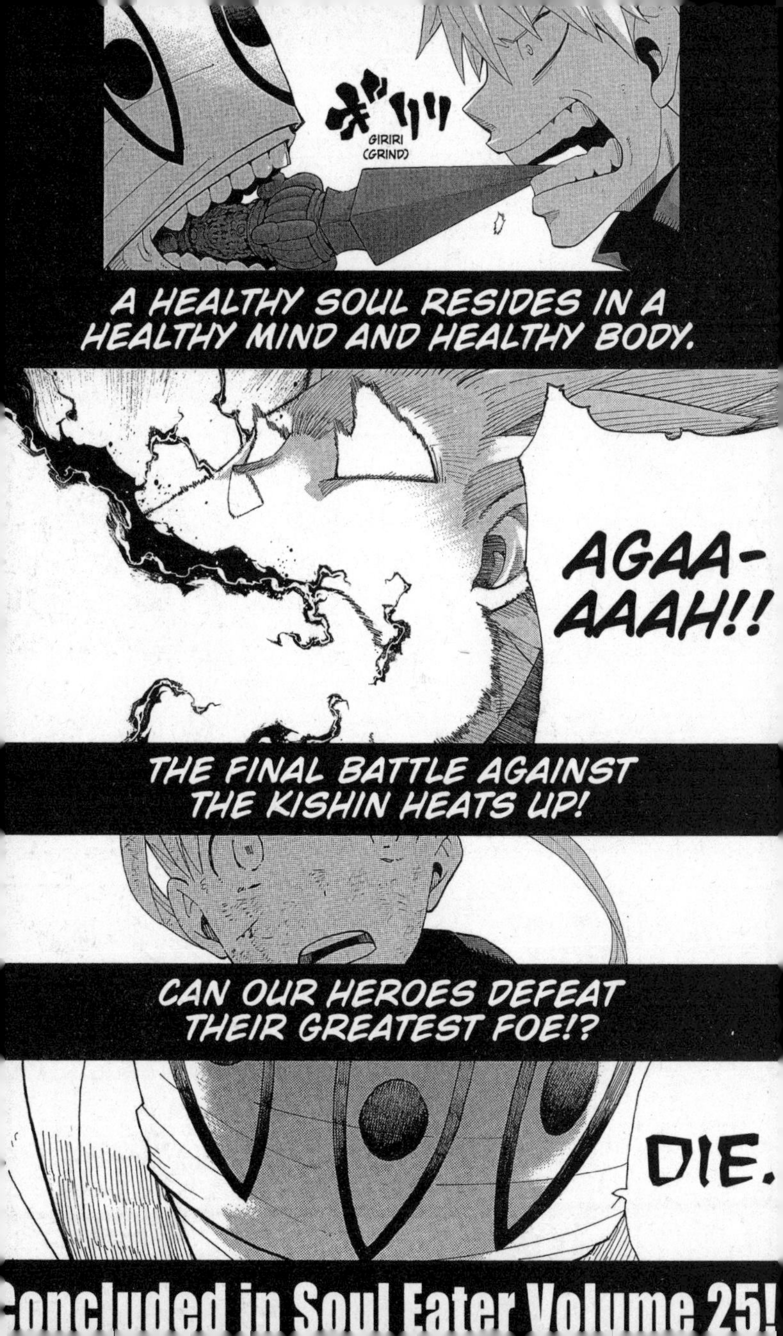
ギリリ
GIRIRI (GRIND)
A HEALTHY SOUL RESIDES IN A HEALTHY MIND AND HEALTHY BODY.
AGAA-AAAH!!
THE FINAL BATTLE AGAINST THE KISHIN HEATS UP!
CAN OUR HEROES DEFEAT THEIR GREATEST FOE!?
DIE.
Concluded in Soul Eater Volume 25!

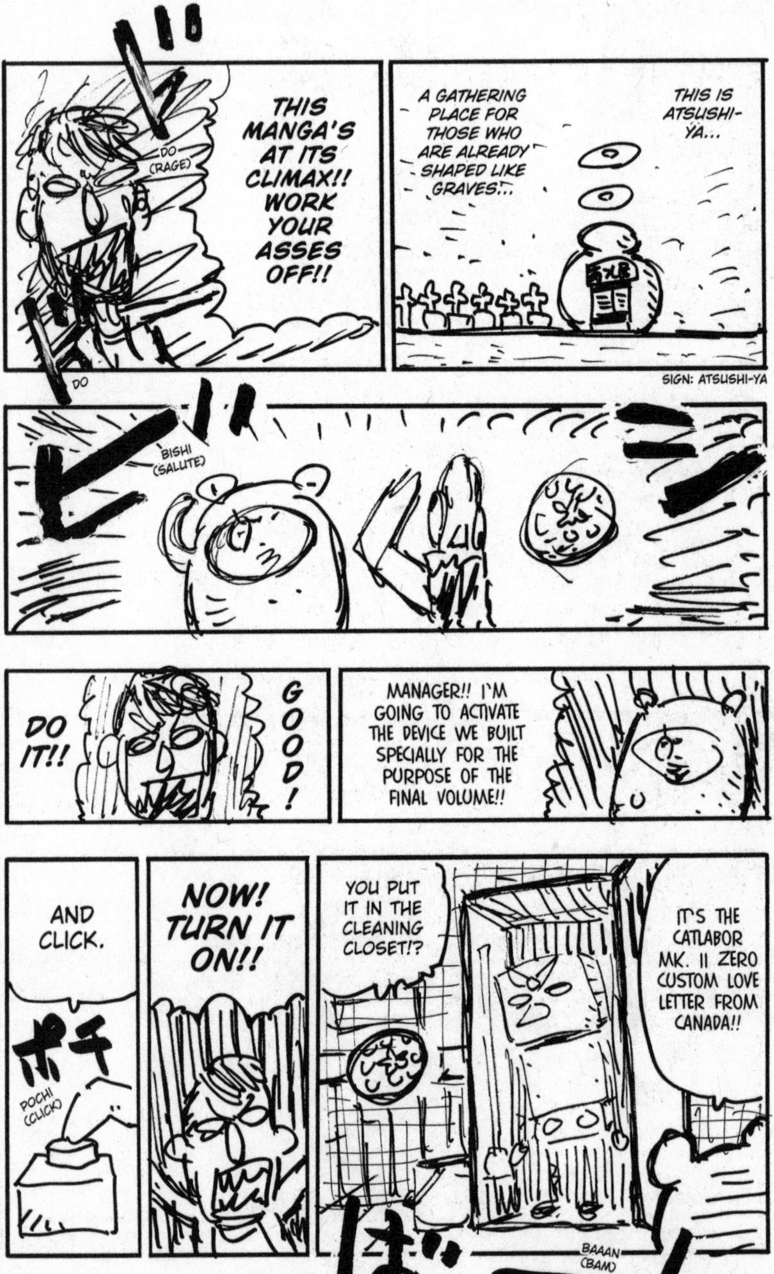
THIS IS ATSUSHI-YA...
A GATHERING PLACE FOR THOSE WHO ARE ALREADY SHAPED LIKE GRAVES...
SIGN: ATSUSHI-YA
DO (RAGE)
THIS MANGA'S AT ITS CLIMAX!! WORK YOUR ASSES OFF!!
DO
BISHI (SALUTE)
MANAGER!! I'M GOING TO ACTIVATE THE DEVICE WE BUILT SPECIALLY FOR THE PURPOSE OF THE FINAL VOLUME!!
GOOD!
DO IT!!
IT'S THE CATLABOR MK. II ZERO CUSTOM LOVE LETTER FROM CANADA!!
YOU PUT IT IN THE CLEANING CLOSET!?
ばーん
BAAAN (BAM)
NOW! TURN IT ON!!
AND CLICK.
ポチ
POCHI (CLICK)

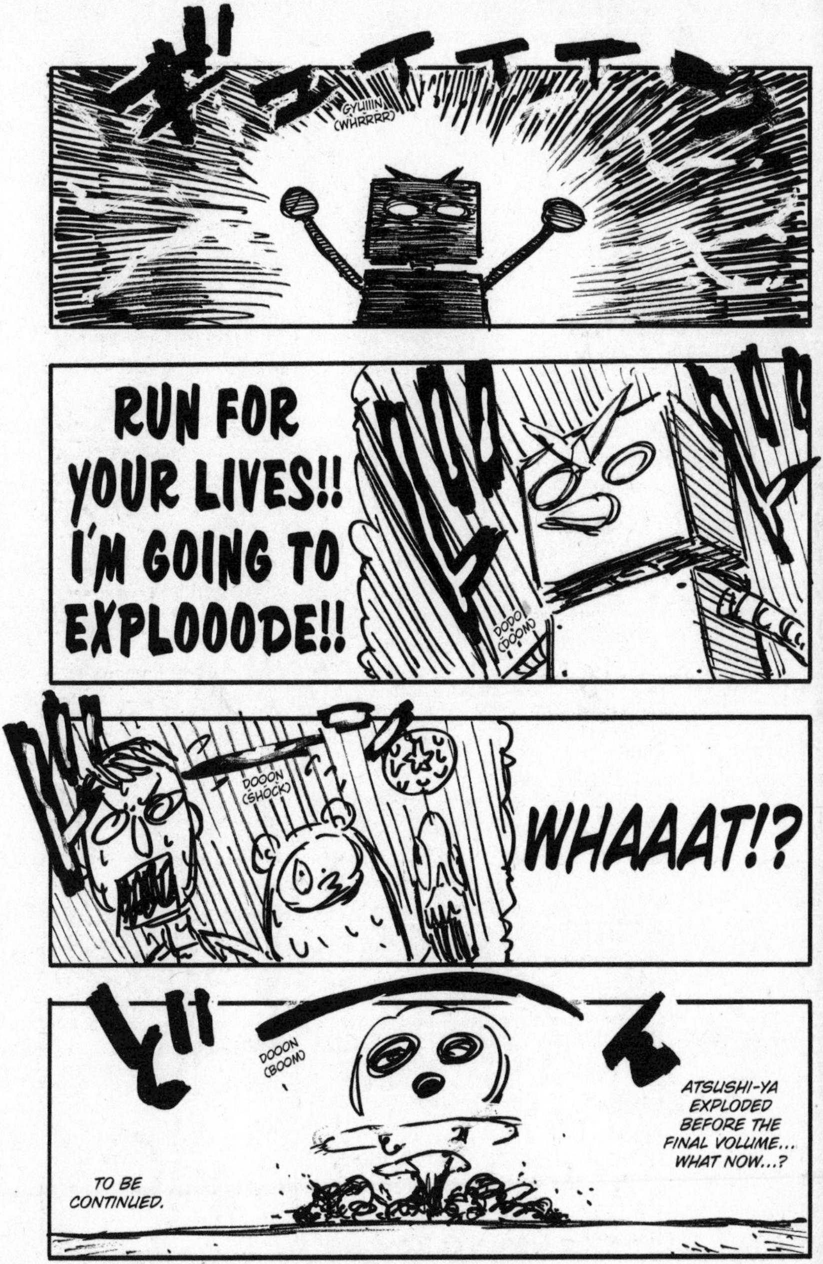
GYUIIIN (WHRRRR)
DODO (DOOM)
RUN FOR YOUR LIVES!! I'M GOING TO EXPLOOODE!!
WHAAAT!?
DOOON (SHOCK)
ATSUSHI-YA EXPLODED BEFORE THE FINAL VOLUME... WHAT NOW...?
DOOON (BOOM)
TO BE CONTINUED.

NOT!

SOUL EATER NOT!

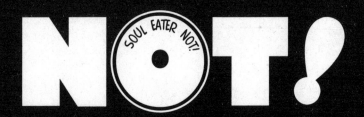

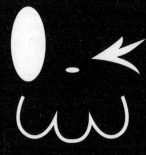

ANOTHER *SOUL EATER*?

IT'S A SAVAGE BUT SUPER-FUN LIFE! ♪

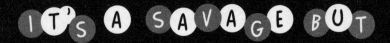

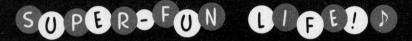

IT'S *SOUL EATER NOT!*

Here's an excerpt from a short story published in Volume 3 of our sister series, *Soul Eater Not!*

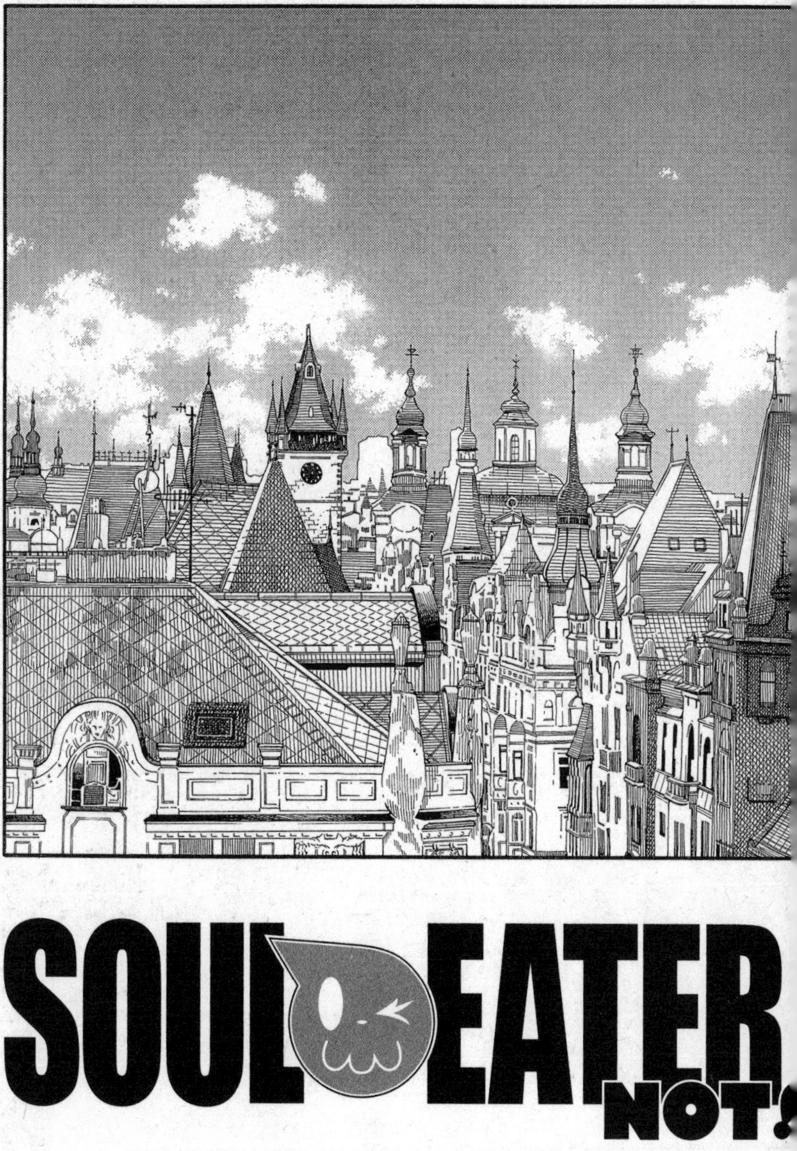

SOUL EATER NOT!

TEXAS HOLSTEIN

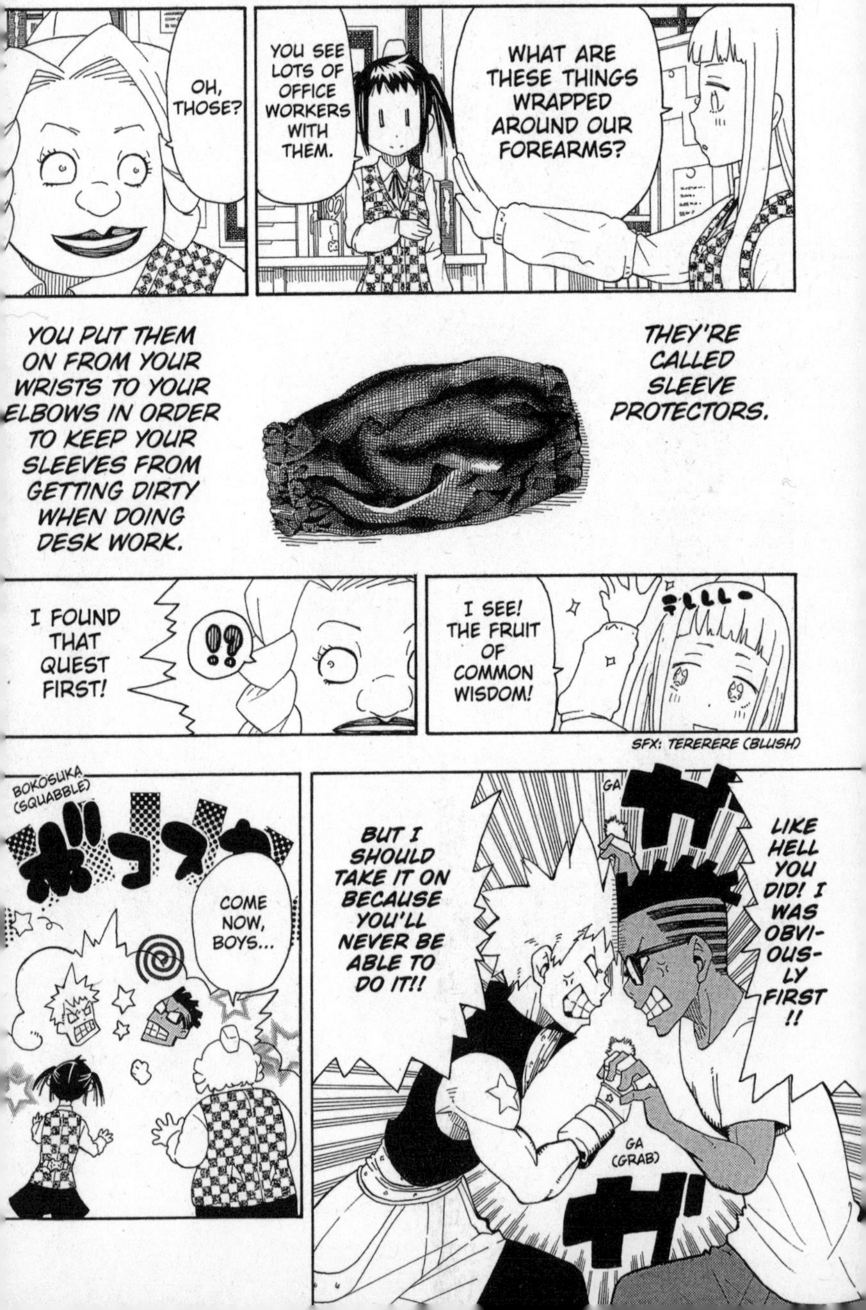
WHAT ARE THESE THINGS WRAPPED AROUND OUR FOREARMS?
YOU SEE LOTS OF OFFICE WORKERS WITH THEM.
OH, THOSE?
THEY'RE CALLED SLEEVE PROTECTORS.
YOU PUT THEM ON FROM YOUR WRISTS TO YOUR ELBOWS IN ORDER TO KEEP YOUR SLEEVES FROM GETTING DIRTY WHEN DOING DESK WORK.
I SEE! THE FRUIT OF COMMON WISDOM!
SFX: TERERERE (BLUSH)
I FOUND THAT QUEST FIRST!
GA
LIKE HELL YOU DID! I WAS OBVIOUSLY FIRST!!
BUT I SHOULD TAKE IT ON BECAUSE YOU'LL NEVER BE ABLE TO DO IT!!
GA (GRAB)
BOKOSUKA (SQUABBLE)
COME NOW, BOYS...

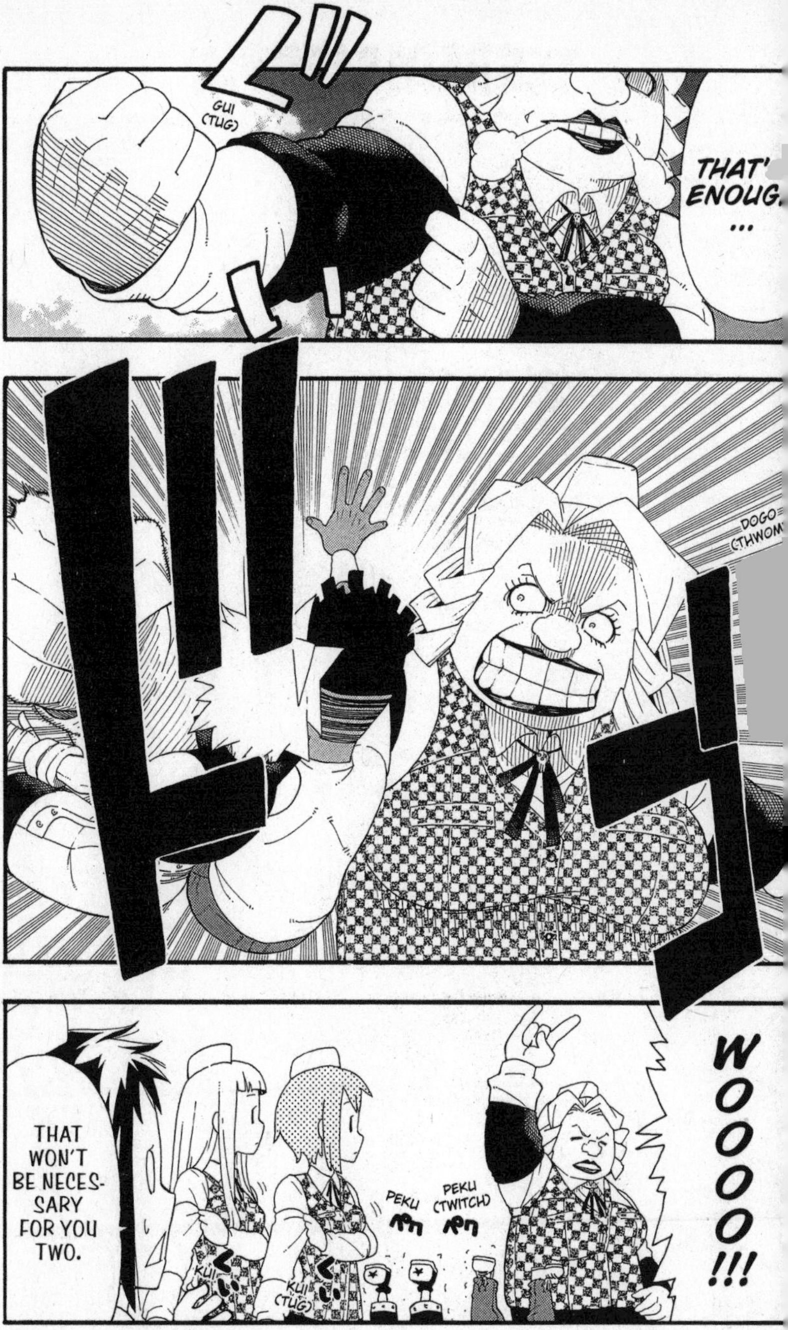
THAT'
ENOUG
...
GUI
(TUG)
DOGO
(THWOM
WOOOOO!!!
PEKU
PEKU
(TWITCH)
KUI
KUI
(TUG)
THAT WON'T BE NECES-SARY FOR YOU TWO.

SPECIALTY

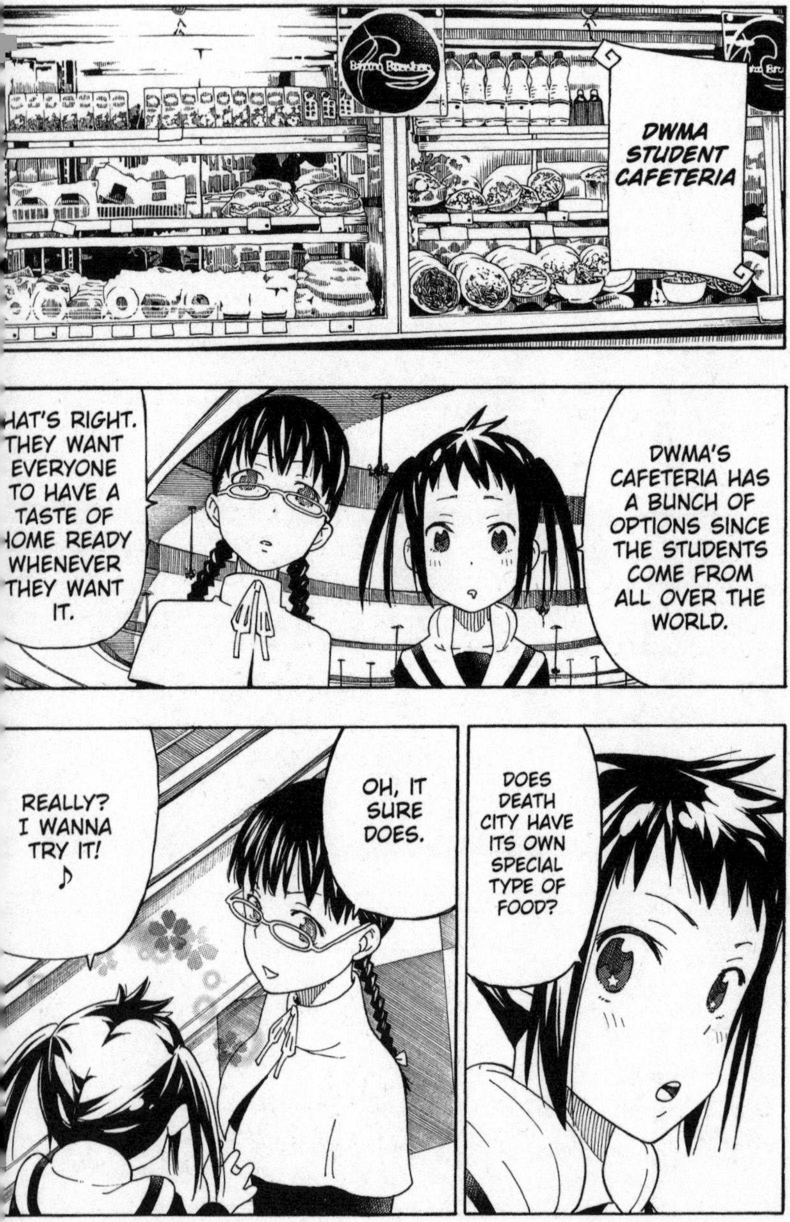
DWMA STUDENT CAFETERIA
DWMA'S CAFETERIA HAS A BUNCH OF OPTIONS SINCE THE STUDENTS COME FROM ALL OVER THE WORLD.
HAT'S RIGHT. THEY WANT EVERYONE TO HAVE A TASTE OF OME READY WHENEVER THEY WANT IT.
DOES DEATH CITY HAVE ITS OWN SPECIAL TYPE OF FOOD?
OH, IT SURE DOES.
REALLY? I WANNA TRY IT! ♪

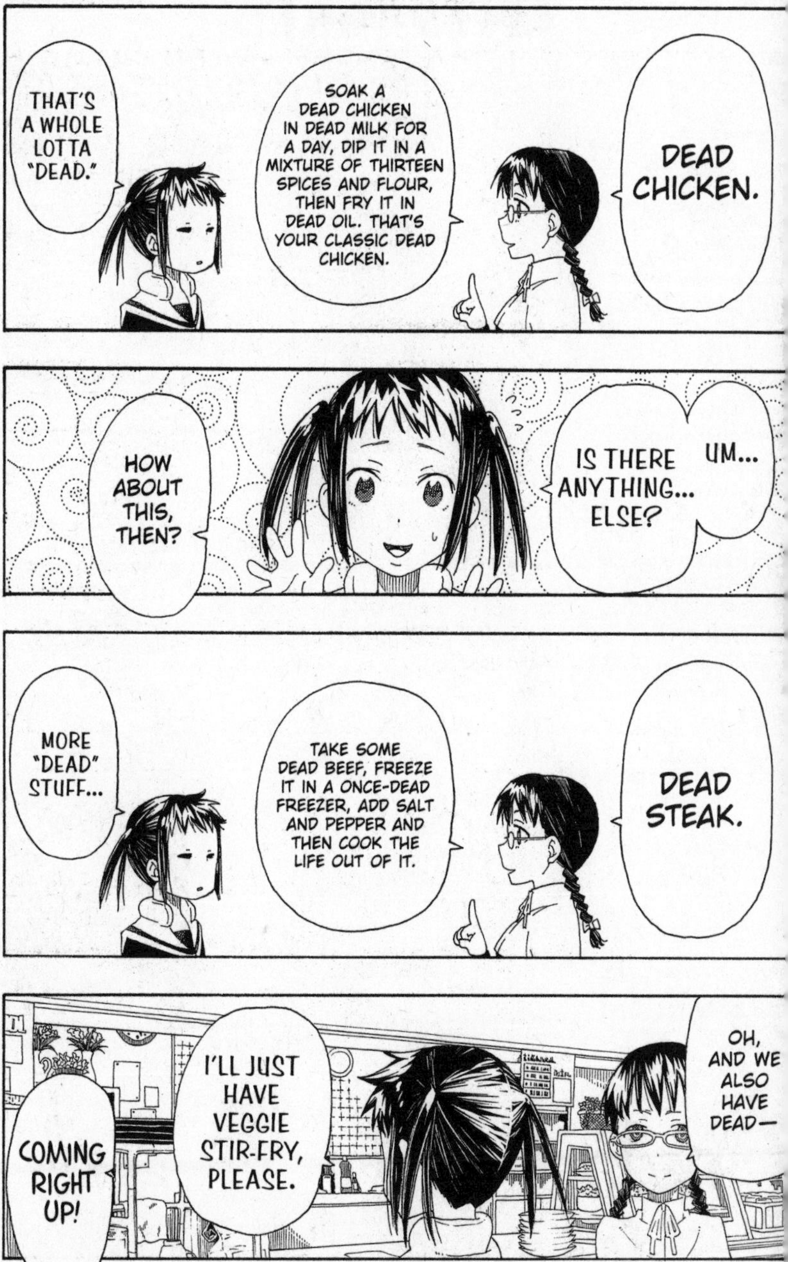
DEAD CHICKEN.
SOAK A DEAD CHICKEN IN DEAD MILK FOR A DAY, DIP IT IN A MIXTURE OF THIRTEEN SPICES AND FLOUR, THEN FRY IT IN DEAD OIL. THAT'S YOUR CLASSIC DEAD CHICKEN.
THAT'S A WHOLE LOTTA "DEAD."
UM...
IS THERE ANYTHING... ELSE?
HOW ABOUT THIS, THEN?
DEAD STEAK.
TAKE SOME DEAD BEEF, FREEZE IT IN A ONCE-DEAD FREEZER, ADD SALT AND PEPPER AND THEN COOK THE LIFE OUT OF IT.
MORE "DEAD" STUFF...
OH, AND WE ALSO HAVE DEAD—
I'LL JUST HAVE VEGGIE STIR-FRY, PLEASE.
COMING RIGHT UP!

AFTER THAT...

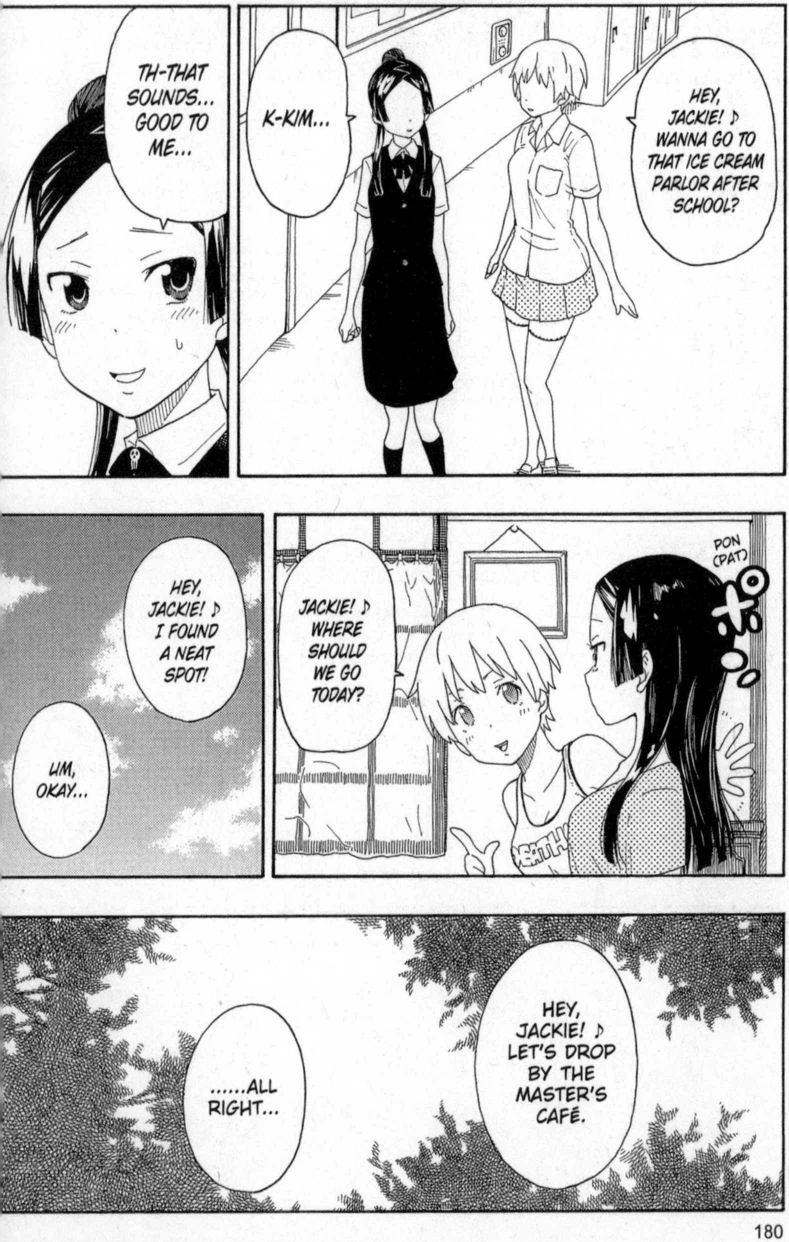
HEY, JACKIE! ♪ WANNA GO TO THAT ICE CREAM PARLOR AFTER SCHOOL?
K-KIM...
TH-THAT SOUNDS... GOOD TO ME...
PON (PAT)
JACKIE! ♪ WHERE SHOULD WE GO TODAY?
HEY, JACKIE! ♪ I FOUND A NEAT SPOT!
UM, OKAY...
HEY, JACKIE! ♪ LET'S DROP BY THE MASTER'S CAFÉ.
......ALL RIGHT...

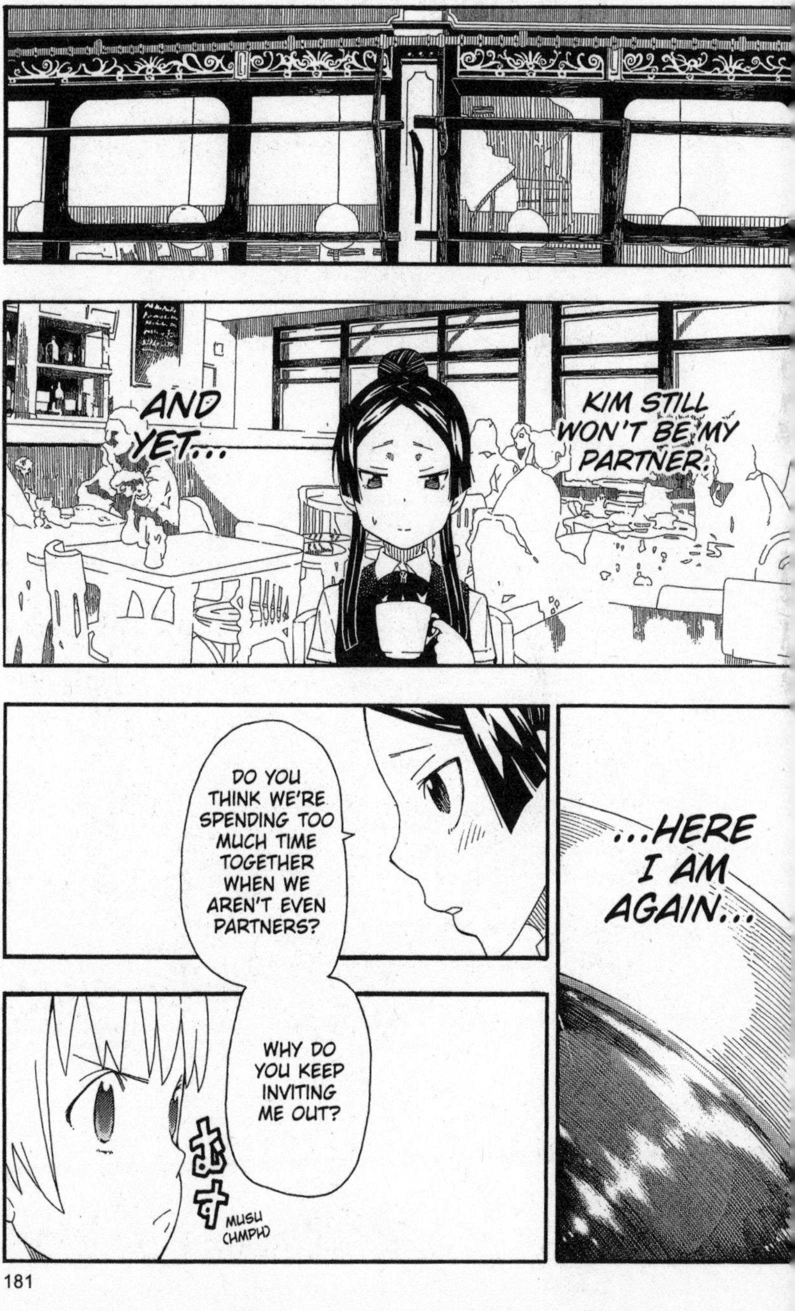

KIM STILL WON'T BE MY PARTNER.
AND YET...
...HERE I AM AGAIN...
DO YOU THINK WE'RE SPENDING TOO MUCH TIME TOGETHER WHEN WE AREN'T EVEN PARTNERS?
WHY DO YOU KEEP INVITING ME OUT?
むす
MUSU (HMPH)

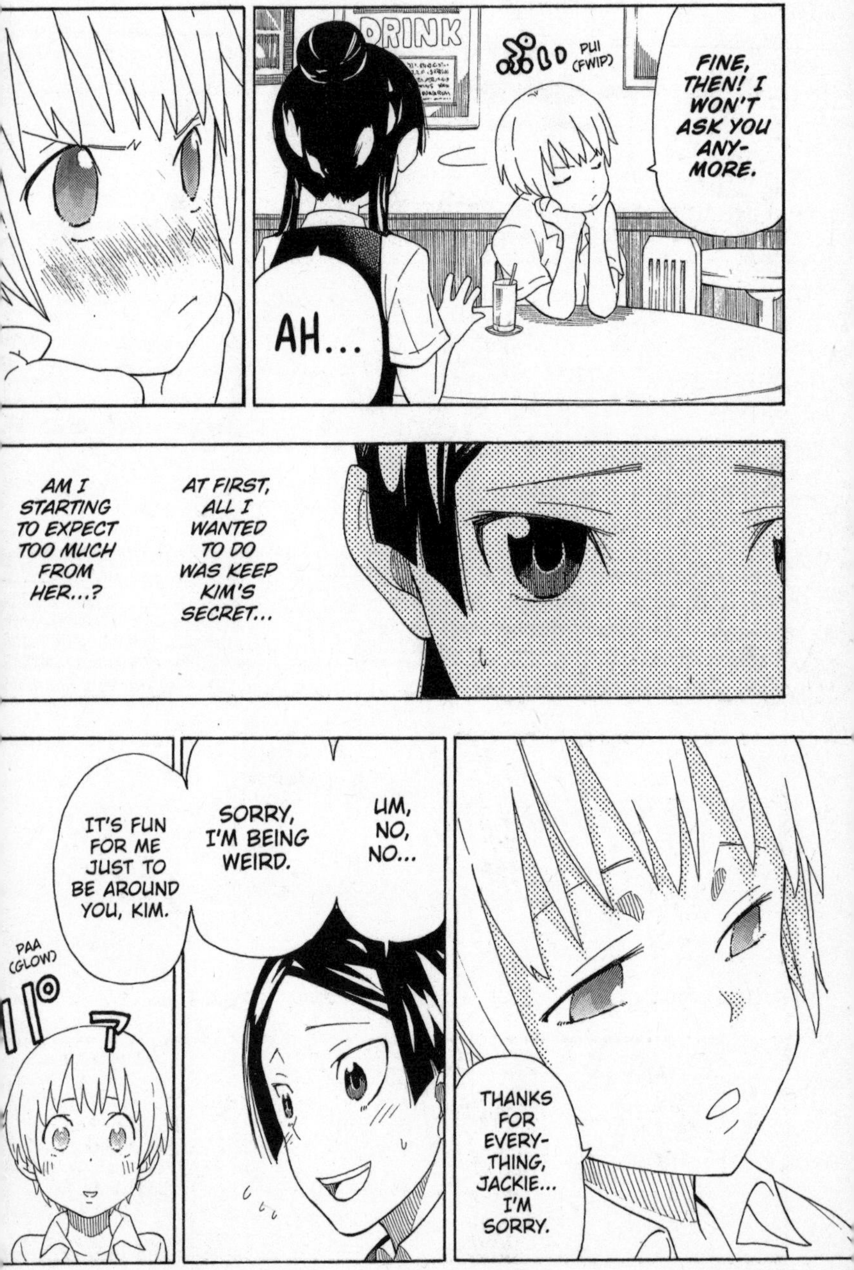

FINE, THEN! I WON'T ASK YOU ANYMORE.
PUI (FWIP)
AH...
AT FIRST, ALL I WANTED TO DO WAS KEEP KIM'S SECRET...
AM I STARTING TO EXPECT TOO MUCH FROM HER...?
THANKS FOR EVERYTHING, JACKIE... I'M SORRY.
UM, NO, NO...
SORRY, I'M BEING WEIRD.
IT'S FUN FOR ME JUST TO BE AROUND YOU, KIM.
PAA (GLOW)

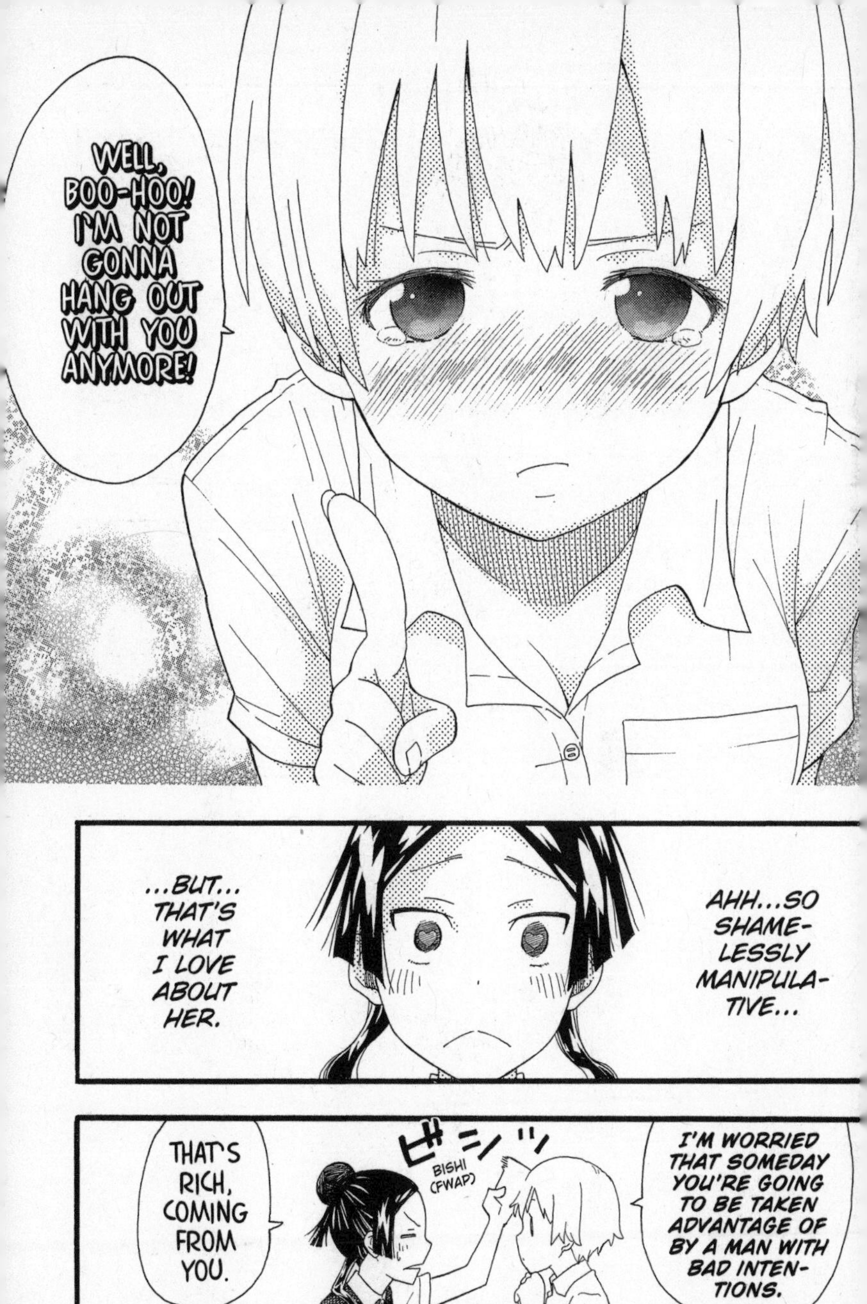
WELL, BOO-HOO! I'M NOT GONNA HANG OUT WITH YOU ANYMORE!
AHH...SO SHAME-LESSLY MANIPULA-TIVE...
...BUT... THAT'S WHAT I LOVE ABOUT HER.
I'M WORRIED THAT SOMEDAY YOU'RE GOING TO BE TAKEN ADVANTAGE OF BY A MAN WITH BAD INTEN-TIONS.
ビシッ
BISHI (FWAP)
THAT'S RICH, COMING FROM YOU.

DEATH CHILD

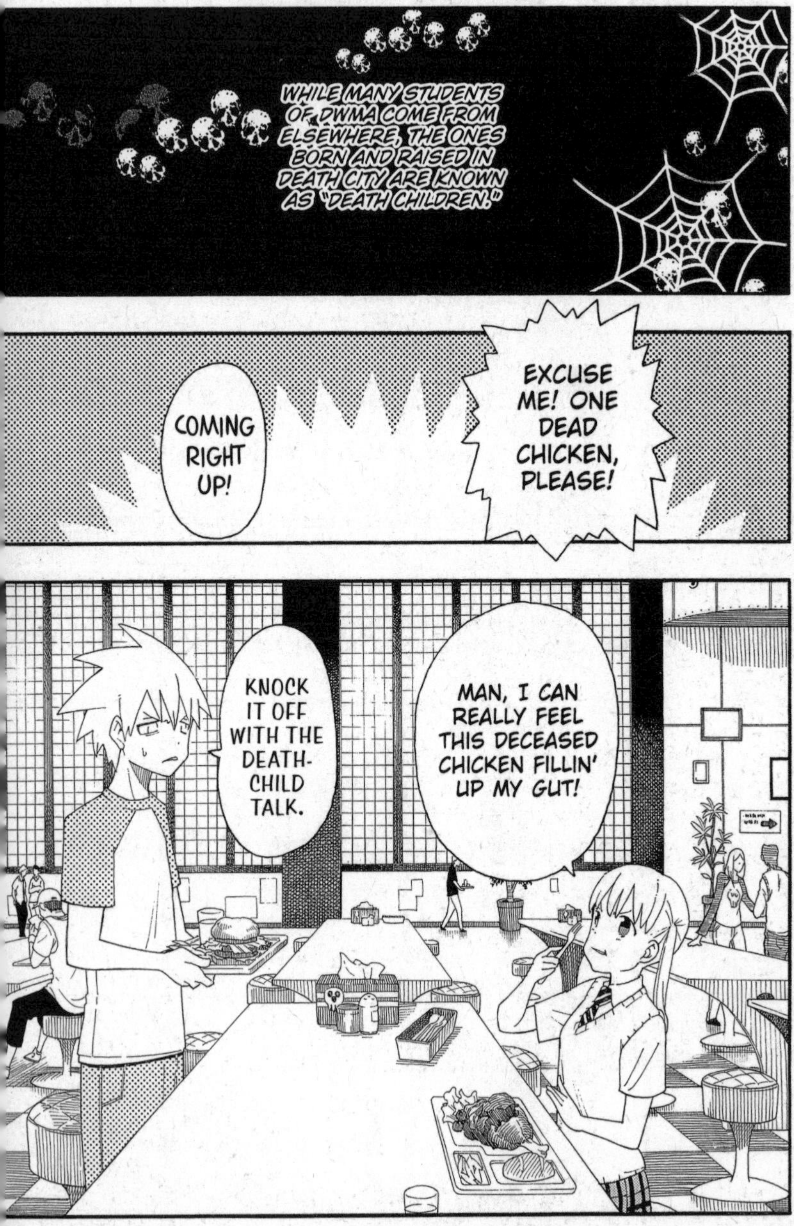
WHILE MANY STUDENTS OF DWMA COME FROM ELSEWHERE, THE ONES BORN AND RAISED IN DEATH CITY ARE KNOWN AS "DEATH CHILDREN."
EXCUSE ME! ONE DEAD CHICKEN, PLEASE!
COMING RIGHT UP!
MAN, I CAN REALLY FEEL THIS DECEASED CHICKEN FILLIN' UP MY GUT!
KNOCK IT OFF WITH THE DEATH-CHILD TALK.

SOUL EATER

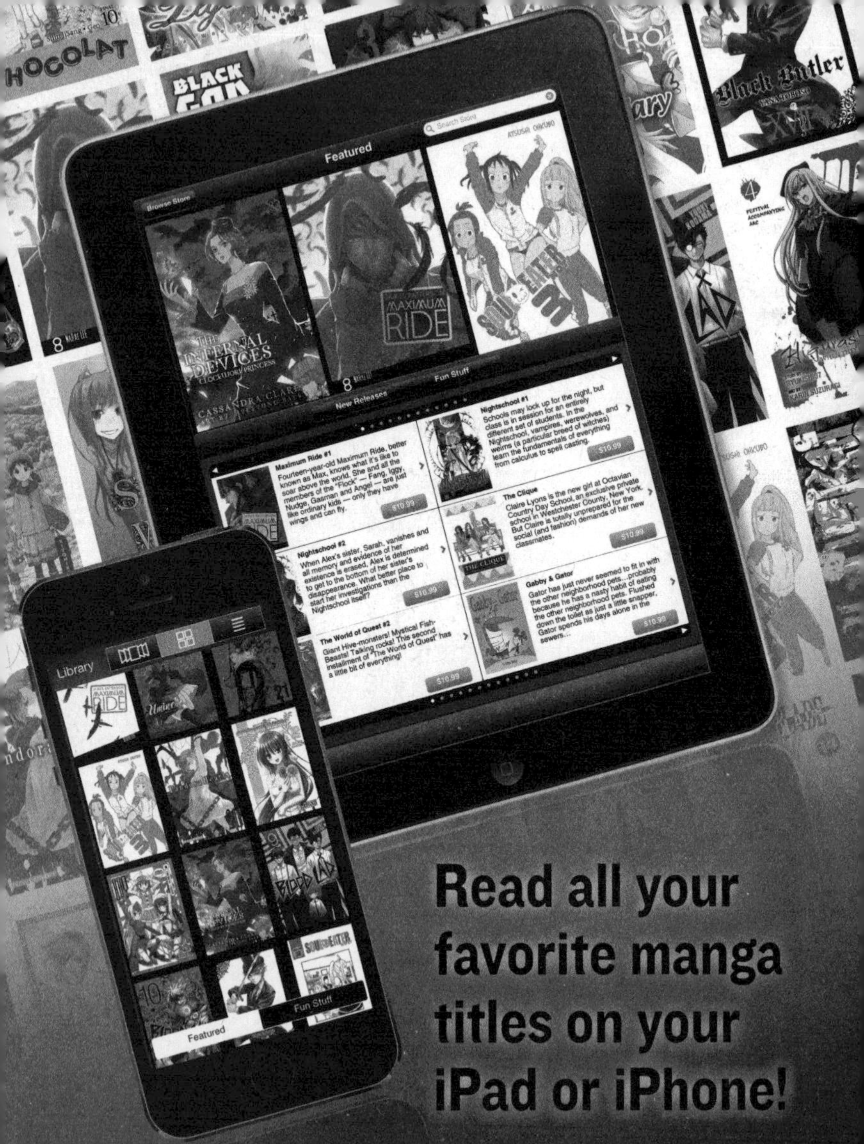
Featured
Browse Store
Search Store
New Releases
Fun Stuff
Maximum Ride #1
Fourteen-year-old Maximum Ride, better known as Max, knows what it's like to soar above the world. She and all the members of the "Flock" — Fang, Iggy, Nudge, Gasman and Angel — are just like ordinary kids — only they have wings and can fly.
Nightschool #1
Schools may lock up for the night, but class is in session for an entirely different set of students. In the Nightschool, vampires, werewolves, and weirns (a particular breed of witches) learn the fundamentals of everything from calculus to spell casting.
Nightschool #2
When Alex's sister, Sarah, vanishes and all memory and evidence of her existence is erased, Alex is determined to get to the bottom of her sister's disappearance. What better place to start her investigations than the Nightschool itself?
The Clique
Claire Lyons is the new girl at Octavian Country Day School, an exclusive private school in Westchester County, New York. But Claire is totally unprepared for the social (and fashion) demands of her new classmates.
The World of Quest #2
Giant Hive-monsters! Mystical Fish-Beasts! Talking rocks! This second installment of "The World of Quest" has a little bit of everything!
Gabby & Gator
Gator has just never seemed to fit in with the other neighborhood pets...probably because he has a nasty habit of eating the other neighborhood pets. Flushed down the toilet as just a little snapper, Gator spends his days alone in the sewers...
$10.99
Library
Featured
Fun Stuff

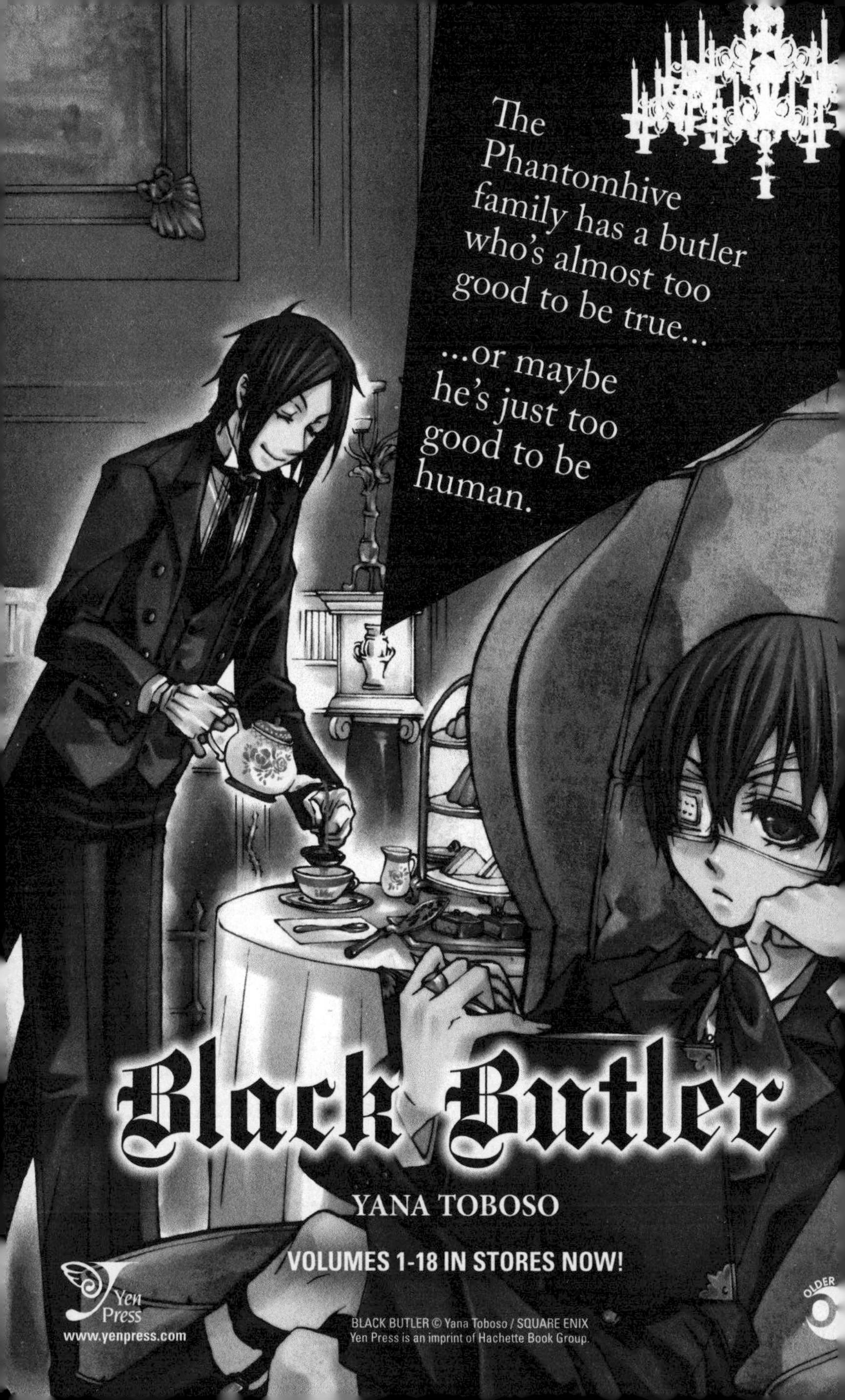
The Phantomhive family has a butler who's almost too good to be true...
...or maybe he's just too good to be human.
Black Butler
YANA TOBOSO
VOLUMES 1-18 IN STORES NOW!
Yen Press
www.yenpress.com
OLDER
BLACK BUTLER © Yana Toboso / SQUARE ENIX
Yen Press is an imprint of Hachette Book Group.

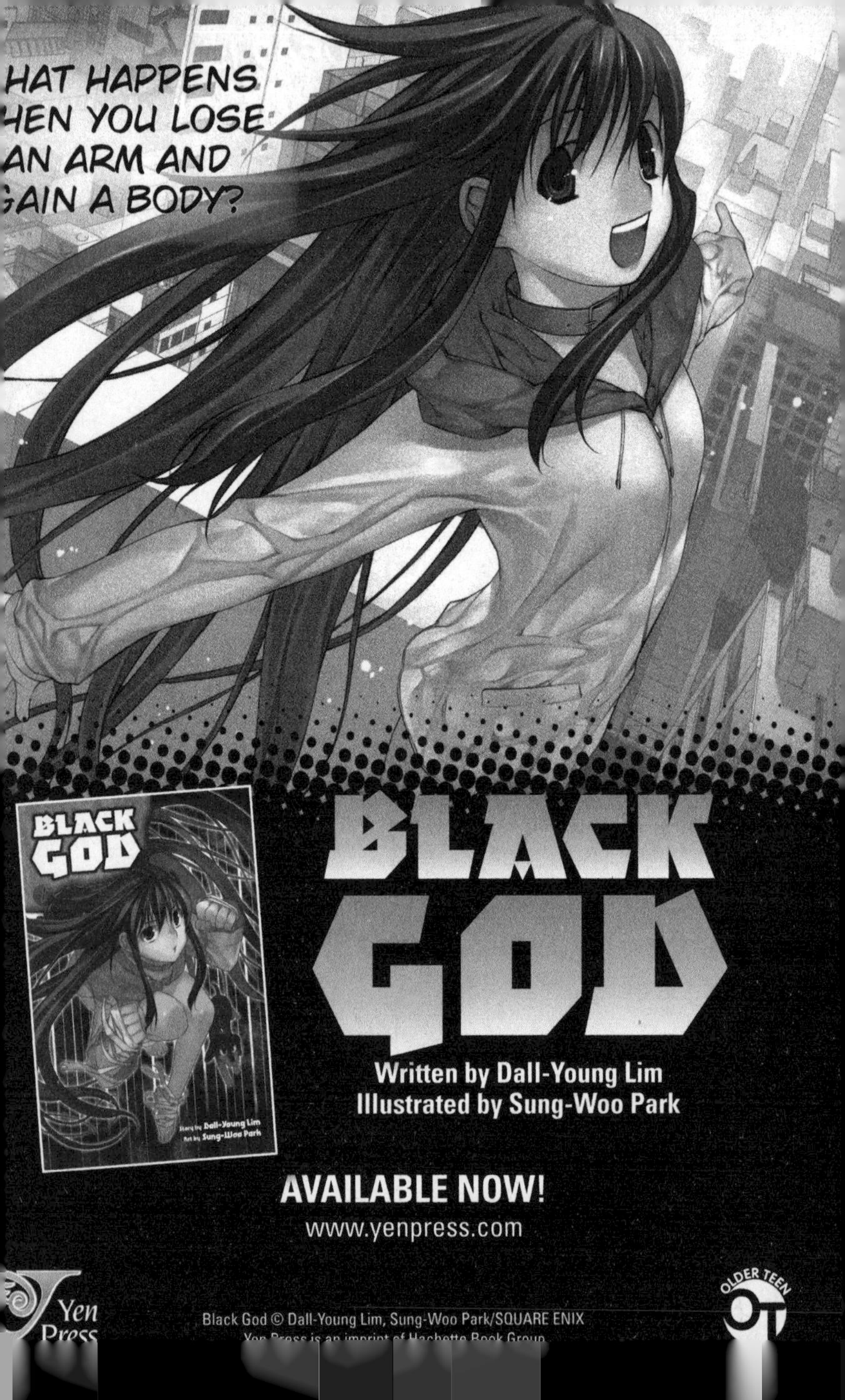
HAT HAPPENS
HEN YOU LOSE
AN ARM AND
GAIN A BODY?
BLACK GOD
Story by Dall-Young Lim
Art by Sung-Woo Park
BLACK GOD
Written by Dall-Young Lim
Illustrated by Sung-Woo Park
AVAILABLE NOW!
www.yenpress.com
Yen Press
OLDER TEEN
OT
Black God © Dall-Young Lim, Sung-Woo Park/SQUARE ENIX

SOUL EATER ㉔

ATSUSHI OHKUBO

Translation: Stephen Paul

Lettering: Abigail Blackman

SOUL EATER Vol. 24 © 2013 Atsushi Ohkubo / SQUARE ENIX.
First published in Japan in 2013 by SQUARE ENIX CO., LTD. English translation rights arranged with SQUARE ENIX CO., LTD. and Hachette Book Group through Tuttle-Mori Agency, Inc.

Translation © 2015 by SQUARE ENIX CO., LTD.

Yen Press
Hachette Book Group
1290 Avenue of the Americas
New York, NY 10104

www.hachettebookgroup.com
www.yenpress.com

Yen Press is an imprint of Hachette Book Group, Inc. The Yen Press name and logo are trademarks of Hachette Book Group, Inc.

First Yen Press Edition: January 2015

ISBN: 978-0-316-37793-5

10 9 8 7 6 5 4 3 2 1

BVG

Printed in the United States of America